W9-BZZ-569

THE BEDFORD SERIES IN HISTORY AND CULTURE

Judith Sargent Murray

A Brief Biography with Documents

l

THE BEDFORD SERIES IN HISTORY AND CULTURE

Judith Sargent Murray

A Brief Biography with Documents

Sheila L. Skemp

University of Mississippi

BEDFORD/ST. MARTIN'S   Boston ◆ New York

For Bedford/St. Martin's

President and Publisher: Charles H. Christensen
General Manager and Associate Publisher: Joan E. Feinberg
History Editor: Katherine E. Kurzman
Developmental Editor: Louise Townsend
Editorial Assistant: Jen Lesar
Managing Editor: Elizabeth M. Schaaf
Production Editor: Heidi L. Hood
Production Assistant: Arthur Johnson
Copyeditor: Linda Leet Howe
Text Design: Claire Seng-Niemoeller
Indexer: Anne Holmes of EdIndex
Cover Design: Richard Emery Design, Inc.
Cover Art: John Singleton Copley, portrait of Judith Sargent, later Mrs. John Murray, ca. 1768. Private collection. Courtesy of the Frick Art Reference Library.
Composition: ComCom
Printing and Binding: Haddon Craftsmen

Library of Congress Catalog Card Number: 97–74971

Manufactured in the United States of America.

7 6 5
f e d c

For information, write: Bedford/St. Martin's, 75 Arlington Street, Boston, MA 02116 (617-399-4000)

ISBN: 0–312–11506–7 (paperback)
ISBN: 0–312–17770–4 (hardcover)

Foreword

The Bedford Series in History and Culture is designed so that readers can study the past as historians do.

The historian's first task is finding the evidence. Documents, letters, memoirs, interviews, pictures, movies, novels, or poems can provide facts and clues. Then the historian questions and compares the sources. There is more to do than in a courtroom, for hearsay evidence is welcome, and the historian is usually looking for answers beyond act and motive. Different views of an event may be as important as a single verdict. How a story is told may yield as much information as what it says.

Along the way the historian seeks help from other historians and perhaps from specialists in other disciplines. Finally, it is time to write, to decide on an interpretation and how to arrange the evidence for readers.

Each book in this series contains an important historical document or group of documents, each document a witness from the past and open to interpretation in different ways. The documents are combined with some element of historical narrative—an introduction or a biographical essay, for example—that provides students with an analysis of the primary source material and important background information about the world in which it was produced.

Each book in the series focuses on a specific topic within a specific historical period. Each provides a basis for lively thought and discussion about several aspects of the topic and the historian's role. Each is short enough (and inexpensive enough) to be a reasonable one-week assignment in a college course. Whether as classroom or personal reading, each book in the series provides firsthand experience of the challenge—and fun—of discovering, recreating, and interpreting the past.

Natalie Zemon Davis
Ernest R. May

Preface

More than Mercy Otis Warren, more even than Abigail Adams, Judith Sargent Murray (1751–1820) was at the center of the post-Revolution discussion concerning the proper role of women in the new Republic. She wrote and published poetry and essays; in addition, two of her plays were produced at the Federal Street Theater in Boston, making her the first American-born woman to see her work performed on that city's stage. In 1798, she published *The Gleaner,* a three-volume compilation of essays, plays, and poetry that included her famous four-part essay, "Observations on Female Abilities."

Judith Sargent Murray's voice dominated the American discussion of women's character and women's future in the post-war years. *The Gleaner* was read on both sides of the Atlantic. It was discussed and debated in genteel circles in her native country and abroad. Her views of gender relations represented the "cutting edge" of what passed for feminism in eighteenth-century America. Whether she talked about intimate or public roles, she wrote with an authority that baffled, even offended, many of her contemporaries. Although some of her views were derivative, Murray was more thoroughgoing than most of her contemporaries in her willingness to challenge the limits that circumscribed even the educated women of her era, pushing her pleas for equality and opportunity as far as any American woman dared to do at the time.

This book attempts to account for Judith Sargent Murray's lifelong commitment to women's rights by examining her own experiences within the intellectual currents that shaped many educated men and women on both sides of the Atlantic at the end of the eighteenth century. It is divided into two sections. The first half, a topically organized biography, examines the contexts within which Murray wrote and analyzes those factors — such as marriage, motherhood, education, literature, religion, and politics — that led her to embrace a definition of women's roles that was clearly advanced for its time. The biography is followed by a series of fifteen documents that allow Murray to speak on her own, unmediated terms, giving students an opportunity to analyze and evaluate her views for themselves. Excerpts include samples of her previously unpublished letters as well as her essays and poetry, all of which address topics discussed in each chapter of the biography.

An examination of the views of Judith Sargent Murray allows students to become familiar with the fascinating story of a woman whose perspective was both representative and unique. It gives them a concrete and meaningful understanding of the changed attitudes toward women that characterized America at the end of the eighteenth century. It also allows them to glimpse the radical potential that lay beneath the new nation's proclamation of the value of independence and equality. When Murray claimed that women could be heads of state and businesspeople, warriors and farmers, she was taking the promise of the American Revolution to its logical—and most extreme—conclusion. She represents both the limits placed on American women and the possibilities to which any American woman might have aspired in the years after the American Revolution. Her work serves to remind us that in the nation's early history, there was a brief moment when gender definitions were loosely defined, when prospects for women were promising, when possibilities seemed limitless.

ACKNOWLEDGMENTS

All books are the product of a community of scholars. This one owes its very existence to one man, the Reverend Gordon Gibson, a dedicated Unitarian-Universalist minister whose persistent detective work led to the discovery of Judith Sargent Murray's papers in a Natchez, Mississippi, home. Thanks to him, the manuscripts now reside in the Mississippi Archives in Jackson, where scholars can peruse their contents and analyze the beliefs and experiences of their incredibly prolific author.

A number of historians have read all or part of this manuscript and helped me reshape it in many important ways. Thanks, in particular, to Carol Berkin at the City University of New York, Nancy Cott at Yale University, Elaine Crane at Fordham University, Edie Gelles at Stanford University's Institute for Research on Women and Gender, Joan Gunderson at California State University, San Marcos, Linda Kerber at the University of Iowa, Anne Ousterhout at Michigan State University, and Rosemarie Zagarri at George Mason University. Both the Philadelphia Center for Early American Studies and the Newberry Library gave me the opportunity to discuss portions of this manuscript with participants in their seminars. The probing questions the work elicited from these intelligent and selfless scholars—especially Wayne Bodle, Richard Dunn, and Al Young—have been of inestimable value to me.

I have been fortunate to have worked with a number of excellent graduate students, who have helped me at crucial stages of the rewriting process: Dan Fountain, Sari Knoff, Lisa Rowlands, and Heather Sanders of the University of Mississippi, Ben Irvin of Brandeis University, and Hedda Lautenschlager at Miami (Ohio) University deserve special mention. Joan Hall, of the University of Mississippi, has pointed me in the direction of a number of literary sources. Martha Oakes, curator of the Sargent House Museum in Gloucester, has provided countless services. I appreciate, in particular, her informative tour of the "mansion house" in the summer of 1996. Thanks, finally, to the Liberal Arts Development Fund, the Graduate School, and the Department of History at the University of Mississippi, as well as to the National Endowment for the Humanities, all of which helped me finance the research trips, writing time, and conference papers that made this book possible.

Many individuals at Bedford Books deserve more recognition than I can possibly accord them. Chuck Christensen encouraged me to write this book. Louise Townsend has, as always, been a careful, intelligent, and skillful editor. Her comments are invariably on target. The interest she has taken in the manuscript and its progress has been phenomenal. Working with her has been a real pleasure. Thanks are also due to Elizabeth Schaaf, managing editor, who oversaw the book's production and to senior production editor Heidi Hood who ably guided the manuscript from final draft to publication. Ellen Kuhl, senior editor in history, prepared the book for publication with efficiency, care, and an eye to every important detail. Linda Leet Howe's careful and meticulous copyediting helped make the manuscript clearer and more readable. Thanks, as well, to Joan Feinberg, Katherine Kurzman, and Donna Dennison.

Sheila L. Skemp

Contents

PART ONE

Judith Sargent Murray

INTRODUCTION

Judith Sargent Murray's World

The American Revolution was only one small episode in a series of democratic movements that led to sweeping political and social change on both sides of the Atlantic in the mid-eighteenth century. Within a few short years Italy, the Netherlands, Poland, and France all experienced dramatic challenges to the legitimacy of the old order, as people throughout the Western world began to demand new relationships between governors and governed, aristocrats and commoners, state and church, men and women. For those who lived through this period of change and instability, it seemed that the Old World was crumbling, if not collapsing all about them, and that the familiar verities around which they had once arranged their lives no longer had the power to claim their automatic allegiance. For some, the innovations they witnessed were exhilarating. Others found them frightening. No one doubted that they were deep and widespread.

In America, the Revolution did not result in the complete destruction of the traditional order. Still, the new nation was founded on the egalitarian principles immortalized in Thomas Jefferson's Declaration of Independence, and if old ways did not die at war's end, they were surely put on the defensive across a variety of fronts. Elites survived, but privilege and deference based on birth or social position were fast becoming things of the past. America's social and political leaders learned that they had to justify themselves and win support from below if they were to exercise power effectively. Slavery, too, outlasted the Revolution, although it began to disappear in the North, but now slaveholders everywhere had to invent a rationale for an institution they had hitherto taken for granted. Traditional definitions of gender were also subject to question. To be sure, old assumptions about the character of women and the roles women should—or should not—play in the public and private domains died hard and many never died at all. But here, too, conventional beliefs were

3

put on notice as men and women alike began examining customary attitudes and practices from new perspectives.

There were no absolutes, no givens in the new Republic. Everything was in flux and virtually no notion could survive unchallenged. Questions about gender abounded. Were women naturally inferior to men, or were women, like men, "created equal"? If women were equal to men, were they still in some significant if undefinable way different from men? If men and women were different, how did those differences lead to changes in the definitions of masculinity and femininity? If they were equal, how did this equality affect public and private relationships between men and women, husbands and wives? Could Americans continue to justify the legal, economic, and social dependence of women? Now that the new nation was composed of citizens instead of subjects, what was women's relationship to the state? Could women be citizens? Could they vote or hold office, or should they exert their influence indirectly, as mothers and wives, teachers and writers? How, in other words, and to what degree, would women participate in formulating and preserving the values upon which the new Republic depended for its very survival?

The questions were myriad. The answers were open to debate. Thus, as one historian has noted, in the period after the Revolution men and women alike engaged in "dialogue, struggle, and contemplation about the meaning of gender and how men and women should relate to each other."[1] One of the most thoughtful and outspoken participants in that dialogue was Massachusetts-born poet, essayist, and playwright, Judith Sargent Murray.

Murray was both a contributor to and a product of the transcontinental conversation about gender issues that dominated public discourse in the late eighteenth and early nineteenth centuries. This conversation often took place in the realm of print, where men and women "talked" to each other in poems, novels, and essays, in magazines, books, and newspapers. In America, it was made possible by the rapid rise in literacy that began in the middle of the eighteenth century.

Like many elite New England women of her day, Murray read eclectically. Even as a girl, she noted with excitement that there were a growing number of women writers in England and on the Continent who were respectable, who were not pariahs or freaks, who wrote for public consumption, who enjoyed the respect of well-educated men and women, and who even supported themselves with the fruits of their labor. The example these women set for Judith Sargent Murray and a significant, if tiny, number of other American women was an inspiration, an indication that what women thought was important.

Murray did not begin writing for publication until 1782, when she agreed to publish her children's catechism, which was designed to help interested parents teach their progeny the tenets of the Universalist faith. Once she had entered the world of print, she never completely turned her back on it. Having "passed the rubicon," as she put it, she finally admitted her "daring ambition" for literary eminence.[2] By 1784, she was sending her essays and poetry to a select number of magazines, which proliferated in New England in the 1780s and 1790s, using the pen name "Constantia." In 1795, she began a short-lived career as a playwright with two comedies, both of which appeared briefly at Boston's Federal Street Theater. Her disappointment at their negative public and critical reception led her to return to poetry and essay writing. In 1798, she published *The Gleaner,* a three-volume collection of her writings that included new and old essays and poems as well as her two plays. After 1798, Murray's efforts to publish diminished but they did not end. Occasionally, she submitted an essay or poem to local magazines, and she wrote a third play that was also a critical failure. But essentially, her efforts to secure fame and fortune with her pen died with *The Gleaner.* Although her withdrawal from the public stage occurred in part for personal reasons, it is not coincidental that her diminished interest in writing coincided roughly with the conservative backlash that America—and especially Murray's native New England—experienced in the wake of the French Revolution. Not until the 1830s and 1840s would American women once again consider the possibility that they might transcend the position to which their society had consigned them at the end of the Revolutionary era.

Judith Sargent Murray wrote on a wide variety of subjects. She discussed politics and manners, religion and morals, money and fame. She had, it seemed, an opinion on everything and was not reluctant to share her views with her reading public. Historians have always been especially interested in her contributions to the national debate on gender relations, and it is clear that this topic was never very far from her mind. Her "Desultory Thoughts Upon the Utility of Encouraging a Degree of Self-Complacency, Especially in Female Bosoms," her "On the Equality of the Sexes" as well as her four-part *Gleaner* essay, "Observations on Female Abilities," all attest to Murray's abiding concern with expanding economic, social, and even political opportunities for women. In many ways, her thoughts on the subject reflected the views of many of her progressive contemporaries. She argued that in intellectual matters, women and men were equal, and while she agreed that they were different in many significant ways, she always sought to emphasize their similarities, their common humanity. Thus, she agreed with those men and women in

America and Europe who argued that women needed to be educated if they were to contribute to their society as good wives and mothers, and as a force for morality and virtue in an uncertain world. She also demanded equality in all private relationships between men and women, especially within marriage.

In many ways, however, Murray's views were exceptional. Arguably, she was surpassed only by English feminist Mary Wollstonecraft in her willingness to examine and probe the limits that circumscribed even the most talented and capable women in the eighteenth century. She entertained the possibility that women might have a direct part to play in the political realm. Her own determination to write about political and military issues indicates her conviction that women need not apologize for their interest in public affairs. She also urged girls to learn to support themselves so that as widows or spinsters they would never have to depend upon the kindness of friends or relatives for their livelihood. While she assumed that most women would marry, she did not believe that matrimony was the only respectable or desirable fate for everyone. She insisted that women, like men, should have the ability to make choices about their lives, to claim for themselves the promise set forth in the Declaration of Independence: the right to life, liberty, and the pursuit of happiness.

Judith Sargent Murray was not a "typical" American woman. Her elite social status in itself set her apart from most other white women. In many ways, her opinions and her story were her own. Moreover, while her views reflected—and surely derived from—the perspectives of prominent writers of her day, they were also a product of her own unique experience and personality. To analyze her philosophy is to probe the outer limits to which any American woman might have aspired in the postrevolutionary age.

This book is divided into two parts. The text is organized topically, not chronologically, as it explores those factors that led Judith Sargent Murray to develop a view of the definition and role of women that was clearly advanced for its time. Chapter one examines the social and intellectual context within which Murray wrote. Chapters two through six discuss specific aspects of her life that led her to embrace gender-based critiques of eighteenth-century society as more-or-less common sense. Her conversion to the Universalist religion, her experiences during the American Revolution, her financial struggles, and her identity as wife and mother all shaped her views on gender relations. Chapters seven through nine analyze Judith Sargent Murray's opinions on women, discussing her views on women's education and women's role in the public sphere, especially in the literary world and in politics. They highlight once again both her representative perspective and her unique contribution to the eighteenth-century debate on women. Part two contains excerpts from Murray's own writing—her poetry, her essays, and her private letters—so that readers can acquire an unmediated acquaintance with Murray on her own terms.

This book is not a comprehensive biography. It only begins to tell the story of one American woman, throwing at least some light on an individual about whom historians have known very little. Until recently, scholars have known Murray only through her published work and one obscure, woefully incomplete, and often inaccurate biography.[3] Her letters, which reveal so much about her rich and full existence and which also provide the link between her private and public life, remained untouched and unnoticed, gathering dust in an old home near Natchez, Mississippi. In the 1990s, thanks to the persistent detective work of Unitarian-Universalist minister Reverend Gordon Gibson, Murray's letterbooks were rescued from oblivion. Historians can now study them, analyze the beliefs and experiences of their incredibly prolific author, and perhaps give Judith Sargent Murray at least some of the recognition for which she hungered.

NOTES

[1] Joan Cashin, "Introduction to Special Issue on Gender in the Early Republic," *Journal of the Early Republic* 15 (Fall 1995), 355.

[2] Judith Sargent Murray to the Rev. William Emerson, 21 Nov. 1805, Judith Sargent Murray, Letterbook, 13:77, Mississippi Archives, Jackson, Miss.

[3] Vena Bernadette Field, *Constantia: A Study of the Life and Works of Judith Sargent Murray, 1751–1820* (Orono: University of Maine Press, 1931).

1

A Sargent of Gloucester

To have been born a Sargent in eighteenth-century Gloucester, Massachusetts, was—in American terms—to be able to claim a long and distinguished heritage. Admittedly, no colonial family could boast of its links to the European aristocracy. At least in the beginning, provincial leaders achieved their status; they did not inherit it. They arrived early and got the best land or settled near the deepest harbors. Wealth, not blood, was the defining characteristic of America's elite. Still, when affluence along with the social and political perquisites that accompanied them were passed down from one generation to the next, those who enjoyed the benefits of their ancestors' good fortune and industry developed a sense of entitlement, a belief that they were somehow different from and superior to ordinary colonists. By at least the first quarter of the eighteenth century, they had begun the process of gentrification, acquiring and displaying those consumer goods that helped set them apart from the rest of the population. The experience of the Sargent family typifies the process by which ordinary Englishmen attained elite status in the New World.

Gloucester never resembled the storybook picture of a New England community, where houses stood in close proximity to one another and to the meetinghouse built on a centrally located village common. Nature forbade such a configuration. Instead, settlers lived in discrete clusters, divided from one another by rock formations that protruded from the soil and by the inlets, coves, and creeks that formed the landscape. Fortunately for his descendants, William Sargent, Judith's great grandfather, settled on Eastern Point, in the southern section of town. In the short run, his choice appeared disadvantageous: The amount of arable land was limited, nor did he have easy access to the thick forests that covered much of the area. So long as Gloucester residents remained committed to farming and milling, the families whose houses were located along the eastern Annisquam river, just to the north of the Sargents' property, retained a slight social and economic edge. It was here that the first meetinghouse was located. It was here, as well, that a reasonably wealthy group of settlers got its start.[1]

By the beginning of the eighteenth century, the balance of power in Gloucester had begun to tip to the south. As the mineral resources in the town's thin and rocky soil were depleted, residents increasingly looked to the sea for their livelihood. The rise in the importance of the coastal and transatlantic trade meant that families living near Gloucester's excellent harbor found themselves in a privileged position. In the 1730s, merchants who sold their fish and timber to nearby Salem, to Boston, and to the West Indies became increasingly wealthy and more connected to the economic, social, and intellectual currents that pervaded the Anglo-American world. While they remained provincial and somewhat suspicious of outsiders, they were much more cosmopolitan than those families that continued to rely on the soil for their living.

Like their neighbors, the Sargents were farmers at first. But eventually they began to concentrate on the seagoing trade to achieve wealth and status. Like all merchants they enjoyed good years and bad. Still, over the long run they prospered. Judith's grandfather, Epes Sargent, was among Gloucester's wealthiest and most cosmopolitan inhabitants. He was one of a handful of men in his generation who attended Harvard. His far-flung merchant ventures took his vessels to Boston, the West Indies, and Europe. He served at one time or another as justice of the peace of Essex County, as a major in the Essex County Militia, and as a deputy from Gloucester to the Massachusetts General Court.

In her youth, Judith was surrounded by successful Sargents, for the residences of her uncles Epes and Daniel sat in plain view of the house of her father, Winthrop. All three brothers were involved in the merchant and fishing industries. Epes, the oldest son and his father's namesake, inherited the Sargent house and land, and by the outbreak of the Revolutionary War he owned more ships than anyone else in the family. Daniel and Winthrop were not far behind. Daniel left Gloucester for Boston in 1778 and became one of the wealthiest merchants in the city. Winthrop began his career on a relatively small scale, but he used his own resources and his family's connections to profitable ends. Each year his ships left port filled with the fish his own sailors harvested as well as the provisions he bought in Gloucester, Salem, and Marblehead. They sailed as far as Lisbon, exchanging fish and provisions for sugar, molasses, rum, and coffee. In good times — and there were many — his profits were substantial.

Almost everyone with whom young Judith Sargent associated in the 1750s and 1760s could claim a similar social and economic background. Although her maternal connections were not quite as impressive as those of the Sargents, her mother's family was also dominated by successful merchants. Judith's great grandfather, Thomas Saunders (or Sanders), did not arrive in Gloucester until 1702. A shipbuilder and the captain of a sloop, he was, says the town's historian, a "man of great enterprise," as was his son Thomas.[2] Judith's first husband, John Stevens, could point with pride to his father, William, who arrived in Gloucester in 1643 and was one of the town's first selectmen. William Stevens died insolvent, but he had been a prominent merchant, and owned a farm at Eastern Point and a house in the heart of town. Clearly, Judith moved in rarified circles.

Gloucester was a secondary port whose inhabitants had turned to the sea only when they could no longer make a living as farmers. Consequently, at least until the mid-eighteenth century, the town's residents were fairly traditional. Their approach to trade was cautious, their material aspirations relatively limited. They avoided debt and tried to settle differences with their neighbors out of court. They viewed with suspicion the individualistic, competitive approach to business that had begun to characterize the major ports. Community obligations and personal relationships remained important to even the most successful entrepreneurs, and townspeople tried to preserve a traditional, organic society based on order, deference, and hierarchy. For Judith, this meant that so long as she remained in Gloucester, an accident of birth gave her social prestige, considerable wealth, and a family heritage of which to be proud.

Despite the intentions of the town's residents, Gloucester became increasingly cosmopolitan in the years immediately preceding the American Revolution. South Gloucester was a point of contact with the larger world, and it was impossible for men engaged in maritime trade to avoid the influence of Boston, and Europe, forever. As they broadened their horizons, members of the elite could not help but notice that however wealthy and aristocratic they might appear in their own community, compared to leading Bostonians they were minor figures and in England they would rank with the lesser gentry at best. They both admired and resented their more worldly and successful neighbors, but as they began to recognize their own limitations, at least some of them chafed at their insularity. Epes Sargent was the first of Judith's uncles to leave Gloucester, although he went under duress, the victim of his loyalist convictions. Daniel soon followed, moving to Boston in 1778, where he turned his mercantile interests to great advantage. Winthrop Sargent lived in Gloucester until he died, but none of his children, who looked upon their ancestral home with fondness, remained there. They were more receptive to new experiences and new ideas than their parents' generation had been.

All but Judith's sister, Esther, were more ambitious as well, determined to make their mark on the wider world.

Judith Sargent Murray's character was shaped as much by her inherited social position as by the changes that occurred in America in the wake of the Revolution. Although her material circumstances altered over the years, she remained proud of her heritage. The family name gave her a sense of security, an identity that comforted her in an increasingly precarious world. Indeed, it should come as no surprise that upon the death of her first husband, John Stevens, in 1787, Judith reverted to her maiden name. When she married again the following year, this time to the Reverend John Murray, she refused to relinquish it. She was fond of the name "Sargent," she explained, and henceforth signed all her correspondence as "Judith Sargent Murray."[3]

If she viewed the world from the lofty position of a Sargent, Judith also saw it through gendered lenses. The superiority she took for granted as a member of an elite New England family was undercut by a society that scarcely noticed, much less valued, the intellectual abilities of women. If she expected automatic respect because of her family name, she quickly learned that as a woman, her opportunities were limited.

Until she was two years old, Judith Sargent was an only child. In 1753, her brother Winthrop was born. While Judith may have been honored to be named after her mother, it was Winthrop who bore the family name. Almost from the beginning, she had to accept the reality that while age claimed precedence over youth in eighteenth-century New England, men—even younger men—were considered superior to women. Judith insisted that she adored Winthrop, and perhaps she did. Nevertheless, the relationship between brother and sister was often strained, and from time to time each sibling struggled to dominate the other.

Under the circumstances, Judith's unsuccessful efforts to obtain what she considered an adequate education had both a real and a symbolic importance. She was clearly intelligent, but this was not a trait her society admired in women. Her parents thought they were being more than generous when they brought a woman to the house to teach their daughter how to read, sent her to a writing school for three months, and asked the Reverend John Rogers—"a superstitious gloomy pastor," Judith later called him—to give her a few "solemn lectures."[4] She also learned to sew, acquired a "general idea" of financial matters, and studied the Bible and the Congregational catechism.[5] That was the extent of her formal schooling.

Her education may have been typical among girls of her social position in the mid-eighteenth century, but for Judith it was not nearly enough. Her later complaint that she grew up as "a Wild and untutored" child of nature was clearly hyperbolic, but she just as obviously wanted more.[6] She begged her parents to allow her to sit in on Winthrop's lessons. She especially wanted to learn Latin, the mark of any genteely educated man, but they stood firm. Her mother and father were "most affectionate," Judith later explained, but they paid "homage at the shrine of fashion." They wanted her to be competent in all areas that were essential for "female life," but they could not imagine to what possible use she would put a knowledge of the classics.[7]

The contrast between her experience and her brother's could not have been more stark. Winthrop quickly abandoned his Gloucester tutors in favor of the superior education he received at the Boston Latin School. From there he went to Harvard, graduating in 1771. Left to her own devices, Judith educated herself, joining the ranks of many girls in England, France, and America who had little or no formal schooling but managed to expand their intellectual horizons on their own.

Despite her complaints about the deficiencies in her education, in many ways Murray was born in the right place at the right time. She lived in a port city, where even prior to the Revolution wealthy Americans had easier access than ever before to the world of print. No American published a novel until after the war, but colonial printers pirated English and continental fiction without compunction as they tried to satisfy a growing demand for the written word. By the mid-1790s, the number of American magazines had grown dramatically. As a result, readers enjoyed the productions of native or European pens, and writers had the opportunity to display their talents and shape public opinion. Booksellers and stationers sold their wares in port cities. Peddlers carried books into the countryside, crossing and recrossing state lines, allowing those who never left their own villages to hear and evaluate the views of men and women from all corners of the Western world. Those who could not afford their own books borrowed them from friends or subscribed to the many lending and circulating libraries that became increasingly prevalent throughout the century.

Publishers soon discovered that women were excellent customers, and many of them began to cater to women's interests, further expanding an already burgeoning market. Women purchased more than half of the novels published in America in the late eighteenth century and wrote over a fourth of them.[8] Many magazines also appealed directly to women, both as writers and readers. For women, the results were not much short of revolutionary. The very process of selecting a book to read became an act of self-assertion. As readers, women were empowered by their realization that literature was theirs to interpret as they pleased. No intermediate authority figure, no preacher, teacher, father, or husband, could tell them how to react to the written word. They were free to explain, condemn, or praise individual books for themselves. And those who were daring or talented enough could even pick up a pen and submit their views to the public on their own terms.

Not everything that young Judith Sargent read was serious, nor did all the books she devoured deal explicitly with gender issues. Especially in her youth, she was an undiscriminating reader. She spent many a sleepless night "weeping over the fanciful embarrassments, and subsequent distresses of some ideal Hero or Heroine, who hath blazed away in the multiplied pages of a romance."[9] Still, her private letters and published essays indicate that she read more than light romances. (See Document 1.) While her references to books on science, philosophy, history, and politics were often superficial and bore the unmistakeable mark of a self-taught pedant, she clearly took many of the lessons she learned to heart. From the beginning, her reading opened a door to a world beyond Gloucester, connecting her to writers on both sides of the Atlantic who thought about issues that mattered to women like herself, and who challenged the conventions that confined women to a narrow intellectual sphere.

As an adult, Judith Sargent Murray claimed to regret the time she spent reading light fiction, although she defended morally unassailable English novelists such as Samuel Richardson and Laurence Sterne. She always insisted that if novels were peopled with virtuous characters whose stories showed young readers how good triumphed over evil, they might, at least in small doses, provide valuable lessons for the unformed mind. As one scholar has suggested, however, the second-rate romances that Murray later condemned might well have had unintended consequences. Indeed, ministers and politicians may have attacked novels so vociferously because they saw them as a subversive influence, a challenge to the patriarchal order.[10]

Novels did give some girls "ideas," and it is at the very least likely that young Judith Sargent's views of women—whether or not she was conscious of it—were shaped by the hours she spent with a romance in her hands. Novels led their readers to exercise their imaginations and to dream of a better life, to grow vaguely dissatisfied with the drudgery that was often their expected lot. While eighteenth-century fiction seems unforgivably didactic and moralistic to a modern sensibility, it offered readers a world filled with interesting characters who enjoyed an exotic existence and whose actions—for good or ill—had a discernable impact on the lives of people around them. Moreover, most novels of the day praised educated women and encouraged girls to write as well as to read, to exert their moral authority, to make choices about their future.

The novels she read as a girl may well have expanded Judith Sargent's intellectual horizons and sharpened her dissatisfaction with a world that taught her not to dream, not to question the social customs that defined her expectations. Admittedly, such an influence is subtle and difficult to prove. Even as a girl, however, Judith became acquainted with a number of English and European writers who challenged traditional assumptions about women more directly than Richardson, Sterne, and their many less talented imitators ever did. While the American debate over women's place became especially lively in the last quarter of the eighteenth century, it had its roots in the not-too-distant past.

A public discussion of gender issues began in England and France as early as the seventeenth century. Perhaps no one was more outspoken on the subject than Mary Astell (1661–1731), whose traditional religious and political beliefs bore a marked contrast to her views on women. Indeed, it is likely that Astell's defense of the established order in church, state, and society helped make her cause respectable. Richardson, Daniel Defoe, and Richard Steele all quoted her with approval, and she was one of the most influential and widely read women writers of her own and subsequent generations.[11] Her *Reflections on Marriage,* published in 1700, called for a marriage based on mutual esteem and rational friendship, while her *A Serious Proposal to the Ladies,* published six years earlier, proclaimed women's intellectual equality with men. It was custom, she insisted, that wrapped women in a "cloud of ignorance" for "from their very infancy [women were] debarred from those advantages with the want of which they are afterwards reproached." Astell maintained that educated women did not threaten male authority. Rather, she said, in words that Judith Sargent Murray would echo like a mantra, learning rendered women more religious, better mothers, and better wives.[12]

There were other women who published their work fully a half-century before Judith Sargent was born. Anne Wharton (1632?–1685) wrote poetry and plays. Anne Finch (1661–1720), a poet and essayist, used the Bible to prove that women and men were equal. Madam de Scudéry (1607–1701), or "Sappho," wrote historical novels peopled by women who were intelligent, well spoken, and above all, rational. Lady Damaris Masham's (1659–1708) *Occasional Thoughts* (1700) described women as victims of male insecurity and advocated better education for women.

The eighteenth century witnessed even more prolific women writers. Lady Mary Wortley Montagu (1689–1762) wrote an essay in 1737 defending women's rights and accusing men of devaluing women's capabilities; men and women, she claimed, were moral equals. Other women—all roughly contemporaries of Judith Sargent Murray—quickly followed in their wake. Anna Barbauld (1743–1824) and Anna Seward (1747–1809) were poets. Hannah Cowley (1743–1809) and Elizabeth Inchbald (1753–1821) were professional playwrights. Inchbald, a paramour of the radical philosopher William Godwin, was also an actress and a novelist who earned a living as a writer. Indeed, she was one of many women during this period who capitalized on the growing transatlantic appetite for fiction. Fanny Burney (1752–1840), Charlotte Smith (1748–1806), Hannah More (1745–1833), and Madame de Genlis (1746–1830) were especially successful novelists, but they were by no means the only women who discovered that they had marketable talent.

The most famous of Judith Sargent Murray's contemporaries was Mary Wollstonecraft (1759–1797), whose *A Vindication of the Rights of Woman* proclaimed women's intellectual equality with men, demanded better educational opportunities for women, and sought to remove all artificial barriers that kept women from achieving their potential. The *Vindication* was published in its entirety in America in 1794, ten years after Murray's first essay on women's issues reached the public eye. While Wollstonecraft attacked the class and the gender inequalities of her day, Murray merely sought equality of opportunity with the men of her own class. Still, although they had profoundly different social visions, in their views of women's attributes and rights the two were remarkably similar.

Not all the women whose work Murray read were feminists, even according to the eighteenth-century definition of the word. Their thinking spanned the ideological spectrum, but their particular beliefs were hardly the point. For many women, simply knowing that a few of their counterparts in England and on the Continent had written for public consumption was an inspiration. Perhaps no one had more influence on aspiring women writers in England and America in the mid-eighteenth century than the Whig historian Catharine Macaulay (1731–1791). Her eight-volume *History of England from the Accession of James I to That of the Brunswick Line* (1763–1783) was a tour de force. Like so many women, Macaulay was self-educated and knew neither Latin nor Greek. Modern feminists would find her quite traditional. Like most of her contemporaries, she expressed no interest in giving women the vote or access to political office, but she believed in women's intellectual equality with men and strongly supported better education for women. She was more important for what she did than for what she said. By writing about public matters in a serious way, by eschewing fiction for history, and by refusing to write under a pseudonym, she was an example to all women who were beginning to demand an equal voice in the literary world.

After the first volume of her *History* appeared, Macaulay never called attention to her sex. Yet everyone who read or heard about her considered her a "woman historian." Some, like Abigail Adams, Mercy Otis Warren, Judith Sargent Murray, and Mary Wollstonecraft, admired her *because* she was a woman. Others, like Hannah More and Lady Montagu, despised all political women and refused to read her work. Nor were the views of her detractors especially surprising. While most people had begun to accept women authors who wrote about "women's issues," such as religion, manners, marriage, or even education, they remained uncomfortable when women entered a traditionally male preserve such as history. Even in the eighteenth century, many continued to believe that women like Macaulay were "unnatural," that they were either sexually inadequate spinsters or scandalous libertines. Yet despite the obstacles she faced, Macaulay was successful and even profited financially from her endeavors. At least three significant women writers—Judith Sargent Murray, Mercy Otis Warren, and Mary Wollstonecraft—claimed to have been inspired by her example.

We know that Judith Sargent (Murray) read widely as a young girl—at least, she was conversant with a wide variety of writers by the time she began to publish her own work. (See Document 1.) She read the Bible, religious literature, and Shakespeare, of course. After the Revolution, she patronized American authors and subscribed to as many homegrown magazines as she could afford. Although she sometimes saw them as rivals, she supported her country's women writers, including Susanna Rowson and Mercy Otis Warren. Still, her reading material never lost its European and, in particular, its English flavor. She praised the work of those seventeenth- and eighteenth-century women whose writing had inspired her own literary efforts. She was familiar with the thought of philosopher John Locke as well as that of the proponents of the Scottish Enlightenment. She enjoyed natural philosophy, history, and biography but preferred drama and especially poetry. She read her share of contemporary "proper conduct for young ladies" books and seldom went anywhere without Lindley Murray's *Grammar* and Doctor Johnson's *Dictionary* at her side. She read both Rousseau and Voltaire, although she had little use for the former. She continued—judiciously, she always maintained—to read novels by men and women, both English and American. And while she thought for herself, her views on everything from the beheading of Charles I to the importance of women's education were shaped by what she read. It is clear that even in her youth, her love of literature led her to consider writing as a serious avocation if not her life's calling.

Judith Sargent Murray's mature sentiments about gender roles were a product of her particular experiences and of the transatlantic literary and philosophical tradition that characterized the Age of Enlightenment. Much of what she argued—about education, about definitions of "masculinity" and "femininity," and about husbands and wives, mothers and daughters—had been said before. It is hardly surprising that she and Mary Wollstonecraft independently came to so many of the same conclusions. Nor does it require much detective work to explain how and why she developed her perspective on women's education long before she read Catharine Macaulay's *Letters on Education*. All three women were part of the same intellectual tradition. They read the same books. They participated in the same debates. They shared many aspirations for themselves and for their sex.

But to say that the ideas promulgated by a Wollstonecraft or a Murray were "in the air" is to beg the question. For every Mary Wollstonecraft or Elizabeth Inchbald, there was a Hannah More or Lady Montagu, who breathed the same air as her more radical counterparts but came to decidedly different conclusions. In Murray's case, arguments for the intellectual equality of women clearly fell on fertile ground. Her privileged position gave her an early and abiding sense of entitlement. Her failure to secure what she considered to be an education commensurate with her own social status angered her as a child and embittered her as an adult.

Judith Sargent Murray once remarked that the American Revolution first led her to question the attitudes toward women that characterized her world. In the sense that the egalitarian message of the revolutionary generation gave her the language with which to articulate her views, this was no doubt the case. Nevertheless, her early experiences surely prepared her to seize that language and to use it for her own purposes. The American Revolution itself, the religious, social, and economic turmoil that swirled about her in the wake of independence, the economic disappointments she endured as a wife and mother, underscored her sense that arbitrary custom had denied her what was rightfully hers. What she had felt as an inchoate sense of injustice as a young woman came into sharper focus in the postwar years, as she struggled to develop a world view that conformed to her own needs. Moreover, it was in the postwar years that Judith Sargent Murray's inherited class position both complicated and reinforced her views of gender.

NOTES

[1]This description of Gloucester draws heavily from Christine Leigh Heyrman, *Commerce and Culture: The Maritime Communities of Colonial Massachusetts, 1690–1750* (New York: W. W. Norton, 1984).

[2]John J. Babson, *History of the Town of Gloucester* (Gloucester: Proctor Brothers, 1860), 241.

[3]Judith Sargent Murray to Winthrop Sargent, 17 May 1780, Judith Sargent Murray, Letterbook, 2:283, Mississippi Archives, Jackson, Miss.

[4]Judith Stevens to Mrs. Goldthwait, 4 Jan. 1778, Letterbook, 1:82; Judith Stevens to Mrs. Pilgrim of London, Old England, 2 Sept. 1786, Letterbook, 3:139.

[5]Judith Stevens to Mrs. Pilgrim, 2 Sept. 1786, ibid., 139.

[6]Judith Stevens to Winthrop Sargent, 28 Nov. 1784, Letterbook, 2:296.

[7]Judith Sargent Murray to Mrs. Pilgrim, 2 Sept. 1786, Letterbook, 3:139, 140; Judith Sargent Murray to Winthrop Sargent, [Sept. 1803], Letterbook, 12:878.

[8]Herbert Ross Brown, *The Sentimental Novel in America, 1789–1860* (Durham, N.C.: Duke University Press, 1940), 21, 22.

[9]Judith Sargent Murray to Mr. Parker, 5 Sept. 1784, Letterbook, 2:263.

[10]See Cathy N. Davidson, *Revolution and the Word: The Rise of the Novel in America,* (New York: Oxford University Press, 1986), 39–47, 72–73.

[11]Janet Todd, ed., *British Women Writers: A Critical Reference Guide* (New York: Continuum Press, 1989), 19.

[12]Katherine M. Rogers, ed., *Before Their Time: Six Women Writers of the Eighteenth Century* (New York: Frederick Ungar, 1979), 28, 31.

2

"The Despotism of Tradition": Universalism Comes to Gloucester

Judith Sargent Murray's first rebellion was not accomplished in the name of women. It occurred in the mid-1770s when, barely twenty-five years old, she rejected the Puritan religion of her American ancestors and embraced a new, radical version of Protestantism known as Universalism. Unlike the Quakers, Universalists did not overtly encourage women to assume an equal role in religious affairs. Still, the connection between Judith's religious conversion and her views on gender relations is clear, along with her growing willingness to discuss those views in a public forum. The egalitarian message of Universalism, although it was seldom expressed in gendered terms, gave her a framework within which she could begin to define and defend her heretofore vague belief that men and women were intellectual and spiritual equals. Moreover, her decision to reject the Massachusetts religious establishment led her to question other social and intellectual conventions. Any argument based on "the despotism of tradition, the prejudices of education, and the predominating sway of revered opinions" was never quite as persuasive to her again.[1] Once she had defied her community in one area, she found it easier to defy it in others, especially when she was convinced that she was acting in accordance with God's word. Her assumption that God was on her side gave her the courage to become a public participant in the transatlantic discussion of gender issues.

Eighteenth-century Gloucester justly revered its Puritan heritage. Admittedly, the little settlement had gotten off to an unpromising start where spiritual matters were concerned. Not until the mid-seventeenth century did the town's inhabitants find sufficient time and money to lay the foundations of a religious tradition their descendants could regard with pride. In 1664, John Emerson, a Harvard graduate, came to Gloucester from neighboring Ipswich. His long and successful pastorate helped unify and stabilize the community, bringing the town's church polity and theology into line with the rest of the Bay Colony. Thereafter, Gloucester's inhabitants clung ferociously to their brand of religious worship, emphasizing congregational autonomy and lay control of doctrine and practice. They neutralized and ultimately marginalized the Quakers, who began appearing among them in the 1660s. Some thirty years later, they survived the witchcraft scare that almost destroyed nearby Salem. By the eighteenth century, the village had every reason to assume that its inhabitants would continue to worship in unison.

The Sargents had strong emotional connections to the First Parish Church. Erected in 1737 on Middle Street, close to Gloucester Harbor, it was within easy walking distance of the Sargents' ancestral home. From the beginning, it served the needs of the merchants who came to dominate the town. Epes Sargent, Murray's grandfather, had been one of the eight influential men who built the church at their own expense. The Sargent pew, where Judith sat each Sunday, served as a reminder of her family's wealth and status. The poor did not own such pews, nor did even the most affluent newcomers. Pew ownership was hereditary and based on lineage as much as economic circumstances. Ownership of a pew in the First Parish Church signified a proud connection to Gloucester's historic roots, a distinction few would give up willingly. Yet in the spring of 1776, Judith, her parents, and her first husband, John Stevens, began the process that led to that very outcome.

It is difficult for twentieth-century Americans to comprehend the full ramifications of the family's decision to leave the First Parish Church. They were abandoning their past, rejecting a tradition that had accorded them a privileged place in the community, and separating themselves from the intricate network of social and spiritual relationships that shaped their world. For church members, the local meetinghouse was the center of religious and civic life. As infants they were baptized there. As adults they participated in the ritual of communion, forging even closer ties between themselves and other members. To sever those ties was to abandon relationships and beliefs that were as much a part of their lives as the air they breathed.

It was more than tradition or a visceral fear of the unknown that deterred most eighteenth-century New Englanders from indulging in sectarian activity. They knew that to do so might put them in economic and legal jeopardy. Anyone familiar with Gloucester's history knew what happened to those who dared to be different. When the first Quakers arrived in town in the mid-seventeenth century, the members of this pacifist sect were so isolated from the rest of society they found it difficult to eke out a living. They were the objects of frivolous lawsuits, they could not secure loans, and townspeople refused to trade with them. Even after the American Revolution, when states in many parts of the country were moving to separate religious and civil matters, Massachusetts continued to grant the Congregational Church special status. While the state constitution of 1780 guaranteed toleration to all Protestant faiths, it also provided tax support for religious institutions, leaving it to local communities, and ultimately to the courts, to decide whether the tax money of members of a particular dissenting sect would be used to support a religious institution whose tenets they rejected.

Despite the very real social, economic, and legal hazards they faced, a tiny group of Gloucester's First Parish congregants began to question the faith of their fathers in the years before the American Revolution. They did so as a result of a chance encounter with an Englishman named Gregory, who introduced them to the sermons of the Welsh minister James Relly (1722?–1778), an early proponent of Universalism. The ships that carried sugar, rum, and coffee to New England ports also brought passengers with new ideas about God and human affairs. Gloucester's Universalist theology was as much a part of the transatlantic world as the views of gender relations that Judith Sargent encountered in the novels, essays, and tracts she read as a young woman.

Universalism was one small part of the eighteenth century's many-pronged attack on Calvinism. Like all members of the First Parish Church, Judith had grown up accepting the Calvinist view of God without question. She believed in original sin, the notion that all humans were tainted with the sin Adam and Eve had committed in the Garden of Eden. She also accepted the doctrine of predestination, the idea that an all-powerful God had already decided who would be saved and who would be damned. According to this doctrine, there was no way that individuals could "earn" salvation. Salvation was a gift from God. Moreover, Calvinists argued that those destined for heaven were a fortunate and undeserving few. The vast majority of humans, they believed, were justly damned.

It was the genius of Relly and his disciple, the Englishman John Murray, to combine aspects of Calvinism with a dramatically new interpretation of the scripture. They believed in original sin and predestination, and agreed that all humans deserved eternal damnation. They contended, however, that because Christ had died for the sins of all, everyone would be saved. From their perspective, it was irrational to imagine that God would consign some undeserving wretches to perdition while saving others who were equally undeserving. Sin would be punished on this earth, they said, not in the hereafter.[2]

To traditional Calvinists, such an inclusive view of salvation threatened all moral order. If everyone went to heaven, they said, if even the most recalcitrant sinner did not fear eternal punishment, then there would be no compelling reason for anyone to obey human or divine laws. Indeed, everything Calvinists knew about Universalism suggested that it promised nothing but "anarchy and confusion." John Murray, its leading light, was an "unlearned teacher" and a foreigner to boot. His American-born imitators were even less educated and more socially suspect. They were all itinerants, "strolling mendicants" who traversed the country-side, interfered with the orderly relationship between established min-isters and their parishioners and kept everything "in one continual hubub."[3]

Although Universalists represented a cross-section of colonial society, the sect's detractors deliberately situated Murray's followers outside the dominant culture, identifying them with other marginal groups: the poor, blacks, and especially women. Many Americans regarded women as innately irrational, emotional, and "disorderly," attributes that in the minds of some observers led almost automatically to unrestrained car-nality. Indeed, one historian has argued that eighteenth-century Ameri-cans saw disorder and femininity as more or less synonomous. Thus, when members of the First Parish Church characterized the Universal-ists as immoral and lawless, the sexual connotations of these terms lurked just beneath the surface. Not only did such accusations tar dissenting sects with the pejorative brush of femininity, but they implied that dis-senting women were particularly likely to succumb to their own lustful natures.[4]

In some ways, it is difficult to understand the attraction that Univer-salism had for someone like Judith Sargent Murray. A product of her sta-tus, place, and time, she always put great store in propriety and decorum. She had no apparent reason to question a social order that operated to her advantage. Moreover, she lived in a world where reputation was a woman's most prized possession, and as the wife and daughter of promi-nent merchants she always strove to live by the rules. In 1774, however, she took her first hesitant steps toward rejecting the religious beliefs of her forebears, thus inviting the censure of friends, relatives, and strangers.

The little group of "Rellyites," as James Relly's Gloucester followers called themselves, may never have done more than meet quietly in their own homes to read the Bible and discuss Relly's sermons had John Mur-ray not decided to come to America. Murray left London in 1770, fleeing his creditors as well as the deep depression he suffered upon the death of his wife and young child. Like many an émigré, he hoped to begin his life anew in a more hospitable land. His timing was perfect—or, as his supporters would have it, providential. He arrived in America just as the colonies were gearing up to defy the power of king and country, and many Americans were particularly susceptible to all manner of anti-authoritarian rhetoric. They were prepared to sympathize with a religion that championed private judgment over received dogma, a "converted" ministry over a high-toned and well-educated clergy. They had begun to question their deference to received orthodoxy and to a religious establishment that promulgated the wisdom of the past. At least a few of them were willing to listen to someone like John Murray, who had no elite credentials and little formal education, but who encouraged them to think for themselves and to trust their own interpretation of the scriptures. They were also willing to form new religious institutions based on their understanding of religious truth.

In the fall of 1774, word reached Gloucester that John Murray was traveling throughout New England preaching the Universalist version of the gospel. Winthrop and Epes Sargent went to Boston to invite the minister to Gloucester. Murray arrived in town on November 3, 1774, remaining there for nine days. The Rellyites were immediately impressed by him, and were delighted when he accepted the offer of the Reverend Samuel Chandler—who was ill at the time—to preach from the First Church's pulpit. Murray was a charismatic speaker. He was short, a little stout, and given to occasional grammatical lapses, but his audiences forgot his rather unprepossessing appearance the moment he began to preach. He had learned his skills from a master, for in England he had briefly worked under the direction of the popular preacher George Whitefield, who had come to America in the 1740s to preach during the Great Awakening, a religious revival that touched all thirteen colonies before it died down. Like Whitefield, Murray spoke extemporaneously, and according to observers there was "something theatrical in his manner." He assumed the characters of various biblical personages and argued with so much certitude, embellishing his sermons with such a mountain of scriptural proof that many listeners found him impossible to withstand.[5]

Judith never forgot Murray's first sermon. He "enlarged my views," she said, "expanded my ideas, dissipated my doubts."[6] Once she had heard Murray speak, there was "no resisting the force of his eloquence."[7] Just two days after he left town, she gathered her courage and composed her first letter to John Murray. In the eighteenth century, women hesitated to correspond with men to whom they were not related. They were even less likely to initiate such a correspondence. Consequently, Judith felt compelled to justify her behavior. If God did not differentiate between men and women, she wrote, then gender differences were mere artificial constructions, and humans could, "with the strictest propriety mingle souls upon paper."[8]

John Murray was as taken with Gloucester as some of its inhabitants were with him. He returned to the community in December, staying with Judith's parents, and thereafter, although he remained an itinerant, Gloucester served as his home base. His supporters begged him to remain with them permanently, but he assured them that Christians did not require the services of a minister. If all were equal before God, then laypeople as well as ministers, women as well as men, could interpret the scriptures for themselves. His followers had to be content with his frequent visits, regretting his absences and rejoicing whenever he reappeared.

In the spring of 1776, the Rellyites seized upon what looked like an ideal opportunity to secure Murray's services permanently. Instead, they succeeded in bringing their differences with most members of the First Parish Church to a head. Samuel Chandler died. The congregation voted to ask the Reverend Eli Forbes to replace him. Twenty-four members of the church sent a delegation to Forbes, begging him to reject the offer, because they hoped to secure the position for John Murray instead. When their ploy failed, a number of them simply stopped attending the First Parish Church.

In February of 1777, the First Parish elders wrote to fifteen of the congregation's most egregious offenders, demanding that they explain their continued absence from church services. The dissenters refused to reply, claiming only that they were acting in "good conscience."[9] Not satisfied, the elders formally suspended eleven women and four men — among them Judith, her parents, and her uncle Epes — from the First Parish Church.[10] The following January, the suspended remnant formed an Independent Church of Christ and designated John Murray as their unsalaried minister. Sixty-one individuals, including Judith and John Stevens, signed the "Articles of Association" creating the first Universalist Church in America. John Murray's arrival in Gloucester had ended forever Judith's deference to the standards and beliefs of her community. Her ties to most members of that community were severed. She had become a rebel against the establishment her forefathers had helped to create.

For the first time in her life, Judith Stevens knew what it was like to be vilified for her personal views. She, whose reputation had always been irreproachable, was now subject to ridicule and slander from people who had once been her friends. The transition from respected insider to marginal outsider was not easy. Whenever she watched hecklers bombard Murray with hostile questions, her "cheeks were alternately flushed and pale," and she could "scarcely breathe."[11] Years later, after she married Murray and moved with him to Boston, she continued to be shunned by those who condemned Universalism. Even some of her own nieces and nephews visited her home with obvious reluctance, and they met John's overtures with a "kind of peevish frigidity," making "severe remarks upon his religious sentiments."[12] Still, the religious views that cost her so dearly in social esteem ultimately gave her the courage to disagree publicly with her detractors. By submitting to God's will as she understood it, she learned to reject the authority and ignore the criticism of mere mortals. She was determined, she said, in words that had a clear double meaning, to "call no *Man* Master."[13]

The members of John Murray's Independent Church of Christ began to experience the full weight of official intolerance in 1781, when they refused to pay taxes in support of the First Parish Church. The tax assessors used the same tactics their ancestors had employed against the Quakers over a hundred years earlier. No one was harmed physically and no one went to jail. Instead the town attacked the dissenters through their pocketbooks. When they withheld their taxes, the assessors seized their goods, taking a "silver tankard from one, spoons from a second, porringers from a third, and a variety of shop goods from a fourth," selling everything at public auction at an "inferior price."[14] In self-defense, some of Murray's followers took legal action, demanding a tax abatement from the First Parish Church.

The legal wrangling over the status of the Independent Church dragged on for years. Each side sued the other. The issue was decided, appealed, and decided again. One side grounded its case on the principle of toleration; the other insisted that it was simply trying to maintain order in a world rapidly careening out of control. In the end, the state legislature intervened, enacting a statute that gave Murray a respite from further legal assaults. In 1792 the Independent Church finally abandoned its scruples against church-state ties and obtained a charter of incorporation from the legislature.

Although the existing record is meager, it seems clear that Judith Stevens had begun to develop her views on women even before she met John Murray. At the same time, the ideology that underlay the American Revolution and the economic difficulties the Stevenses suffered between 1776 and 1786 surely helped shape her perspective. Her Universalist faith enabled her to structure and legitimize her stance on gender relations. Perhaps as important, in John Murray she found a mentor who was generally sympathetic to her views. He resented his own father, who had been severe and demanding by the standards of any age, and questioned his mother's deference to her husband's authority. "She believed," he wrote, "as most good women *then* believed, that husbands ought to have the direction, especially in concerns of such vast importance as to involve the future well-being of their children."[15] He thought he would have been better served had his mother listened to her own conscience and refused to acquiesce to her overbearing husband. In Judith Stevens, he found a woman eager to ignore traditional views of both gender and religion. Indeed, for her the two were inextricably connected. She challenged the dead hand of custom that in New England made Puritanism the law of the land and that throughout the Western world accorded women limited rights and opportunities.

Universalism gave religious legitimacy to Judith Sargent Murray's desire to oppose "the despotism of tradition" in every sphere.[16] Her rejection of arbitrary custom led her to support toleration that, not surprisingly, first found its voice in a demand for religious liberty. Only when the "shackles of superstition" were destroyed, she argued, and bigotry no longer existed in any form, could true religion thrive.[17] Judith saw the entire course of history as an object lesson in the virtues of toleration, even as she insisted that most religious debates revolved around arbitrary constructions of faith that emanated from humans, not from God. She admired Mary, Queen of Scots because she stood up to those, like that "severe reformer [John] Knox," who favored the *"horrid barbarity of devoting men to death, merely for an opinion."*[18] She saw Charles I of England as a victim of religious, not political persecution, and she praised Henry IV of France who granted toleration to Catholics rather than demand his subjects' adherence to his own Calvinist faith. She also condemned John Winthrop, first governor of the Bay Colony, for his religious bigotry, even as she expressed a cautious hope that in her own "enlightened age," the "broad base of Religious Liberty" would eventually triumph.[19]

Judith's religious convictions also gave her the ammunition to challenge the power of tradition as it shaped the role of women. She believed that society's view of the ability, character, and rights of women derived from habit and superstition, not nature or God. What humans made they could surely change. She was eager to attack the custom of wifely deference to a husband's opinions and despaired of women who, "like Milton's Eve, [seemed] rather to prefer receiving knowledge from her husband, than from a more elevated source."[20] It was dangerous, she thought, for a woman to abandon her religious scruples for anyone. What should a woman do, she asked rhetorically, if fate united her to an "unprincipled libertine?" When "can we be allowed to exercise our reason, if not in matters between God, and our own consciences?"[21]

Like all Christians, Judith believed that the spirit and the mind were separate from and superior to the body. The body was merely a shell, a temporary house for the soul. It was the eternal and genderless soul, which mobilized and controlled the body, that would ultimately prove its superiority on the day of judgment. For women the implications of such a bifurcated perspective were profound. If mind or spirit was the defining characteristic of all humanity, then in all important areas women were equal to men. Judith readily conceded that men had the advantage over women where physical strength was concerned, but this was an ephemeral animal quality. Indeed, she pointed out, lions and tigers were stronger than even the most powerful man, yet no one claimed that their strength endowed them with superiority.[22] If women were men's spiritual equals, then they could fairly claim equality. It was "lordly Man," not the Lord himself, who robbed "half the world of what great Nature gave."[23]

In theory, no Puritan would have argued with Judith's emphasis on the spiritual equality of men and women. Universalist doctrine, however, was also more egalitarian in practice than traditional Puritanism had ever been. Its very essence derived from a belief in human equality. It assumed that Christian and heathen, young and old, male and female were all related—and that all would be saved.[24] God's benevolence, Judith maintained, knew "no bounds," for all people, of whatever "sect, age, country or even sex" were part of "one grand, vast, and collected family of human nature."[25]

Like all Protestants, Universalists valued individual interpretation of the Bible. Because many of their leaders had little formal schooling, they were perhaps more willing to accept the consequences of their belief that everyone could understand scripture without the aid of a liberal education. Judith relished the opportunity to argue for the biblical justification of her belief in the spiritual equality of women. She was particularly eager to demolish the old Puritan view that Eve bore special responsibility for original sin; Adam was in fact weaker and more morally reprehensible than Eve. It took, she said, "the deepest laid Art of the most subtle fiend that inhabited the infernal regions," to convince Eve to eat the forbidden fruit. Moreover, Eve's motive for disobeying God—a thirst for knowledge—was surely laudable. Adam, however, had no such excuse. He willingly consigned the entire human race to everlasting torment because he was "overcome by the influence of softer passions, *merely by his attachment to a female—a fallen female.*" Had he resisted Eve's blandishments, he would have deserved credit for manly firmness. Instead, he deserved nothing but contempt.[26] (See Document 14.)

Judith Sargent Murray's views on women might well have remained private, had she not been encouraged by her co-religionists, especially John Murray, to begin writing for a public audience. She had always enjoyed writing but had assiduously avoided the spotlight. The letters and poems she wrote with such abandon were meant only for the quiet pleasure of friends and family. Murray, however, thought her efforts deserved a wider audience and proudly shared her work with friends as he traveled about America in search of religious converts. Although Judith professed to be embarrassed by his efforts on her behalf, she soon began to relish the praise. The more applause she received, the more she wanted, and she began to admit that if she could "make a choice among the various honours which the present state of existence [could] confer," she would select the "literary crown." Yet, she thought such a lofty goal fanciful and insisted that she had neither the courage nor the talent for the public domain.[27]

In 1782, Judith took her first, tentative step toward a career as a woman of letters knowing that many would find her efforts unseemly. More and more American women were beginning to write for public consumption, but even those who dared to share their thoughts with complete strangers hesitated to comment on controversial subjects. Most preferred to write poems praising the American war effort or extolling the joys of motherhood. Only her belief that she was serving God gave her the courage to publish for the first time, and she did so with serious misgivings.

Judith and her first husband had no children of their own, but they did have a hand in raising two young girls, distant relatives of John Stevens. The primary responsibility for their care fell to Judith, who took her duties seriously. Above all, she wanted the girls to understand the precepts of her own faith. To that end, she devised her Universalist catechism, a summary of religious doctrine designed to instruct neophytes in the rudiments of the faith, sometime before 1782. (See Document 2.) She showed the catechism to her mother, who suggested that she forward a copy to the Universalist minister Noah Parker of Portsmouth, New Hampshire. To Judith's surprise, Parker urged her to publish it.

At first, she refused. She had more than enough excuses at hand. She owed all her ideas to John Murray; there was nothing in the catechism she could claim as her own. When she showed her draft to less sympathetic critics, they pointed out its many errors, and she regretted more than ever the deficiencies in her education.[28] Her Universalist friends persisted. If she failed to use her talent to further true religion, they argued, she was thwarting God's designs. When John Murray added his voice to the chorus, she capitulated, insisting only that the catechism be published anonymously. As she prepared the manuscript for publication, she remained astounded at her own audacity.[29] (See Document 3.)

A cursory perusal of the catechism's preface reveals something of her ambivalence. It reveals, as well, that her reluctance to publish derived to a large extent from her fear that as a woman entering the public domain she was going well beyond her proper sphere. She worried not only about her own reputation but also about the damage to Universalism if critics seized on her writing as evidence that the sect encouraged disorderly women to behave inappropriately. Nevertheless, although she feared that her detractors would accuse her of "Arrogance, heresy, Licentiousness, etc. etc.," she published the catechism and defended her actions on three grounds: as a mother, as a woman, and as a Christian.[30]

Judith claimed that she was fulfilling her motherly duty to her two young charges, insisted that women were equal to men in spiritual matters, and argued that as a Christian she was obliged to utilize her God-given ability in the service of true religion. She also maintained that she sought to avoid all theological controversy, but her protests strike a false note. It is fair to argue that she was not as reluctant to confront those who criticized her religion or to claim credit for her efforts as she professed to be. Although she published the catechism anonymously, she confessed in the first sentence of the preface that she was a woman. At least in Universalist circles, this admission identified her as the author. In addition, if she were truly afraid that critics would seize upon this issue, why did she announce that she was a woman at all? Why did she feel compelled to use her first publication to defend women's right to write for public consumption?

All we know is that Judith Sargent Murray clearly linked religion and gender in her own mind by the time she began writing the catechism. Talented, ambitious, and eager for recognition, at least at a subliminal level, she realized that her religious obligations provided an opening to the public domain. She longed for the distinction her talent as a writer might earn, yet she shrank from exposing herself to the criticism of a censorious world.

Once she had set her mind to the task, Judith proceeded with an energy and a determination that would characterize her literary endeavors for years to come. While she continued to apologize for her audacity, she clearly enjoyed the praise the catechism won. Only Winthrop Sargent's disapproval of what he saw as his sister's unseemly behavior marred her pleasure. Having ventured into the world of public discourse, she discovered that there was no turning back. The delights of earthly fame led her on. If religion had launched her as a writer, the promise of honor, glory, and eventually, profit gave her the incentive to continue.

NOTES

[1]Judith Sargent Murray, *The Gleaner: A Miscellaneous Production in Three Volumes* (Boston: L. Thomas and E. T. Andrews, 1798), 1:182.

[2]"An Appeal to the Impartial Public by the Society of the Christian Independents Congregation in Glocester," n.d., in Richard Eddy, *Universalism in Gloucester, Massachusetts* (Gloucester: Procter, 1992), 142.

[3]"An Answer to a Piece Entitled 'An Appeal to the Impartial Public by the Society of Christian Independents Congregating in Glocester,' " October 1785, in Eddy, *Universalism in Gloucester,* 171, 174, 175.

[4]Susan Juster, *Disorderly Women: Sexual Politics and Evangelicalism in Revolutionary New England* (Ithaca: Cornell University Press, 1994).

[5]Quoted in P. Elton Carpenter, "John Murray, and the Rise of Liberal Religion" (master's thesis, Columbia University, 1937).

[6]Judith Stevens to John Murray, 14 Nov. 1774, Judith Sargent Murray, Letterbook, 1:13, Mississippi Archives, Jackson, Miss.

[7]Judith Stevens to Aunt E._____S_____, 10 Apr. 1778, ibid., 107.

[8]Judith Stevens to John Murray, 14 Nov. 1774, Letterbook, 1:13.

[9]Eddy, *Universalism in Gloucester,* 112.

[10]It is not clear why John Stevens's name is not on the list. He did, however, join the Universalists when they formed their own church.

[11]Judith Stevens to John Murray, 8 Aug. 1778, 17 Sept. 1778, Letterbook, 1:140, 156.

[12]Judith Sargent Murray to her Sister S_____, 26 Feb. 1805, Letterbook, 10:988.

[13]Judith Stevens to John Murray, 25 June 1785, Letterbook, 2:344.

[14]Judith Stevens to Mrs. Gardiner, 4 Apr. 1788, Letterbook, 3:290.

[15]John Murray, *The Life of Rev. John Murray with a Continuation by Mrs. Judith Sargent Murray,* ed. Rev. G. L. Demarest (Boston: Universalist Publishing House, 1869), 16.

[16]Murray, *The Gleaner,* 1:182.

[17]Ibid., 44; Murray, "On an insult offer'd to our friend," Judith Sargent Murray, Poetry, 1:248, Mississippi Archives, Jackson, Miss.

[18]Murray, *The Gleaner,* 2:143.

[19]Judith Stevens to Mr. Right, a Native of Copenhagen, 1 July 1785, Letterbook, 2:349, 350.

[20]Judith Stevens to John Murray, 12 Aug. 1779, Letterbook, 1:199.

[21]Judith Stevens to Mrs. Barrell of Old York, 31 Jan. 1784, Letterbook 2:193.

[22]Judith Stevens to Mr. Parker, 16 Dec. 1780, Letterbook, 1:305.

[23]Judith Sargent Murray, "Dissimilarity of Minds," Poetry, 1:305.

[24]Judith Sargent Murray, "Christmas Day," Judith Sargent Murray, Repository, 145–153, Mississippi Archives, Jackson, Miss.

[25]Murray, *The Gleaner,* 1:159.

[26]Judith Stevens to Mrs. Goldthwait, 6 June 1777, Letterbook, 1:63; Judith Stevens to Mr. Parker, 16 Dec. 1780, ibid., 305.

[27]Judith Stevens to Mr. Sewell, 15 July 1781, ibid., 339, 340.

[28] Judith Stevens to Winthrop Sargent, 12 Oct. 1782, Letterbook, 2:71; Judith Stevens to Mr. Parker, 31 Jan. 1782, ibid., 1.

[29] Judith Stevens to Mr. Parker, 18 Apr. 1782, ibid., 4; Judith Stevens to John Murray, 28 June 17[82], ibid., 36.

[30] Judith Sargent Murray, *Some deductions from the system promulgated in the page of divine revelation, ranged in the order and form of a catechism, intended as an assistant to the Christian parent or teacher* . . . (Norwich, Conn.: John Trumbull, 1782), iii.

3

Earning the "Laurel Wreath":
The Revolutionary Years

In later years, as a published poet and essayist who had seen two of her plays performed at Boston's Federal Street Theater, Judith Sargent Murray credited the American War of Independence for forcing her to question the legal, political, and economic limitations American women endured throughout the eighteenth century.[1] She may have given the Revolution too much credit: The sense of injustice she experienced as a girl along with her religious beliefs provided a solid emotional and intellectual foundation for her views. Yet it was within the context of America's revolutionary tradition that she challenged the gender-based strictures that defined her world.

Women have always been affected by war. Occasionally they have seized the opportunities created by wartime exigencies to enter the public sphere, calling into question, however fleetingly, traditional stereotypes about their abilities and their role. Just as often, however, war has reinforced gender differences, reminding men and women alike that the battlefield is a male preserve and that heroic self-sacrifice and patriotism are the province of men. The American Revolution simultaneously undermined and realigned, reinforced and challenged traditional gender definitions. If it told women that they could not enter certain spaces or have certain experiences, it provided them with the occasion to criticize male behavior from their own perspective. While it did not encourage them to believe in their own right—or their own ability—to enter the public sphere, it did give women like Judith Sargent Murray a sense of their own worth. Moreover, war taught many women to privilege their own gendered values over the "republican virtue" that so dominated eighteenth-century public discourse.

Women's experience in the American Revolution demonstrates yet again the two-faced nature of war. On the one hand, this conflict was fought and won primarily by men at a time when women's political role was marginal at best. No woman sat in the Pennsylvania State House in Philadelphia as the Second Continental Congress declared the independence of the American colonies. Slogans such as "no taxation without representation" meant little to those who could not vote in provincial elections, in town meetings, or even in their own churches. On the other hand, a war fought in the name of equality and fundamental human rights, a war that challenged ascribed status and demanded the right to "life, liberty and the pursuit of happiness" for all people, should have had some relevance to women.

In fact, the founders seldom acknowledged the full implications of their own rhetoric. While they talked of equality, slaveholders kept black men and women in bondage. Although they praised the virtue of independence, most American men continued to view even propertied women as dependent. They had rebelled against a king and rejected governmental patriarchy in favor of republican principles, yet they took for granted a family structure based on deference. The Revolution may have been a turning point in the nation's history, but in the lives of most women its promise remained unrealized.

Some historians have contended that despite its limitations, the Revolutionary War was a consciousness-raising event for many women. The egalitarian rhetoric of revolutionary leaders, the argument goes, led women to question their subservient status. Their wartime experiences enhanced their self-esteem. When their husbands marched off to battle, they stayed behind to struggle with day-to-day problems and make ends meet. As they learned how to survive on their own, they grew more confident in their abilities and took pride in the sacrifices they made for their country. As a result, some of them argued that their political opinions should be taken seriously. They began, as one young enthusiast put it, to feel "Nationly," to believe that, as women, they were an important— if still a subordinate—part of the body politic.[2]

Whether or not the American Revolution was a liberating experience for some women, it remains true that women won few political, legal, or economic victories as a result of the war. The very fact that men did the bulk of the fighting while women remained at home, reconfirmed the notion that helpless women needed men to protect them. Moreover, not all women responded to wartime challenges with equal success. If some gained self-respect by managing their own affairs, others floundered and ended up living off the charity of others. Even the redoubtable Abigail Adams, who became a successful merchant and "farmeress" while her husband tended to public affairs, did not relish her newfound independence. Many women were like Adams, viewing themselves as "deputy husbands" who were merely standing in for their menfolk until life returned to its natural rhythms. They resented their husbands' absences and their extra duties. For them, war was a burden, not an opportunity.[3]

In many ways, the American Revolution did not dramatically alter Judith Stevens's life. Her husband joined the Gloucester Committee of Safety, but he did not enlist in the Continental Army. If he was seldom home, it was because the demands of trade required prolonged absences. For Judith, the daughter as well as the wife of a merchant, this was the normal state of affairs, and she was no more lonely or worried about her husband during the war than she had been before hostilities commenced.

Like most patriotic women, she probably did her part to support colonial boycotts of British goods. Indeed, the war transformed the meaning of many traditional domestic tasks: When Judith sewed homespun clothes or refused to buy English imports, she acted politically. Still, her support for independence was dignified and circumspect. She did not participate in the spinning bees that made some women feel so "Nationly." Nor did she join those women who accompanied their husbands to the front, cooking, cleaning, nursing, and even taking up arms themselves. It is quite impossible to imagine the proper Mrs. Stevens joining a crowd to protest coffee prices or to attack a shopkeeper for violating strictures against trade with the British. Some women published patriotic poems and essays, but Judith expressed her views to friends and relatives, in particular, her brother Winthrop.

Nevertheless, Judith Stevens did not escape the vicissitudes of war. Because the battle for independence was waged on American soil, homefront and battlefield were sometimes perilously close. As women went about their daily tasks, trying to maintain a normal routine in abnormal times, they were seldom free of worry. New England coastal areas were vulnerable to enemy attack, and anyone who lived in the region could tell lurid tales of women who fell victim to British inhumanity. Judith was not alone in her belief that the British intended to "lay [American] Sea Ports to ashes," and on more than one occasion she and her mother fled Gloucester for the relative safety of the interior.[4] At war's end, Judith witnessed some of the consequences of British hostilities for herself. In Groton, Connecticut, sixty-two women had been made widows in a single hour of fighting. In New Haven, the British had destroyed even the featherbeds—some 850 in all—in what she described as gratuitous maliciousness on the part of an immoral enemy.[5]

When she was not worrying about imminent danger, Judith faced the financial hardships that accompanied war. She complained of rising costs and scarce supplies, and spent many a "wearisome day" going from shop to shop in the "vain hope" of finding the barest necessities. What she found was often outrageously priced, due, as she sardonically commented, to "the blessed effects of our paper currency."[6] Women might not risk their lives on the battlefield, but they did have their own burdens to bear. In ancient Rome, she pointed out, the Senate honored the economic sacrifices women made for their country. If frugality and simplicity were hallmarks of republican virtue, then American women, acting as prudent housewives, were surely doing their part to preserve the moral foundations of the fledgling nation. Yet in America, she said, women seldom won public praise for their private sacrifices.[7]

Judith's economic position was made even more bleak by her husband's precarious finances. Merchant activity was always risky, but in time of war, the perils of commerce were magnified. Disruptions in trade often led to a disastrous combination of depression and inflation. Although John Stevens enjoyed some success during the war, Judith had good reason to blame his eventual bankruptcy on the Revolution.

Judith also despised the constant reminders of war that disturbed her once tranquil village. The "frequent alarms, drums beating, bells ringing," she said, the sight of men bearing "instruments of death," utterly transformed her little town.[8] Above all, she worried about her brother Winthrop, an officer in the Continental Army. Her dreams were haunted by images of his death, and when occasional rumors filtered into Gloucester indicating that her nightmares had become a reality, she endured days of agony before learning that the "premature intelligence" of her brother's death was false. Every account of a battleground "purple with human gore" convinced her anew that he was among the war's casualties.[9]

When she was not worried about his welfare, she missed Winthrop's companionship. One of his nephews, she said, always spoke of his uncle as though he was "perhaps on the moon."[10] It was almost impossible to communicate with Winthrop in any regular fashion. Bad weather, bad luck, or wartime dislocation meant that her letters were often delayed or lost, and whenever her brother failed to answer immediately, she always assumed the worst.

Judith Stevens, like most of her family, was a patriot. Her parents and husband favored independence. Winthrop was a Continental officer. John Murray, an Englishman, also did his part, serving as chaplain for the First Rhode Island Regiment until ill health forced him to resign. Yet although Judith sympathized with the American war effort and prayed for a patriot victory, she was not anti-British. Indeed, she never embraced the Revolution with unqualified enthusiasm and often wished that the "unnatural contest" could have been avoided.[11] As the wife of a merchant, as a Universalist, as a woman, and as an aspiring writer, she expressed her doubts about the conduct of a war that mocked her sense of morality and justice, and destroyed her chance for fame.

Many New England merchant families watched the coming of independence with mixed emotions. They resented British attempts to tax the colonies and feared the loss of liberty threatened by Parliament's encroachments, but they had been raised to believe that England meant "everything great, everything good."[12] Their commercial ties to the mother country also gave them pause, and while most threw their support to the Revolution they regretted its necessity.

Judith Stevens tended to judge abstract political issues in terms of their effect on her family and friends. When she criticized the war effort to Winthrop, reminding him that "the contending parties are the offspring of some happy brother and sister like you or me" and bemoaning the tears of parents who wept to see their children destroying one another, she was not indulging in sentimental rhetoric.[13] Her uncle Epes Sargent, one of the staunchest supporters of the Gloucester Universalists, was a loyalist, and she had watched with sadness as he and his family were driven from town by the "gothic Mob," forced "to wander in a state of exile, far from their peaceful home." She regarded the American Revolution as a *"Civil War"* that pitted brother against brother, and she was all too familiar with the pain of such divisions.[14] (See Document 4.)

Judith's religious convictions also caused her to question the morality of war. Universalists placed special emphasis on the spiritual equality and interconnectedness of all humans. If God made no judgments based on race or gender, neither did he evaluate people in terms of their national origins. Judith always maintained that as a *"Citizen of the World,"* she was related to "every son and daughter of *humanity."* She found it unthinkable to view any country—even England—with a prejudiced eye. Then too, she argued, individuals could not claim credit or accept blame for the virtues and vices of their own country.[15] Besides, she said, no doubt thinking of John Murray, she could not help but revere "the many worthies who drew their first breath upon the chalky shores of Albion."[16]

Judith's fondness for her uncle and her Universalist convictions inspired her sympathy for those who remained loyal to England. Her own experience as a religious dissenter and the value she placed on religious tolerance led her to demand tolerance for political dissenters as well. "Mere sentiment," she argued, "mere opinion, these ought never to be subjected to human jurisdiction, for the free born soul will ever assert its right."[17]

The abortive effort of a rump session of the Committee of Safety to banish John Murray from Gloucester in 1777 confirmed Judith's commitment to tolerance. Although Murray had served the American forces as a chaplain, the Committee pretended to believe that he was a British spy whose presence endangered American liberty. His friendship with known loyalists, men like Epes Sargent, bolstered their case. But no one seriously believed that Murray's politics were at issue. It was, rather, his "very erroneous principles," which his enemies believed threatened the "morals of the people," that led the Committee to demand his ouster. Murray ignored the Committee's order, insisting that he had broken no law and would be bound by no earthly authority. God alone, he said, could remove him from Gloucester, Massachusetts.[18]

Judith admired John Murray's defense of civil and religious liberty and in her own small way imitated his example. She never passed up an opportunity to defend the rights of American loyalists, even to total strangers. In the spring of 1775, as she conversed with a man she met on a trip to Boston who questioned Epes Sargent's patriotism, she explained demurely, "I do not constitute myself a judge of the contest so unhappily subsisting." As for "the terms *Whig* and Tory," she claimed, "I am free to own I do not understand them." Yet she felt perfectly qualified to assess her uncle's character and insisted that his virtues were unsurpassed by anyone in Gloucester. While she did not deny her uncle's English sympathies, she believed he should be judged by more important criteria.[19]

Judith was even more outspoken after she visited the former residence of Sir William Pepperell, who had led the colonial forces against the French at Louisburg in 1745 during King George's War. He had once been hailed as an American hero, but his descendants were not so lucky. Because they opposed independence, they were stripped of their property and forced to return to England in disgrace. They were punished, Judith insisted, "merely for dissenting," not because they had actively undermined the American war effort.[20] How, she asked, "doth it square with rectitude to wrest property from individuals, merely because their ideas do not exactly coincide with our own?"[21]

Judith Stevens's often tepid support of the American Revolution, and her staunch defense of civil liberties were an outgrowth of her family connections, her religious views, and her admiration for John Murray. It was as a woman and an aspiring writer, however, that she made her most trenchant criticism of the war effort, questioning the hierarchical construction of gender relations in a nation founded on egalitarian principles.

Judith's interest in the war was prompted by her concern for the moral welfare of her brother Winthrop. She had supported his decision to join George Washington's army and believed that his wartime experience would refine his judgment and supplement his formal education with an appreciation of the ways of the world. The war, she assured him, will "ripen your knowledge beyond your years."[22] His valor on the battlefield would earn him not only "pecuniary advantages" but the admiration of all Americans.[23] He would wear the "laurel wreath," and fame and fortune would be the reward for his sacrifices.[24] War called on men to risk their lives for their country, but it offered them boundless opportunities in return. Judith sincerely hoped her brother's head would be crowned with the laurel wreath. Nevertheless, her letters to him reveal an undercurrent of envy and resentment that grew stronger as the war progressed. (See Document 5.) She, too, hungered for fame and adulation, but as long as the war continued, her chances of achieving recognition of any kind were minimal.

The patriot movement was grounded at least in part in classical republicanism, which assumed that a nation's welfare was determined by the moral character of its inhabitants, even as it described virtue in traditionally masculine terms. For republicans, "manly" attributes—physical strength, bravery, independent and uncorrupted patriotism, and the willingness to sacrifice one's life for the good of the country—defined virtue and guaranteed its practioners the right to citizenship. Cowardice, idleness, luxury, and dependence, the polar opposites of republican virtue, were associated with women. In a world that defined virtue in public, active, and militaristic terms, and where the surest route to honor was through war, women could not hope to be considered political—or even significant—beings.

Americans had placed a high value on republican virtue prior to 1776. The war simply underscored its significance. Whenever Judith Stevens compared her own situation to that of her brother, she was embarrassed and resentful, wondering how he could be interested in anything that emanated from her "female pen." (See Document 5.) He was "actively engaged in struggling for the sacred rights of Mankind,"[25] while she lived in a "confined situation."[26] We are, she wrote, "encircled by one Eternal sameness. I can only dwell on what you already know, and how fatiguing the dull repetition."[27] Winthrop might think of the little village of Gloucester with nostalgia, remembering it as a veritable Eden. His sister knew better. "The manners of the inhabitants," she complained, "render the picture of one day, the delineation of a Century. Revolutions are hardly to be expected among us, we take our sense of public matters from our superiors and we can scarcely boast an idea of our own."[28]

When Judith tried to transcend the domestic sphere to discuss polit-

ical or military matters, even John Murray greeted her efforts with
paternalistic amusement, joking that she was in danger of becoming a
"female politician," an unnatural species he viewed as an "amphibious
animal."[29] Judith may have tried to characterize such comments as
good-natured jibes, but they obviously rankled. She hoped that her
brother, at least, would not yield to prevailing prejudice and assume that
because she cared about her country she had traveled "out of her
sphere." For, she asked, "are not our sex interested as wives, as Mothers and as friends" in the fate of the men they have sent into battle? Do
they not rise and fall, she wondered, with those to whom they are
bound? Did women not have the right, even the duty, to inquire about
America's prospects?[30] But that was surely the point: In Judith Stevens's
world, women's "interest" in public affairs was determined by their connections with independent men as "wives, as Mothers and as friends,"
not as citizens.

Judith harbored no subliminal wish to become a soldier, although in
essays she wrote after the war, she pointed out that women were physically and emotionally capable of donning a suit of armor and slaying the
enemy in a righteous cause. "Courage is by no means *exclusively* a masculine virtue," she insisted, citing countless examples of women throughout history who had exhibited "heroic firmness" on the battlefield.[31] Still,
she had no desire to follow her brother to the front. Her role as she saw
it was not to enter the fray but to monitor those who fought in her country's name and advocate changes in the nature of warfare itself. She
wanted soldiers and officers to adhere to the moral values that women
held dear. A self-proclaimed critic of the war, she turned her "inferior"
womanly status into an asset. As a disinterested outsider, a spectator who
had no stake in defending her country's conduct, she felt that she was in
a better position than her brother to perceive the immorality that per-
meated military culture.

Judith insisted that soldiers should adhere to the highest principles,
and she despised—perhaps she did not understand—the compromises
that public men, especially military men, made in politics and war. She
demanded a level of purity from soldiers and statesmen that most men,
including her brother, saw as impossible to attain and irrelevant to their
purposes. As the hostilities between England and America dragged on,
Judith's letters, essays, and poetry became preoccupied with images of
death and deplored the "rude effects of savage war."[32] When she thought
of the laurel wreath her brother might wear she envisioned it "steep'd in
blood." She warned Americans not to "gloat upon the carnag'd brave,"
for, she asked,

What can trophied wreaths supply
To drown the desolating cry
That o-er the enpurple'd fields afar
Proclaims the dread destructive pow'r of war?[33]

War involved not glory but the "slaughter" of "millions," millions, more-over, who shared "kindred blood, from kindred veins."[34] Nor were sol-diers the only casualties. "Defenceless" civilians could be destroyed by the savagery of the battlefield. And when that happened,

With wild distraction shrieking females fly,
And little suff'rers join the gen'ral cry.[35]

Every American victory created "desolate widows," "destitute orphans," "bereaved friends" and "aged Parent[s]" who would mourn the loss of their loved ones forever.[36]

Much worse, and more threatening to American virtue, was the way war coarsened and corrupted the spirit of every soldier. Camp life was rough and unseemly. Soldiers and officers alike cursed, drank, and failed to keep the sabbath. Judith was outraged when she heard about an Amer-ican victory off the coast of Massachusetts in 1779. Word had it that the victorious Americans had sailed their vessel under false colors, luring the "brave English sailors" into a deadly trap. She was repelled by the ploy and mourned her country's failure to measure up to the example of a more heroic age. "I sigh," she said, "for the superior heroism of those ancient times." Now "deceit is deemed a virtue" and he "who can most success-fully dissemble is the most renowned."[37]

If soldiers suffered no moral qualms in combat with the enemy, they were equally cavalier in their treatment of one another. Her own brother was a demanding officer who insisted upon strict obedience to his orders and swiftly punished those who failed to comply. Judith sympathized "with those unhappy beings doomed to suffer the severity of military dis-cipline." How, she wondered, could those who claimed to fight for liberty ask their own men to surrender one of the "dearest prerogatives of nature?" Admitting that by commenting on military matters she had "wandered from [her] proper sphere," she was nonetheless convinced that anyone, even a woman, could see that harsh punishments often transgressed the bounds of justice.[38]

The more she saw of war, the more she recognized the worth of tra-ditionally defined feminine values. "Our sex," she wrote with pride, "is form'd for tenderness and love."[39] With effort, she thought, men, even sol-diers, could emulate their female counterparts. If women could not join men in war, they could feminize the war effort. She refused to believe that "tender passions" were incompatible with military endeavors.[40] (See Document 5.) Surely, she argued, compassion "is not altogether confined to the female bosom."[41]

In time, Judith began to doubt even her own brother's ability to resist the corrupting influences of war and urged him to quit the "ensanguined paths of death" altogether.[42] Was it not possible, she asked, for the true patriot to "hasten to that retirement which awaits him in the bosom of his friends? to books and all those contemplations which may free him for better days and more effectual exertions?" Why, she wondered, was the willingness to sacrifice one's life for one's nation deemed the highest mark of patriotism when it was possible to serve in so many other, perhaps more noble, ways?[43]

Judith drew a sharp contrast between war and peace, the battlefield and domestic pleasures. The soldier hoped for the chance to dazzle the world with his battlefield exploits. The wife, the parent, the sister, the child longed only for his safe return. Society mocked those who stayed at home because of their "womanish fear," but she thought it was the soldier whose values were misplaced.[44] If women could not—and should not—engage in military activities, this might be all to the good. They, not their soldier husbands, kept God's moral order alive.

In many ways, Judith's condemnation of war echoed the views of all women troubled by wartime immorality. But when most women anticipated the end of hostilities, they hoped simply to turn back the clock, resume their old habits, and forget the war. As a writer, however, Judith Stevens wanted more than a return to the life she had enjoyed before the Revolution. If her wartime experience magnified the arbitrary limits she faced as a woman, only in peacetime, she was convinced, would she find a socially acceptable way to gain the recognition she desired.

"From conspicuous rewards of merit," Judith observed, "the female world, seem injudiciously excluded. To man the road of preferment is thrown open—glory crowns the military hero." Women, on the other hand, enjoyed nothing but "*secondary* or *reflected* fame." She longed for a society that rewarded the virtue "natal in the female bosom,"[45] but she knew that women's special attributes would not receive recognition while the war continued. As long as her compatriots valued republican virtue, men's military exploits would garner admiration while women's more private and mundane sacrifices would go unnoticed.[46] War served as a reminder that women were weak and defenseless, that they depended on men to protect them. And if Americans believed that women contributed nothing important to the war effort, no one would argue that they deserved the political or economic fruits of victory.

Judith knew that her own chance would come only when the war ended. Then the line separating male and female spheres would become more permeable and less invidious. Softer values would prevail for men as well as for women. Order would return, and reason, not brute force, would rule. The arts and sciences would be celebrated. Poetry would take its rightful place beside military exploits in defining the character of the new nation. Historians would celebrate American victories so that future generations would appreciate and imitate the sacrifices made in their name. America would become venerated, not for its military might but for the goodness of its citizens and the superiority of its literature. "Writers of every Class," wrote Judith, and presumably of both sexes, would "wield the pen." "Imagination" would "mark the historic page." Talented women, too, would earn their laurels.[47]

NOTES

[1]Mary Beth Norton, *Liberty's Daughters: The Revolutionary Experience of American Women, 1750–1800* (Boston: Little, Brown, 1980), 238.

[2]Quoted in ibid., 169.

[3]Edith Gelles, *Portia: The World of Abigail Adams* (Bloomington: University of Indiana Press, 1992), chapt. 3. For a characterization of the notion of "deputy husband," see Laurel Thatcher Ulrich, *Good Wives: Image and Reality in the Lives of Women in Northern New England, 1650–1750* (New York: Knopf, 1980), 36–50.

[4]Judith Stevens to Judith Sargent, [?] Jan. 1776, Judith Sargent Murray, Letterbook, 1:28, Mississippi Archives, Jackson, Miss.

[5]Judith Stevens to Winthrop Sargent, 23 June 1786, Letterbook, 3:98; Judith Stevens to Judith Sargent, 5 July 1786, ibid., 115.

[6]Judith Stevens to Winthrop Sargent, 8 Sept. 1779, Letterbook, 1:232; Judith Stevens to John Murray, Summer 1777, ibid., 67, 69.

[7]Judith Sargent Murray, *The Gleaner: A Miscellaneous Production in Three Volumes* (Boston: L. Thomas and E. T. Andrews, 1798), 2:119.

[8]Judith Stevens to Judith Sargent, [?] Nov. 1775, Letterbook, 1:26; Judith Stevens to John Murray, 17 June 1775, ibid., 19.

[9]Judith Stevens to Winthrop Sargent, [?] Nov. 1777, ibid., 78.

[10]Judith Stevens to Winthrop Sargent, 3 July 1778, ibid., 123.

[11]Judith Stevens to John Murray, 1 Oct. 1775, ibid., 25.

[12]Judith Stevens to Winthrop Sargent, 28 Oct. 1781, ibid., 358.

[13]Ibid.

[14]Judith Sargent Murray, "Reflections during a fine Morning, upon existing circumstances," 1775, Judith Sargent Murray, Repository, 18, 20, Mississippi Archives, Jackson, Miss.

[15]Judith Stevens to Miss Pierce of Plymouth, England, 16 July 1788, Letterbook, 3:333; Judith Stevens to Mrs. Pilgrim of Old England, 31 Oct. 1784, ibid., 291.

[16]Judith Stevens to John Murray, 11 Aug. 1778, Letterbook, 1:143.

[17]Murray, "Reflections during a fine Morning, upon existing circumstances," 1775, Repository, 20.

[18]John Murray, *The Life of Rev. John Murray, Preacher of Universal Salvation, Written by Himself, With a Continuation, by Mrs. Judith Sargent Murray,* ed. Rev. G. L. Demarest (Boston: Universalist Publishing House, 1869), 322–324.

[19]Judith Stevens to John Murray, 17 June 1775, Letterbook, 1:16–18.

[20]Judith Stevens to John Murray, 27 Aug. 1779, ibid., 222. Judith's father had accompanied Pepperell on the Louisburg expedition, a fact that no doubt increased her interest in the fate of his family.

[21]Judith Sargent Murray, Journal, 18 Oct. 1786, Letterbook, 3:169.

[22]Judith Stevens to Winthrop Sargent, 3 July 1778, Letterbook, 1:122.

[23]Judith Stevens to Winthrop Sargent, 5 Apr. 1779, ibid., 174.

[24]Judith Sargent Murray, "Line addressed to my mother upon the death of the last of her brothers who died abroad attended only by a nephew," 2 Nov. 1782, Judith Sargent Murray, Poetry, 1:45, Mississippi Archives, Jackson, Miss.; "News from my Brother," ibid., 247.

[25]Judith Stevens to Winthrop Sargent, 25 Feb. 178, Letterbook, 1:88.

[26]Judith Stevens to Winthrop Sargent, 1 Dec. 1779, ibid., 262.

[27]Judith Stevens to Winthrop Sargent, 5 Apr. 1780, ibid., 271.

[28]Judith Stevens to Winthrop Sargent, 1 Dec. 1779, ibid., 262.

[29]Judith Stevens to John Murray, 31 Aug. 1778, ibid., 151.

[30]Judith Stevens to Winthrop Sargent, 25 Feb. 1778, ibid., 88.

[31]Murray, *The Gleaner* 3:192, 193.

[32]Judith Stevens to John Murray, 30 Nov. 1780, Letterbook, 1:298.

[33]Murray, "Vanity," Poetry, 4:43.

[34]Murray, "On the ill-fated Penobscot Expedition," Letterbook, 1:192.

[35]Murray, "Upon the approach of the Chatham Man of war to our harbour's mouth — May 4, 1782," Letterbook, 3:155.

[36]Judith Stevens to John Murray, 16 Sept. 1779, Letterbook, 1:234.

[37]Judith Stevens to John Murray, 16 Sept. 1779, ibid., 234, 235.

[38]Judith Stevens to Winthrop Sargent, 20 July 1781, 25 August 1781, ibid., 342, 346.

[39]Murray, "Sentiments," Poetry 1:136; Murray, "A Party of Pleasure," Repository, 361.

[40]Judith Stevens to Winthrop Sargent, 25 Feb. 1778, Letterbook, 1:90.

[41]Judith Stevens to Winthrop Sargent, 25 Aug. 1781, ibid., 346.

[42]Judith Stevens to Winthrop Sargent, 1 Sept. 1781, ibid., 347.

[43]Judith Stevens to Winthrop Sargent, 25 Aug. 1781, ibid., 346; Judith Sargent Murray to Winthrop and Judith Sargent, 12 Oct. 1788, Letterbook, 3:350.

[44]Judith Stevens to Winthrop Sargent, 25 Aug. 1781, ibid., 346.

[45]Murray, *The Gleaner,* 2:217.

[46]Murray, *The Gleaner,* 3:88.

[47]Murray, "On reading the institution of the Cincinnati, January 28, 1784," Poetry, 3:182.

4

The Fruits of Independence:
Women and Property in the Republic

If money is power, then eighteenth-century women were powerless creatures indeed. When patriotic men entered the war with England to defend their own property, they expressed no interest in expanding property rights for women. As a result, although women made a few haphazard gains during this period, most continued to exist in a state of "enforced dependence."[1] In a society that linked independence with citizenship, women's subordinate economic position had serious political ramifications.

Eighteenth-century women — especially married women — had little control over their own economic status. Men drew up wills and disposed of property. Some husbands and fathers were generous; others were not. In either case, women were the passive victims or beneficiaries of decisions made by men. If they suffered as a result of their dependence, they did not see their individual grievances as grounds for protest. Even fewer discussed their views in public. Instead, they endured their lot in silence or complained privately to friends. They seldom generalized from their own experience or demanded changes in the rules, although their society claimed to value equality, independence, and self-reliance.

In writing publicly about her own life in order to discuss the general economic plight of women in American society, Judith Sargent Murray was rare. She transcended her particular circumstances, regarded her problems as women's problems, and employed Revolutionary rhetoric to claim the fruits of independence for her sex. Her own chronic financial difficulties reaffirmed how important it was for women to be self-sufficient.

Nothing in her formative years prepared Judith Sargent Murray for a life of material privation. She grew up in a family that took its wealth for granted, and as long as she remained in her father's house her needs and most of her desires were satisfied. When she married John Stevens in 1769, she assumed that she would continue to be comfortable. Stevens had enough money, she said, "that in almost any business, supposing but moderate success, would have secured a competency."[2] Admittedly, John's father had died insolvent, and just a year before their marriage Stevens sold most of his father's estate to satisfy creditors. But Judith knew too much about the uncertainties of trade to be unduly concerned. John Stevens came from a family whose status equaled that of her own. Intelligent, charming, and at age twenty-eight, ten years older than his young bride, he presented a picture of reassuring solidity. Unfortunately, bad luck, wartime exigencies, and poor judgment combined to destroy his prospects.

Even before the winter of 1786, Judith Stevens had been uneasy about her husband's affairs, but although she begged him to confide in her, he resolutely refused to divulge the extent of his difficulties. "The fear of breaking my peace," she explained, "hath induced Mr. Stevens to draw a veil before my eyes."[3] In January, while Gloucester was celebrating the New Year, she learned just how deeply in debt her husband was. Her father informed her that Stevens's creditors had gone to court to demand payment of his arrears. If he failed to comply, he would go to prison. In the meantime, he could not leave town.

John Stevens had experienced financial difficulties before the American Revolution, and only his father-in-law's generosity had enabled him to stave off bankruptcy. During the war, he turned to privateering, a lucrative but highly risky operation, using his ships to attack enemy vessels and dividing the captured prizes with his crew. At first he prospered, doing so well that he was able to build a three-story "mansion" overlooking the harbor. It was, said one admiring visitor, the "largest and most elegant house in town."[4]

Although she enjoyed their prosperity, Judith disapproved of privateering. She believed that her husband's profits were tainted, since they often came at the expense of honest and industrious citizens. Still, she could hardly argue with success. And as she explained to a friend, "Mr. Stevens hath never allowed me to interfere in his business."[5] Nor was he obliged to do so under the doctrine of "coverture," which denied married women any independent legal or economic status. Once they were married, husband and wife were legally one person. "He" always spoke for "them" and, at least theoretically, represented "their" best interests. Not only did a woman lose her own name when she married, she also lost the right to sue or be sued, to make contracts without her husband's permission, to devise wills, and to own property. Any personal property she brought to her marriage became his. She was, in the parlance of the day, a "femme covert," which meant that legally she did not exist.

This was especially the case in Puritan New England, where the legal system was designed to maintain the strength of loving families. Lawmakers argued that any practice that allowed a wife to pit her will against her husband's inevitably led to divisiveness. A husband and wife, they said, had identical interests, and husbands could fairly speak for both. In an ideal marriage this might have fostered the common good, but in an imperfect union, or one in which the husband, like John Stevens, was not a prudent businessman, coverture made it difficult for a woman to look out for her own interests. The system was designed in part to bolster male power, but its supporters also believed that it protected women, who were too weak and irrational to make intelligent decisions about financial matters. Women were like privileged children in need of protection, not responsible adults.

In many ways, coverture was simply a legal reflection of traditional beliefs and practices. Indeed, customary attitudes were probably more important than legal strictures in defining the relationship between husbands and wives. No court prevented John Stevens from consulting Judith or following her suggestions. Convention and pride, however, often kept husbands from involving their wives in what they saw as their own affairs. Thus, Judith had no choice but to acquiesce to her husband's decisions, even if she considered them immoral or unwise.

At war's end, John Stevens's privateering fortunes collapsed, and he returned to conventional trading. Unfortunately, Gloucester suffered a prolonged postwar depression. Taxes soared. The fishing industry was moribund. Trade remained chancy. Many people left the town altogether, and those who remained roamed the "deserted village" watching abandoned houses disintegrate before their eyes and shaking their heads as brambles and weeds reclaimed once well-tended gardens.[6] Despite this gloomy outlook, John Stevens attempted to defy the odds, investing in one unsuccessful venture after another, borrowing money to fit out his vessels when he had no liquid resources of his own. Throughout the 1780s, his position declined as his expenses grew.

When he was in Gloucester, John Murray stayed with the Stevenses. Judith's aunt, Sarah Allen, and her son lived with them for a while and tried to help defray their own expenses, but Judith was mortified to accept payment for services she would once have rendered in the name of hospitality. When another aunt, Maria Sargent, invited her to Boston, Judith refused. Maria and her husband, Daniel, moved in the best circles, and Judith thought it unseemly to be seen in such rarified company when her husband's prospects were so bleak. Their interests, she said, adopting the language of coverture, were "one." Moreover, she did not want to give John's creditors any excuse to complain. If she frequented the "Beau Monde," she asked, would she not "put it in the power of ill nature, or perhaps *justice,* to make the most mortifying comments? Delicacy forbids it."[7]

In 1786, with her father's disclosure of the extent of her husband's debts, Judith's world collapsed. The humiliation she suffered was excruciating in a small town like Gloucester, where everyone knew everyone else's business. Whenever she left home she feared the whispers of rumormongers. When she had defied the orthodoxy of the First Parish Church, she had been proud to face mean-spirited gossips. This was different. In her world, a man who refused to pay his debts was little more than a thief. To be married to such a man, no matter how well-meaning his intentions, was to be tainted by his shame. Her only recourse was to withdraw from society. She did not even visit her parents until the "shades of evening so far prevailed, as to veil [her movements] from every curious eye."[8]

John tried to find a way out of his difficulties. He could not pay his debts unless he could recoup his losses. To do this, he had to invest what money he had in yet another trading venture. He also needed to seek permission to leave Gloucester, and for this he had to persuade his creditors to sign a "Letter of License" granting him permission to make another voyage. If even one individual refused to sign, his hands would be tied. The task of contacting each creditor was painful. John Murray, who considered himself almost a member of the family, agreed to take the Letter of License to Boston. Although Judith knew it was "presumptuous" for a wife to interfere in her husband's affairs, she wrote to some of Stevens's creditors asking their indulgence.[9] She was always careful, she said, to appeal "in such terms as became my sex."[10] Occasionally she even used her gender to her own advantage. When she asked Benjamin Russell, editor of the *Columbian Centinel,* for his assistance, she coyly explained that she hoped he would "tolerate from a female pen, what [he] might justly hold Mr. Stevens inexcusable for soliciting."[11]

The Stevenses also tried to protect their remaining assets. At some point, Judith's father assumed legal ownership of their house in an effort to keep it in the family. He also advised John to "sell" their furniture to Judith's brother. Although Winthrop had no intention of taking possession, the two men solemnly exchanged receipts in front of witnesses. With some justice, John's creditors cried foul, claiming that he intended to defraud them of what was rightfully theirs.

Judith's behavior caused further difficulties. Despite her claims to the contrary, she was proud of her social position, and during the first years of her marriage she had slipped easily into the role of a prosperous merchant's wife. Even after her husband's business began to flounder, she continued to wear expensive clothes. Not one of her "superfluities," she protested, came from her husband's pocket; they were the result of her father's largess. She promised, moreover, that until John was debt-free, she would not "derive the smallest support from his exertions."[12] Still, it was galling to see Judith Stevens dressing well and living in an elegant house while her husband claimed he could not pay his arrears. Not surprisingly, while many of John's Boston creditors signed his Letter of License, most of his Gloucester creditors dug in their heels.[13]

By the end of January, the Stevenses were living in a state of seige, cowering in their house behind bolted doors. The sheriff announced that their goods and estate had been attached. He also served a writ of attachment on Winthrop Sargent, Sr., accusing him of hiding some of his son-in-law's assets. The ordeal took its toll. Judith trembled at every sudden noise. She became so edgy that when her father came to call, she imagined that one of her husband's creditors was mimicking his voice in an effort to gain entrance to the house. I feel, she wrote to a friend, as though "the enemy is constantly laying in ambush for our destruction."[14]

In the spring of 1786, John Stevens ignored both courts and creditors, and made a last desperate effort to regain his independence. Borrowing one of his father-in-law's ships, he fled his house through a back window and sailed for the island of Saint Eustatius in the West Indies, where he hoped to recoup his losses. Judith disapproved of John's decision, but she was powerless to stop him. "My opposition has been strong," she wrote to her brother Winthrop, "and although I am now *silenced,* I am not, however, convinced of its utility." John hoped she would be able to fend off his creditors once he was out of reach. "And," she added, "the poor man flatters himself, that in the course of a few months, he shall be able to return blest with liberty and competency."[15]

Whenever Judith heard from her "exile" he was optimistic, but she had ceased to accept his rosy predictions at face value. Her husband was, she conceded, "rashly enterprising," and he indulged in the "most hazardous expedients." She even considered following him to Saint Eustatius to "council and restrain him." She had once trusted her husband's judgment. Now, she imagined that her business instincts were shrewder than his.[16]

By failing to support his wife and by losing his own independence, her husband was emasculated in the eyes of society. Despite evidence to the contrary, eighteenth-century observers tended to evaluate economic failure not as an outcome of impersonal market forces but in moral terms. They saw a debtor as self-indulgent and profligate (characteristics usually associated with women). If a man fled his creditors instead of standing before them to pay his debts, he was the worst kind of character. It is hardly surprising that Judith publicly defended her husband's intentions as honorable but felt that he had committed "some dark crime."[17]

Judith Stevens never saw her husband again. In the early spring of 1787, John fell ill, dying on March 8 before he could return home. Judith was stunned by the news and distressed to discover that her once wealthy husband had not even left her with a "competency." Indeed, she told a relative, "I have scarce anything which I can call my own."[18]

American law took great pains to protect widows. When a man died, his widow received whatever real property she brought to her marriage — her "dowery." She also enjoyed "dower rights," which meant that if her husband died without a will, as John Stevens did, she received one-third of his personal property outright. This might include livestock, furniture, clothing, or dishes. She also enjoyed one-third to one-half of his real property — usually land and the house — "for her use" during her own lifetime.[19] Upon her death, that property went to her children; if the marriage was childless, it reverted to her husband's family. A widow's share of her husband's real property was meant to guarantee her security, not to give her independence. Thus, she could not sell it or alter it in any way that might decrease its value. If her husband died insolvent, his creditors could seize neither her real property nor the goods she brought to her marriage. They could, however, confiscate the personal property she had inherited.[20]

Judith knew that many women became destitute when a husband died. By the last quarter of the eighteenth century, especially in coastal regions where the ratio of men to women was increasingly skewed, a widow's future was bleak. If she was under thirty and, like Judith, had no children, her chances for remarriage were reasonably good. Most women were in their fifties when their husbands died, however, and few of them remarried. Under the best circumstances, the death of a husband was traumatic. A widow suffered emotionally as she faced an existence bereft of the companionship of a man whose affection she cherished. As head of an "incomplete family," she also faced the loss of a way of life or worse, dependence upon her husband's often misplaced confidence in their children for her subsistence. In some cases, she was no longer even mistress of the house she and her husband had once shared. Often she simply exchanged one dependent status for another, less satisfying one. Judith Sargent Murray did not exaggerate when she claimed that "a state of widowhood whatever may be the situation of the bereaved female is, in many respects, desolate, and forlorn."[21]

In the months following her husband's death, Judith complained bitterly about her financial circumstances. Yet if her situation was hardly grand, she was by no means destitute. At the very least, she had a roof over her head. Still, when she learned that her father intended to divide the deed to "her" house among all his children, she was upset. She had assumed that the entire house would be hers, and thought his decision unjust. To meet her expenses, she took in needlework, sold some of her furniture, which technically belonged to her brother, and seriously considered taking in boarders.

Winthrop urged her to move in with their parents, but Judith steadfastly refused. She claimed to adore them but had no wish to live with them. For the first time in her life, she was an independent woman. I have, she explained, my own "mode of appropriating my hours," as well as "my beloved *retirement*, my *books*, and my *pen*." She no longer had access to accustomed luxuries, but her ability "to preserve a *kind of independence*" partly compensated for their loss.[22]

She soon discovered that her husband's death had done nothing to halt the demands of his creditors. When her cousin Epes warned her that she faced "perpetual Law Suits" if she made no effort to satisfy them, she decided to cut her losses.[23] Even then, she was determined to keep her books. She had begun building her library when she was seven years old and to her its value was "incalculable." Moreover, she insisted, implicitly denying the tradition of coverture, all humans had an innate "fondness for property." She would give up some of what she thought was rightfully hers, but she would do everything to keep the rest for herself.[24] In the end, she invited her husband's creditors to share in an equitable division of her personal property. The probate judge divided it down to the last "joined china tea cup."[25] By 1790, she had met her obligations to the best of her ability, although she still owed John Stevens's creditors over one thousand pounds. The entire "heart affecting business" was over.[26]

Judith's struggles with her husband's creditors left an indelible mark. For the rest of her life she was obsessed with financial security. Scattered among her essays are sympathetic stories of worthy and blameless debtors. She condemned anyone whose troubles were the result of idleness or extravagance and agreed that debtors should make every effort to reimburse their creditors. At the same time, she heaped praise on creditors who exhibited compassion toward deserving supplicants. Her novel-like story of "Margaretta," which formed the bulk of the "Gleaner" essays she began submitting to the *Massachusetts Magazine* in 1792, was one of many in which she contrived a happy ending for a family facing economic disaster. (See Document 6.) She described the case of Edward

Hamilton, Margaretta's husband, whose unsuccessful merchant ventures led him into bankruptcy and shame. Like John Stevens, Hamilton decided to leave the country in an effort to redeem his economic fortunes. Just as he was preparing to sail, however, a wealthy stranger, Margaretta's long-lost father, materialized and helped him pay his creditors. In her own life, of course, no such benefactor appeared, and Judith remained keenly aware that, in the real world, innocent debtors were often helpless to avert disaster.[27]

Although she never faced bankruptcy again, Judith's financial troubles did not end. Her marriage to John Murray in 1788, less than two years after her first husband's death, did little to guarantee her security, much less her prosperity. By his own admission, John Murray was "never sufficiently sensible of the value of money to retain it in [his] possession."[28] In England, he had seen the inside of debtor's prison. Until he and Judith married, he had refused to accept a salary from his Gloucester congregation, relying on God to tend to his needs. Only his obligations to his new wife forced him to accept a yearly stipend, and even then his finances remained precarious. At times, Judith could not suppress her irritation at her husband's lackadaisical approach to his affairs. "I regret," she told him, "that you are not more uniformly attentive to your interest—at times you appear anxious, and sufficiently economical—but you seem to have no *fixed plan*."[29]

If Murray lacked worldly wisdom, he was at least less determined than John Stevens had been to handle his family's finances. This was no small blessing for Judith Sargent Murray. "How sweet is the reflection," she rejoiced, "that I do not run even the smallest risk of offending the Lord of my wishes, by . . . dictating in his pecuniary concerns."[30] Judith responded enthusiastically to the challenge of ordering her family's affairs. "The pleasure I derive, upon each revolving week," she said, "from appropriating the stated stipend, in a manner which shall answer our various exigencies, none but those who are attached to order, will conceive."[31]

The more involved Judith became in financial affairs, the more resentful she was of the legal strictures all women endured. When, for instance, she sought a buyer for some Ohio land she had inherited from her father, she complained because she could not sell anything without her husband's approval. "The law," she fulminated, "acknowledges no *separate* act of a *married* Woman."[32] Judith became even more frustrated as the result of a protracted dispute with a Philadelphian, Samuel Jackson, over her investment in a land venture known as the Population Company of Pennsylvania. Jackson was so confident of the company's prospects that he promised to reimburse the Murrays out of his own pocket should anything go wrong. When the investment failed to achieve its promise and Jackson refused to make good on his assurances, Judith was convinced that he had cheated her. She wanted to begin legal proceedings against him immediately, but she needed her husband's permission to do so and John would not allow her to consult a lawyer. Even more frustrating, Jackson refused to deal with her directly, and would speak only to her husband about the matter. The property in question, she cried, is "mine by a double right." As her father's daughter, she held it by the "right of Nature." It was also hers by "the sanction of my husband, who guaranteed to me the sole and separate use thereof." Thus, she asked Jackson, how can you say "that you owe Mr. Murray, in other words, that you owe me nothing?"[33] She knew the answer to her question even before she asked it. Jackson feared nothing "from a Woman's pen." Six years later, she was still trying to retrieve what she believed she deserved, convinced that only the "serious remonstrances of a determined Man" would make Jackson heed her pleas.[34] By then, John had died, her brothers were tired of her complaints, and she had to concede defeat.

Judith never regretted her second marriage, but she often chafed at her financial insecurity and was always "anxious about pecuniary matters."[35] In 1793 she entertained brief hopes for John's prospects when he became minister of Boston's Universalist Church. Judith had always claimed to prefer the little village of Gloucester to the dubious pleasures of the *"beau monde,"* but after her parents' death she was ready to set foot upon a larger stage. With a mixture of trepidation and excitement, she agreed to sell the Gloucester house, a third of whose profits belonged to her, and leave her childhood home.

Unfortunately, the Boston church seldom met its financial obligations to the Murrays. The city's economic fortunes fluctuated throughout the early nineteenth century, and members of the upwardly mobile but hardly affluent Universalist congregation often found it difficult to support their minister. From the beginning, Judith grumbled that her husband's weekly stipends came much too irregularly.[36] Even when he received it, his salary was not substantial. Moreover, Boston was expensive, rents were high, and John was determined to find accommodations that compared favorably to the Gloucester mansion. In the end, the Murrays leased a house at Number 5 Franklin Place, part of a new complex of buildings located in South Boston. Designed by the architect Charles Bullfinch, the homes were "spacious, lofty, commodious, and elegant," and "finished in the modern taste." Moreover, everyone who was anyone — at least in polite Federalist circles — lived in the southern part of the city. The house was clearly more than a struggling minister's family could afford.[37] When the Franklin Place proprietors kept raising the rent, the Murrays decided to buy their residence, using the money from the sale of the house in Gloucester plus funds borrowed from a "Widow Woman" to purchase the mortgage.[38]

Although Judith pretended indifference to material matters, she was clearly concerned about them, at times obsessively so. She had grown up in comfort. Both her brother Fitz William and her sister Esther's husband, John Ellery, were successful merchants. Her brother Winthrop became the first territorial governor of Mississippi, married advantageously, and presided over a large plantation near Natchez. Many of her other relatives enjoyed a style of living that was little short of opulent. Judith found it humiliating to watch every penny and frightening to imagine that when she and her husband died, their daughter, Julia Maria, might have to rely on the charity of relatives. "I tremble," she said, "under the apprehension of leaving a female orphan, to the frigid sympathies of an unfeeling world."[39]

In reality, however, Judith was never as poor as she claimed to be, and many of her difficulties were of her own making. She always had at least one servant. The house on Franklin Place was surely a luxury, and the Murrays spent as much on their daughter's education as all but the wealthiest parents: They bought a piano for Julia Maria, sent her to writing school, and provided dancing, music, and French lessons. Moreover, Judith's complaints about her poverty must be considered in context. She was always proud that she was Judith *Sargent* Murray and inevitably compared her standard of living not only to the one she had enjoyed as a girl but to that of her wealthier relatives. She admitted as much to Winthrop in defending herself against his accusations that she complained too much about money. She knew, she said, that she was not poverty-stricken. Still, she pointed out, "We are the children of the same Parents, and my wishes for *ease* and *affluence* are similar to your own."[40] She was not really dissimulating when she claimed she had cut her expenses to the bone and given up every conceivable luxury. Compared to her siblings, she was economical indeed.

Judith constantly devised schemes for reversing her fortunes. She bought stocks and investment funds, generally keeping John in the dark about her ventures. Her husband, she explained, was "unacquainted with the nature of public stocks," and left such matters in her hands.[41] In 1795, she decided to use her literary talent to make money. Until then, she had published her essays and poetry without remuneration. But worries about her daughter's future led her to write for profit. Two plays, *The Medium,* and *The Traveller Returned,* resulted. Produced by Boston's Federal Street Theater in 1795 and 1796, respectively, they were greeted with a tepid critical and popular response. The theater, it appeared, was unlikely to earn her either glory or riches.

Undaunted, she returned to her essay writing, compiling *The Gleaner,* a three-volume "miscellany," which she published in 1798. She used the profits from its sale to pay off the mortgage on Franklin Place, but the work did not earn enough money to warrant a second printing, and the effort paid no other dividend.

Judith's financial concerns produced unpleasant side effects. She quarreled with everyone about money matters. When she took care of Winthrop's children and stepchildren, most of whom boarded with the Murrays at one time or another, disagreements over finances invariably arose. She also bickered with Esther and Fitz William, accusing them of cheating her out of some £50 of her dower.[42] The controversy with Samuel Jackson was another protracted example of Judith's determination to get "justice, justice, justice," despite her belief that the law "was not designed for integrity."[43]

Nor should her touchiness over money matters come as a surprise. As one historian has pointed out, it was difficult for women to make ends meet, especially in a society that neither prepared them to deal with the complexities of the business world, nor allowed them to enter that world on an equal footing. Their fear of insolvency and their sense of inadequacy bred insecurity, and they argued over trifling amounts of money.[44] Having once been "doomed to drag the Debtor's length'ning chain," Judith lived in constant fear that she would repeat the experience.[45]

In 1801, John Murray suffered a stroke, and lost the use of his right hand. Eight years later, he had a second, more debilitating seizure. This time he was totally paralyzed, and Judith and Julia Maria could not care for him without help. At first the Universalists were generous, possibly because they assumed that John's death was imminent. They hired a nurse and promised to continue his salary, although they had no legal obligation to do so. John's economic relationship with his church was unusual. Most Massachusetts ministers were guaranteed a lifetime stipend, but Murray refused anything but a yearly contract. Judith feared that when her husband's contract came up for renewal, the congregation might let it expire.[46] She had reason to worry. Beginning in the spring of 1810, the church began to renege on its promises, and in 1812 a "fearful majority" of the members voted to reduce Murray's pay by more than half.[47] In 1814, they threatened to cut him off altogether.

On the morning of September 3, 1815, almost six years to the day after his second stroke, John Murray died. Judith Sargent Murray was a widow once more. John had drawn up a new will the previous year giving her all his property outright.[48] The will also had symbolic importance, for it did not limit her inheritance to a widow's third, nor did she hold her husband's estate for life only. Moreover, the house was paid for. The interest on her investments approached seven or eight hundred dollars a year, and she continued to hope that she could sell copies of *The Gleaner* as well as the biography of her husband upon which they had labored during the last years of his life.[49] Still, Judith insisted that her resources were insufficient.

She remained in Boston until 1818, increasingly depressed and worried about her circumstances. She was "weary of conjecture, struggling to keep hope from expiring, and frequently loathing life, with all which it can bestow."[50] Her sister, Esther, was dead. She quarreled frequently with Winthrop. Fitz William never wrote and seldom visited. Still, she enjoyed flashes of her old optimism and even toyed with the idea of moving to Ireland. Her friends thought the notion "romantically fanciful," but she had always envied her brothers' trips abroad, and she retained a lingering desire to follow in their footsteps.[51] She never did indulge her fancy, but her final journey did not lack adventure. In 1818, Julia Maria traveled to Natchez to join her husband, Adam Bingaman, a Mississippi planter. After much hesitation, Judith decided to accompany her daughter. Like so many widows of the period, she spent her last years in some one else's house.

Despite her precarious economic position, Judith Sargent Murray identified with the interests and values of New England's merchant community. A strong supporter of the Federalist party, she never abandoned her belief in order, stability, and hierarchy. If she did not embrace all the egalitarian implications of the American Revolution, she did claim that "independence" was essential to the basic humanity of every person. At a time when Americans viewed even single women as dependent creatures who by definition had no political existence, her effort to claim independence for members of her sex was radical. "A spirit of independence has been regarded as natal in the bosom of Americans," she said, and she left no doubt that she spoke not simply of colonial independence from England, but of economic independence for women as well.[52]

When women married, they exchanged their dependent position as daughter for a similarly dependent status as wife. Their standard of living was determined by their husbands' successes or failures. A woman's contributions to the family economy were private, passive, and indirect.

She was a prudent consumer and used her skills in the service of the household, but she aspired to nothing more. Remembering her own experience as she helplessly watched her first husband's business flounder and fail, Murray thought that a woman's idleness was at the very least a waste of valuable resources. "The *united efforts of male and female*," she said, "might rescue many a family from destruction."[53] She knew that even the best families faced potential adversity. "Writs of attachment; irritated creditors; and sheriff's officers" could disturb the tranquility of any home. A good wife had to be prepared for such contingencies.[54]

Unfortunately, society prepared women for dependence, not self-reliance. Young girls were taught to see marriage as their only means of advancement, and once married, they assumed their husbands would provide for them. Because they could not earn their own fortune, they ceased even to improve themselves. Many abandoned any pretense of industry, order, or economy; few had any idea of how to "procure for themselves the necessaries of life."[55]

Although Murray believed that married women should be able to help their families economically, she was even more determined that single women—whether widowed or never married—should be equipped to be financially independent. She knew that most single women endured material hardship because they had few resources or skills. For them, independence was often a cruel mockery, for without training or opportunity they could not earn a living. They were the mere "sport of contingencies."[56]

Murray knew from experience how ill-prepared most women were to fend for themselves. When John Stevens died, she had been immobilized with fear. "Dependence," she had told her brother, "with all its train of mortifications stare[s] me full in the face."[57] Years later, as she watched John Murray's health deteriorate, she again faced the fact that she had few resources or remunerative skills. She was simply a housekeeper, she told a friend, and while she dreaded accepting the charity of her relatives, she could conceive of no realistic option.[58] "Would it were the custom," she cried, "to qualify women for exertions, which would enable them to bring forward even in a state of widowhood the children whom they had introduced into being."[59]

While Judith Sargent Murray went further than most of her American contemporaries in proclaiming the value of economic independence for women, she remained a prisoner of her time. In theory, she believed that women were capable of anything and argued that they should aspire "to the loftiest heights."[60] When she spoke of employment opportunities for women, however, her vision was limited, and her views paradoxical.

Her glowing description of contemporary women in *Gleaner* essay No. 91 underscores both the breadth of her perspective and its limitations (See Document 7.) Although she claimed that men and women were intellectual equals, she could not envision a world where male and female roles were interchangeable. She had no desire to "create that confusion" that would result from the "mingling of those departments, now so advantageously, and so properly assigned to the male and female world."[61] If she praised a strong and intelligent "farmeress," she also pointed out that the woman was tender, affectionate, and faithful. Although she lauded the success of a widowed "she-merchant" from St. Sebastian, she did not believe that most women should aspire to a commercial career because she did not want them to lose their "feminine" attributes.[62] Even Murray's literary creation, Margaretta Hamilton, despite her superior education and character, did nothing practical to help her husband when he faced the demands of his creditors. Margaretta "contributed" not by getting a job or even taking in sewing, but by agreeing to give up her servants and live with her parents to cut down on expenses. Her sacrifices may have reflected her "fortitude," but this was a moral virtue, not a useful skill.[63] (See Document 6.)

The experiences of Murray's own friends illustrate the difficulties women faced when they tried to attain the independence she advocated. What little work was available to women in the eighteenth century was low skilled and poorly paid, and most professions were closed to them. Murray knew several who were teachers or governesses, and she praised the historian Mercy Otis Warren, whose "merit" allowed her to attain a *"noble independence"* as a writer.[64] Nevertheless, although she hoped that women on their own would not be *"necessarily* condemned to laborious efforts, or to the drudgery of that unremitted sameness which the routine of the needle presents," most of her acquaintances survived their years alone by sewing or taking in boarders.[65]

Nor did Murray protest the laws and customs that narrowed women's career choices. She seemed to think that if women were educated, their problems would somehow be resolved. She advocated an ambitious curriculum for young women, which included encouraging them to learn Latin and Greek, but she never believed women would use their education — as men did — to become doctors, lawyers, or ministers. Nor did she wonder how a knowledge of the classics would enable women to earn a competency when they were barred from the professions. A world peopled with women politicians and ministers, carpenters and sailors was simply beyond her ability to imagine.

Reality always impinged on Murray's rhetoric, and she often shrank from following her own logic to its obvious conclusions. At times she even rejected the painful lessons of her own experience. In 1816, as her brother Winthrop contemplated preparing his will, he sought his sister's advice. Judith had once argued that everyone—even women—had an innate desire to protect property, yet her advice to him was traditional: If I had a large estate to devise, she wrote, I would leave it to my wife for her use so long as she remained a widow, but I would leave strict instructions about the estate's disposal after my wife's death. For "who can say," she demanded, "what wonderful effects may be produced upon the mind of a lovely, tender, caring Woman, and that Woman a fond Mother?"[66] In the end, Judith Sargent Murray was unable to reject completely the assumptions on which coverture was based. In theory, she agreed that women were capable of handling their own affairs, but in reality she doubted that many of them were prepared to do so.

NOTES

[1]The phrase is Marylynn Salmon's; see *Women and the Law of Property in Early America* (Chapel Hill: University of North Carolina Press, 1986), xv.

[2]Judith Stevens to Madam Walker, 8 Oct. 1783, Judith Sargent Murray, Letterbook, 2:171, Mississippi Archives, Jackson, Miss.

[3]Judith Stevens to Winthrop Sargent, 5 Jan. 1786, Letterbook, 3:36.

[4]Excerpt from Susan Lear's diary, quoted in Emma Worcester Sargent, *Epes Sargent of Gloucester and His Descendants* (Boston: Houghton Mifflin, 1923), 51.

[5]Judith Stevens to Madam Walker, 8 Oct. 1783, Letterbook, 2:171.

[6]Judith Stevens to Winthrop Sargent, 15 Sept. 1783, ibid., 169.

[7]Judith Stevens to Maria Sargent, 15 June 1784, ibid., 237.

[8]Judith Stevens to John Murray, 14 Jan. 1786, Letterbook, 3:40.

[9]Judith Stevens to Mr. _____ of _____, 31 Jan. 1786, ibid., 55; Judith Stevens to Mr. Russell, 31 Jan., 1786, ibid., 58.

[10]Judith Stevens to Winthrop Sargent, 28 Mar. 1786, ibid., 77.

[11]Judith Stevens to Mr. Russell, 31 Jan. 1786, ibid., 59.

[12]Judith Stevens to Mr. _____ of _____, 31 Jan. 1786, ibid., 55; Judith Stevens to Mr. D. Rogers of Gloucester, 5 Mar. 1786, Letterbook, 3:72.

[13]Judith Stevens to Mr. Pierce of Gloucester, 6 Mar. 1786, ibid., 75.

[14]Judith Stevens to Madam Walker, 31 Jan. 1786, ibid., 53.

[15]Judith Stevens to Winthrop Sargent, 21 Apr. 1786, ibid., 81.

[16]Judith Stevens to Winthrop Sargent, 5 Aug. 1786, ibid., 130.

[17]Judith Stevens to Madam Walker, 31 Jan. 1786, ibid., 53. See also Toby L. Ditz, "Shipwrecked; or Masculinity Imperiled: Mercantile Representations of Failure and the Gendered Self in Eighteenth-Century Philadelphia," *Journal of American History* 81 (1994): 51–80.

[18]Judith Stevens to Mrs. Gardiner, 15 Aug. 1786, Letterbook, 3:214.

[19]She would obtain the larger amount if the marriage was childless.

[20]While most men died intestate, a sizable minority left wills. The terms of those wills generally followed the outlines designated by intestate laws. A widow could contest any will that left her with less than her dower rights, but in many cases, especially if the family had

an adult son, the husband might simply instruct the son to take care of his mother's needs so long as she lived. Wills varied greatly, but the general trend throughout the eighteenth century was in the direction of less autonomy—that is, more dependence—for women.

[21] Judith Sargent Murray to Mrs. W_____ of Philadelphia, 13 June 1792, Letterbook, 8:50.

[22] Judith Stevens to Winthrop Sargent, 17 Jan. 1787, 18 Apr. 1788, Letterbook, 3:257, 298; Judith Stevens to Mrs. Barrell of Old York, 12 Sept. 1787, ibid., 231.

[23] Judith Stevens to Winthrop Sargent, 22 Sept. 1788, ibid., 345.

[24] Judith Stevens to Winthrop Sargent, 15 Jan. 1787, ibid., 193.

[25] Judith Sargent Murray to [?], 10 Sept. 1807, Letterbook, 14:74.

[26] Judith Stevens to Winthrop Sargent, 22 Sept. 1788, Letterbook, 3:345. In fact, as late as 1807, stray creditors showed up to make claims on her estate. Judith Sargent Murray to [?], 10 Sept. 1807, Letterbook, 14:73–75.

[27] Murray, *The Gleaner: A Miscellaneous Production in Three Volumes* (Boston: L. Thomas and E. T. Andrews, 1798), 1:223, 274–85.

[28] John Murray, *The Life of Rev. John Murray, Preacher of Universal Salvation, Written by Himself, With a Continuation, by Mrs. Judith Sargent Murray,* ed. Rev. G. L. Demarest (Boston: Universalist Publishing House, 1869), 75.

[29] Judith Sargent Murray to John Murray, 29 Jan. 1791, Letterbook, 5:349.

[30] Judith Sargent Murray to John Murray, 11 May 1789, Letterbook, 4:32.

[31] Judith Sargent Murray to Mr. J_____ T_____, 5 Sept. 1798, Letterbook, 10:146.

[32] Judith Sargent Murray to Winthrop Sargent, 23 Nov. 1791, Letterbook, 5:362.

[33] Judith Sargent Murray to Samuel Jackson, 28 Sept. 1809, Letterbook, 15:141, 142.

[34] Judith Sargent Murray to Winthrop Sargent, 15 Feb. 1814, Letterbook, 18:70.

[35] Judith Sargent Murray to John Murray, 2 Dec. 1789, Letterbook, 4:62.

[36] Judith Sargent Murray to the Mother of Mr. Murray, 10 Aug. 1798, Letterbook, 10:263.

[37] Judith Sargent Murray to Winthrop Sargent, 24 Sept. 1794, Letterbook, 9:492.

[38] Judith Sargent Murray to Winthrop Sargent, 24 Apr. 1797, ibid., 611.

[39] Judith Sargent Murray to [?], 18 Feb. 1812, Letterbook, 17:80.

[40] Judith Sargent Murray to Winthrop Sargent, 28 Sept. 1817, Letterbook, 20:63.

[41] Judith Sargent Murray to [?], 21 Dec. 1808, Letterbook, 15:79, 80; Judith Sargent Murray to Mr. Parkman, 20 Aug. 1808, ibid., 39, 40; Judith Sargent Murray to [?], 17 Sept. 1810, Letterbook, 16:n.p.

[42] Judith Sargent Murray to Fitz William Sargent, 4 Nov. 1806, 18 Nov. 1806, 31 Mar. 1810, Letterbook, 14:35, 36, 38–39, n.p.

[43] Judith Sargent Murray to Mr. and Mrs. Jackson, 7 July 1810, Letterbook, 16:79, 80.

[44] Lee Virginia Chambers-Schiller, *Liberty a Better Husband: Single Women in America: The Generations of 1780–1840* (New Haven, Yale University Press, 1984), 44.

[45] Judith Sargent Murray to Mr. J_____ G_____, 5 Sept. 1798, Letterbook, 10:146.

[46] Judith Sargent Murray to Winthrop Sargent, 1 Nov. 1809, Letterbook, 15:158, 159; Judith Sargent Murray to Fitz William Sargent, 20 Jan. 1810, Letterbook, 16:[4, 5].

[47] Judith Sargent Murray to Winthrop Sargent, 8 May 1812, Letterbook, 17:102.

[48] Judith Sargent Murray to Winthrop Sargent, 6 Aug. 1814, Letterbook, 18:107.

[49] Judith Sargent Murray to Winthrop Sargent, 23 Sept. 1816, Letterbook, 20:32, 33.

[50] Judith Sargent Murray to Winthrop Sargent, 30 July 1815, Letterbook, 19:141.

[51] Judith Sargent Murray to [?], 16 Mar. 1818, Letterbook, 20:81.

[52] Murray, *The Gleaner,* 3:243, 245.

[53] Ibid., 220.

[54] Murray, *The Gleaner,* 2:302.

[55] Murray, *The Gleaner,* 1:168.

[56] Murray, *The Gleaner,* 3:196.

[57] Judith Stevens to Winthrop Sargent, 29 Jan. 1784, Letterbook, 2:186.

[58] Judith Sargent Murray to [?], 6 June 1810, Letterbook, 16:n.p.

[59] Judith Sargent Murray to Maria Sargent, 16 Mar. 1793, Letterbook, 8:101.

[60]Judith Sargent Murray to Mr. Redding of Falmouth, England, 7 May 1801, Letterbook, 11:288.

[61]Ibid., 287.

[63]Murray, *The Gleaner,* 1:279.

[64]Murray, *The Gleaner,* 3:184.

[65]Murray, *The Gleaner,* 1:69, 70; 2:258; Judith Sargent Murray to Miss N_____, 17 Sept. 1800, 3 Nov. 1800, Letterbook, 11:191, 220.

[66]Judith Sargent Murray to Winthrop Sargent, 27 Jan. 1816, Letterbook, 20:4, 5.

5

The Bonds of Matrimony

Most eighteenth-century women defined themselves in terms of their roles as wives. Probably even more than their religious beliefs, it was their domestic relationships that shaped their daily lives and gave them their identity and sense of purpose. In common parlance and even in law throughout the seventeenth and eighteenth centuries, the words "wife" and "woman" were more or less interchangeable. A good woman was by definition a "good wife"; a woman who never married was a "spinster," which in the seventeenth century carried connotations of sinfulness, immorality, and a threat to the social order. A century later, however, it implied only that an unmarried woman was an object of scorn or pity. Thus it is not surprising that as Judith Sargent Murray began to explore her own views about women's nature and role, she did so within the context of marriage. If, after all, women were not equal in their own homes, they would never be able to demand political or economic rights.

Murray's perspective was influenced by a variety of sources, including the subtle but important modifications in attitudes toward the institution of marriage on both sides of the Atlantic by the latter half of the eighteenth century. In America, the ideology of the Revolution, with its emphasis on equality and independence, gave special meaning to those changed attitudes. The novels and essays Murray read as a girl were influenced by—and helped legitimate—this new view of marriage. Judith Sargent was by no means the only American girl whose love affair with the printed word led her to desire more of married life than economic security. Finally, her own experiences as a wife called traditional practices into question, imbuing her with the conviction that her views had merit.

In a society whose institutions assumed that women were naturally dependent, Judith Sargent Murray was keenly aware of the central importance of marriage in determining a woman's chances for security, status, and happiness. Still, while she railed against the limitations imposed by traditional views of marriage, she harbored ambivalent attitudes about an institution she both valued and questioned. She defended the worthiness of the single life yet praised marriage as the highest form of human happiness. She was contemptuous of any union not founded on mutuality and equality while advocating wifely submission and holding women responsible for the success of most marriages. Murray's conflicting views were not the product of muddled thinking or hypocrisy but a reflection of the limits within which all women operated in postwar America. Her willingness to demand publicly that women enjoy the promise of the American Revolution revealed her as more radical than most of her contemporaries. Yet her statements often have a deceptively modern ring, and her respect for propriety, order, and decorum limited her vision.

To say that Judith's first marriage was unhappy would be an exaggeration. John Stevens may have been a poor businessman, but he did his best to provide for his wife's material welfare. Although he apparently had little interest in literature, he was genuinely proud of Judith's talent as a writer and encouraged her to publish her children's catechism. He may not have been a soulmate, but he shared his wife's commitment to the Universalist faith. All the same, Judith Sargent Murray's first marriage did not achieve her ideal. Indeed, she may have been thinking of her own situation when she warned her brother that an unhappy couple could find the bonds of wedlock "infinitely more galling than those worn by the slaves confined to the turkish Galley."[1]

Judith was only eighteen when she married John Stevens. He was twenty-eight. On average, women in the mid-eighteenth century married at the age of twenty-three, men slightly older. Judith never explained her reasons for marrying so young, but the match probably surprised no one at the time. John was handsome and amusing, and had excellent prospects. Moreover, the Sargents and Stevenses shared a similar social background, which everyone agreed was the best foundation for a good marriage. By the eighteenth century, Gloucester's merchant elite formed a tightly knit network, bound together by an intricate web of family relationships. In this sense, Judith was following time-honored practice when she accepted John's proposal.

Although she never openly criticized her husband, Judith occasionally hinted that she regretted her marriage, admitting that her youth and inexperience had clouded her vision and that her "false calculations" had resulted in disappointment.[2] She never ceased reminding anyone who would listen that women should avoid early marriages, for she was convinced that with maturity came a measure of wisdom. She was also frustrated by John's tendency to exclude her from his financial decisions, to view her with paternalistic tolerance rather than as an equal. Judith was aware of John's finer qualities and respected his integrity, but from the beginning her feelings for her husband were marked by friendship, not passion, Until she married John Murray she had assumed that she was simply "*incapable* of *love,* as traced by the pencil of the Poet."[3]

There had been a time, of course, when young brides expected neither equality nor romantic love in a marriage. At least by the middle of the eighteenth century, however, first in Europe and then in America, upper- and middle-class women celebrated the attributes of what historians call the "companionate marriage." Simply put, this was a shift from the patriarchal, deferential model of the past toward equality, autonomy, and mutual affection. Although few marriages lived up to the companionate ideal, many women hoped to achieve it; these expectations led to greater disappointment when they failed to do so. The colonies lagged behind England and Europe in accepting these new attitudes, but the ideology associated with the American Revolution both accelerated and legitimated a process already underway. Indeed, as one historian has argued, companionate marriage was the ideal metaphor for the age. Egalitarian, affectionate, and above all voluntary, it provided an appealing image for a nation founded on republican principles and promised to be an ideal training ground for the virtuous citizen.[4]

The notion of voluntary marriage based on mutual affection nowhere received as much attention or had as great an impact as in eighteenth-century novels. The books Judith Sargent read in her youth had their effect. Like many girls, she had been entranced by tales of dashing lotharios who swept virtuous heroines off their feet with promises of eternal bliss. Such stories recognized the value of feeling or "sensibility," encouraging women to seek emotional fulfillment, not simply economic security. Judith may well have been describing herself when she wrote of a young girl who was "accustomed to devour *indiscriminately*" every novel she could, and who consequently acquired such a fanciful view of love that she spent her life searching for a mythical "*belle passion.*"[5]

Everyone in the eighteenth century was obsessed with the institution of marriage. Novelists and playwrights, essayists and poets all had something to say on the subject. They began with their views of courtship, a time when young people—especially young women—made the most important decision of their lives. For obvious reasons, Americans emphasized the value of the free choice of bride and groom. The more they claimed an inalienable right to the pursuit of happiness, the more they insisted that parents who imposed their will on their adult children were tyrants. But while arguing that men and women should choose their own spouses, they advised the inexperienced to heed the advice of their loving parents. They knew only too well that when men and women exercised control over their own marital choices, they gained power and autonomy but risked failure and disappointment.

Judith Sargent Murray supported the modern view of courtship. She was at one with her contemporaries in her opposition to arranged marriages. Indeed, she argued that parents should not try to influence their children's choices, although she did believe that mothers and fathers should give their offspring general rules of conduct to help them assess the merits of potential spouses. Beyond that she resolutely refused to go. Not only did parental interference threaten to produce a loveless marriage, but efforts to meddle in matters of the heart would very likely backfire. *"Opposition,"* she observed, "generally begets *opposition.*"[6] In most cases, it was wiser for parents to stand back and hope for the best.

Although she warned mothers and fathers not to dictate to their children, Murray also urged young people to heed parental advice. Like many Americans, she had internalized the lessons of Samuel Richardson's novel *Clarissa*. Clarissa's downfall occurred, on the one hand, because her tyrannical parents tried to force her to marry for money instead of for love, and on the other, because she decided to disobey her parents and elope with the wicked Lovelace, whose machinations ended in her ruin and death. The moral was clear: If parents should not be tyrants, neither should children be rebels. The story of Margaretta in *The Gleaner* was an object lesson for both parents and children: it taught the former how to lead their charges along the path of virtue, while advising the latter to honor their parents' wisdom. Murray's "modern" conviction that young people should assume control over their own romantic affairs was subverted by her sense that parents ultimately knew best.

Murray's own experience demonstrated that courtship was a time of danger as well as potential happiness. Young people could be fooled, as she herself had been, by "specious appearances."[7] Still, there was hope. If her first marriage taught her about the pitfalls facing a credulous girl, her second was in most respects a textbook case of the ideal. Judith was in her midthirties when she realized that her "sentimental, virtuous friendship" with John Murray had evolved into something quite different, that she had "become a slave to the most impetuous of all passions."[8] Emotions were fine in their place, of course, but given free rein they could lead to disaster. Fortunately, the relationship between Judith and John was based on rational friendship as well as romantic love. The two had known each other for over a decade and under such natural circumstances that they had no reason to employ the *"little arts"* that so often marked superficial courtships. (See Document 8.) Theirs was an honest relationship, the only kind that would enable husband and wife to pass their days "in a state of delightful equality."[9] Their religious views were identical. Their attraction was based on a judicious mixture of esteem and respect, rationality and passion. Indeed, only her brother Winthrop's angry denunciation of the marriage spoiled what would have been a joyous event.

Winthrop's reaction was testimony to what every eighteenth century woman knew. Unmarried women, even respectable widows like Judith Stevens, had to guard their reputations more carefully than men did. This may have been especially true for women who joined the "disorderly" Universalist Church, whose views, said its detractors, virtually guaranteed licentious behavior among its adherents. Unfortunately, Judith gave her enemies an excuse to criticize her, and they seized upon it with ill-concealed glee. When John Murray continued to live in Judith's house after her first husband's death, "malicious hearts" spread rumors about the couple, even hinting that they had been having an affair before Stevens died.[10] When the titilating gossip reached Mississippi, Winthrop railed against the man who had placed his sister in so "improper" a position.[11] Judith tried to convince Winthrop of her innocence, regretting that the world would "not allow a single Woman, an intellectual connexion with an individual of the opposite sex."[12] Her efforts were to no avail. In a society where women owned little property, their reputation was their most valuable asset. Thus they had to guard themselves, giving whisperers no opportunity for slander. They could not permit a suitor the "smallest *personal* liberty." Even a kiss on the hand might lead a man to assume he could go much further. To fail to reprove him could destroy a woman's standing in polite circles.[13]

In time, Winthrop came to accept his sister's marriage. Still, the experience had been painful, and thereafter Judith seized every opportunity to decry her society's sexual double standard. She knew that people accepted in men what they condemned in women. Nevertheless, "Unblemished virtue is in my estimation as essential in a man, as in a woman, and as *man is commonly the primary aggressor,* I regard a *male prostitute* with even greater detestation than I do an abandoned female."[14] If she sometimes used views of gender differences for her own ends (men were the "primary aggressors"), at other times she refused to admit that such differences existed. Indeed, most gender definitions were based on custom, not nature, and thus were subject to change. What humans had created they could abolish. Although Murray was reluctant to urge women to ignore custom, her argument that these rules had no natural basis was unusual, and its implications radical.

Murray even toyed with the idea that women were not obliged to accept a passive role in the ritual of courtship. "Custom," she explained, "hath erected around our sex barriers which we may not leap with impunity. Man, so says the despot, must make his approaches, proposals must come from him, while we do with apparent reluctance accede to his wishes." She admitted that women risked criticism by deviating from time-honored practice but thought that in some circumstances a woman might ignore convention and propose to her lover instead of waiting meekly for him to take the initiative.[15] Her play *The Traveller Returned* provided a case in point when the pretty and vivacious Harriot Montague initiated a romantic rendezvous with Alberto Stanhope, even though she acknowledged that she was not acting "strictly speaking within the line of discretion."[16] Harriot was clearly a positive character, and in the end she was rewarded for taking charge of her own courtship.

In her *Gleaner* essays, especially the story of Margaretta, Judith Sargent Murray warned her readers about the dangers inherent in courtship, thus implying that care, rationality, and good judgment might help anyone avoid those dangers. Ironically, when she tried to guide her own daughter along the hazardous path leading to matrimony, she failed abysmally. Only in the world of her imagination, where she could create characters who conformed to her bidding, was she able to guarantee a happy ending. Julia Maria's experience was proof that the most dutiful daughter and the most prudent mother could not guard against all eventualities.

In 1807, young Adam Bingaman left his parents' plantation in Natchez, Mississippi, and traveled east to Boston. He remained there five years, living much of the time with the Murrays on the advice of Judith's brother Winthrop. From the beginning, mother and daughter were impressed by their new boarder. On the face of it, Adam was an ideal marital prospect. He was handsome, intelligent—he graduated at the top of his Harvard class—moral, and apparently wealthy. If he and Julia Maria forged an attachment based on reason as well as passion, their marriage could easily result in the proverbial happy ending about which mother and daughter dreamed. Adam was as taken with Julia Maria as she was with him. Although Judith insisted that their thoughts toward one another were as "pure as the visions of a slumbering Cherub," she watched anxiously over the young people, even insisting that Julia Maria sleep with her every night.[17] She knew that even one "single inconsiderate act" could destroy her daughter's reputation.[18]

In the fall of 1812, Adam graduated from Harvard and left for Mississippi, promising to remain there only briefly before returning to Boston to study law. He had already informed his parents of his plans to marry

Julia Maria and they had given him their blessing. Once he was home, however, he seldom wrote and seemed in no hurry to leave Mississippi. According to Winthrop, the Bingamans—acting like the parents of the tragic "Clarissa"—were pressuring Adam to marry someone who could add slaves and land to the family estate. But Richardson's Clarissa was in better circumstances than Julia Maria. In the winter of 1813, she confessed to her mother that she and Adam had secretly married before he left for home. The couple had obviously consummated their wedding vows, for by January it was clear that Julia Maria was pregnant. Judith was stunned, but determined to make the best of it. When Adam returned to Boston in May, she and John announced the marriage in the newspapers. A month later, Julia Maria gave birth to a girl, Charlotte Bingaman.

Even then, the couple's affairs remained unsettled. Adam had decided that Natchez promised him a better future than Boston. Julia Maria had no desire to leave Massachusetts, and her mother was distraught at the thought of losing the company of her only child. In the end, Adam left for Mississippi, promising either to return quickly or to make arrangements to have his wife and daughter join him. There matters stood for five years. Julia Maria remained in Boston, visited only occasionally by her husband. Mortified by her anomalous position, she became a virtual recluse. Mother and daughter lived in a constant "state of corroding suspense," and Judith thought that she herself was becoming a "confirmed maniac."[19]

Julia Maria finally joined her husband in Mississippi. She had little choice. "The Law," Judith pointed out bitterly, "has placed the destiny of my only child, and now of a darling grand child, in his power—he can, if he pleases, remove them *forever* from my view."[20] When a husband commanded, a wife had to obey. Her new home was not kind to Julia Maria. She survived Mississippi's sultry climate for only four years, dying in 1822, two years after her mother.

Not all courtships ended in disaster; not all marriages were unhappy. Fortunately, her own second marriage allowed Judith Sargent Murray to experience the pleasures of wedded bliss. As a result, while she never ceased warning of the possibility of an unfortunate union, the letters, poems, and essays she wrote after 1787 were more positive than her earlier writings.

Murray had firm notions about the components of a good marriage, notions that in most ways were unexceptional. No one, she said, should marry for money or status, nor should anyone be seduced by outward appearances or unchecked passion. Wealth without love made no one happy. Even when individuals were "rolling in affluence," if they married "in violation of their reluctant hearts," they would be "the most wretched of the wretched."[21] Beauty faded. Only the mind improved with age. If passion was important, it had to be carefully balanced with reason. Love could be trusted only "when the sensations of the heart, generally the offspring of impassioned fervour, [were] meliorated by reason, and authorized by judgment."[22] Still, although she stressed the importance of reason, reminding her readers that the strongest passion was short-lived at best, Murray argued that love remained essential. This was especially true for women, because, as Murray delicately explained, without love it would be torture for a woman to submit to the "indulgences" that were part of married life. Only love would enable her to yield herself to her husband "with sweet reluctance." Without it, her "every concession" would lead to "the keenest disgust."[23]

Murray, like other proponents of companionate marriage, argued that mutuality and equality were the keys to a happy union. "Mutual esteem, mutual friendship, mutual confidence," and above all, *"mutual forbearance"* were needed if a couple was to survive the difficulties that were bound to arise in even the happiest marriages.[24] In the long run, esteem—respect and admiration—was more enduring than romantic love. Equality, too, was essential. Ideally, husband and wife should be approximately the same age and share similar social and economic backgrounds. It was for this reason that Eliza Clairville, the destitute heroine of Murray's play *Virtue Triumphant,* refused to marry the wealthy Charles Maitland. I cannot, she explained, marry any but "the *equal* of my *humble family and lowly fortune.*"[25] More important than age or status were shared interests and beliefs—especially religious beliefs—and congenial minds.

The notion of equality in marriage was always problematic. Most Americans believed that they had a natural right to rebel against the king, but they did not think women possessed a similar right to rebel against their husbands. In an otherwise egalitarian, individualistic, and competitive society, marriage remained as the single most important institution to embrace the values of paternalism, self-sacrifice, and deference. Moreover, most eighteenth-century commentators saw marriage not as a relationship between two equal and autonomous individuals but as a melding of opposite and complementary characteristics. Men's rationality checked women's emotionalism, while a wife's emotional and moral nature softened the aggressive and competitive tendencies of her husband. Together, man and woman created an institution that was perfectly balanced.[26]

Even when both partners embraced the egalitarian ideal and tried to arrive at decisions jointly, the process often resulted in discord. Ultimately, of course, if husband and wife disagreed, the husband's views generally prevailed. A wife's influence depended upon her husband's indulgence. She could use her powers of persuasion to gain her point, but if he refused to listen to her, she had little alternative but to submit to his will. As Abigail Adams pointed out, a husband's power over his wife was an invitation to abuse. "Unlimited power in the hands of the Husbands," Adams wrote, was dangerous, for "all men would be tyrants if they could."[27]

Murray's own experience led her to argue more forcefully for the virtues of egalitarian marriage than did most of her contemporaries. Her willingness to sit back as John Stevens made one disastrous business decision after another had served no one's interest. More important, as a religious dissenter, she had learned to question traditional authority in matters of conscience. She could not imagine that God thought wives should embrace false doctrine simply for the sake of marital peace. A woman's opinions, she insisted, were her own. For a woman to submit to her husband's beliefs was to submit to tyranny.[28]

Despite her admiration for women who cherished their own opinions, Murray could not entirely ignore her society's emphasis on the value of wifely submission. In 1790, for instance, when John Murray considered job offers from Universalist congregations in Boston and Pennsylvania, Judith admitted that she preferred to remain in Gloucester. Nevertheless, the choice was not hers to make. "As a Wife," she explained, "it doth not become me to direct."[29] Years later, even as she sympathized with her daughter's distress at the thought of leaving Boston, she counseled wifely submission. "No one," she said, "will controvert a husband's right to rule."[30]

If Murray believed that women had to follow their husbands to the ends of the earth — or even to Mississippi! — she also assumed that wives were more responsible for creating the conditions for a good marriage than husbands. A prudent wife made her husband's happiness the focus of her married life. In *Virtue Triumphant,* Judith wrote of the experience of Augusta Bloomville, who married a man she did not love. As a result, Bloomville neglected her wifely duties, engaging in a meaningless round of parties and encouraging mild flirtations with other men. Her aunt, the virtuous Matronia, berated Bloomville, insisting that her own as well as her husband's happiness depended upon her willingness to reform. You must, she lectured, "let your husband's wishes become your future study, and rectitude shall once more crown your hours."[31]

Murray had words of wisdom for husbands as well as wives. A husband, she told Winthrop, should "spread over every amiable foible, the mantle of love," gently correcting his wife's little errors and accepting those weaknesses he could not change.[32] Still, she knew that in most marriages it was the wife who adapted and submitted. In the story of Margaretta, Mr. Vigillius praised his wife for her willingness to defer to his wishes "with that kind of acquiescence, which [the male] sex is so fond of considering as the proper characteristic of womanhood."[33] In fact, Murray's view of the "proper characteristic of womanhood" was complicated. She attacked the stereotype of the acquiescent woman and advocated wifely subservience. At times, she argued for both positions simultaneously.

This was surely the case in her *Gleaner* essays, when she described a crisis in the fictional marriage of Margaretta and Edward Hamilton. (See Document 9.) When Margaretta suspected that her husband had fallen in love with his ward, Serafina, she redoubled her efforts to please him. Her stepmother approved her strategy, even implying that Margaretta might be to blame for Edward's faithlessness. "I am not," she said, "an advocate for undue gentleness, or submissive acquiescence; such conduct may border upon meanness; a woman should be *just too, she should reverence herself.* . . . But custom hath established a certain order in society, and custom is a despot, whose chains I am fearful, it will be vain that an individual will assay to bury."[34] Clearly, the stepmother's message was self-contradictory. Custom was a despot. It was a human creation; it was often wrong. Women were equal to men and had no obligation to be subservient to them. Yet she did not advise her stepdaughter to rebel against tyrannical tradition, even though at some level she thought Margaretta had the right to do so. Custom, in the end, had to be obeyed.

In her insistence that most differences between men and women were cultural rather than natural, Judith Sargent Murray moved a considerable distance toward the destruction of the philosophical foundation upon which traditionally defined gender roles rested. In this, she echoed the views of the English feminist Mary Wollstonecraft, situating herself at the cutting edge of eighteenth-century "feminism." She was even more radical — at least in comparison to her American contemporaries — when she argued that marriage was not a goal toward which all women should strive. Women, in other words, could be women without being wives. In the heady days after her marriage to John Murray, she joyouslyly proclaimed to her friend and fellow writer, Sally Barrell, "I confess I have never yet conceived of a state, this side immortality, more marked by felicity, than a union founded upon a judgment, formed under the auspices of reason."[35] But if the unhappy memory of her first marriage faded, it never disappeared. Murray never forgot that for women, there was a fate worse than the single life. Marriage, she insisted, should be a choice, not an inevitability.

Murray railed against those misguided individuals who saw the *"old maid"* as a "contemptible being," even as she admitted that women were more likely than men to leap headlong into a disastrous marriage.[36] Women were not inherently weaker or more foolish than men. But their socialization, not to mention sheer economic necessity, made most girls feel that they had no other option. They were, Murray observed, "bred up with one particular view, with one monopolizing consideration, which seem[ed] to absorb every other plan."[37] Moreover, because as women they could not expect either to inherit their fortune or to earn it, they saw marriage as the only means to advance their prospects—or to survive. Custom and fear prompted many a girl to throw herself away on the first man who asked for her hand.

If Murray encouraged women to view marriage as a contingency rather than a necessity, her thinking here, as in so many other instances, was contradictory. Her plays, in particular, sent mixed messages to the audience. Both included characters who questioned the necessity of marriage. In both, her heroines seriously entertained the possibility of a single life, arguing that their happiness did not depend upon marriage. Yet in the end, the audience was meant to feel relief when the obstacles to marriage disappeared for Emily, in *The Traveller Returned,* and for Eliza, in *Virtue Triumphant.* A good marriage remained preferable to the single life. A happy ending, her plays implied, was a happy marriage.

Perhaps at no time were Judith Sargent Murray's views more unambiguously traditional than in her discussion of divorce. In many states after the Revolution, it became easier for a woman to obtain a divorce from her husband. This was especially true in New England, where the Puritans had always looked on marriage as a civil contract, not a religious sacrament. With independence, legislators in Massachusetts and Connecticut further loosened restrictions on divorce. In Massachusetts, for instance, women as well as men could sue for divorce on the basis of adultery. While they could not obtain a divorce for cruelty, desertion, or nonsupport alone, each of these complaints, when infidelity was added to the mix, gave wives cause for dissolving their marriages. Still, social opprobrium and economic necessity made most women think carefully before obtaining a divorce.

Although she sympathized with women who suffered in unhappy marriages, Murray drew the line at divorce. For her, once a couple entered the bonds of matrimony, the relationship was "indissoluble."[38] When she visited neighboring Connecticut in the fall of 1790, she was horrified at the ease with which its inhabitants ended their marriages. They could separate, she reported, for the flimsiest of reasons. If the courts failed them, they could apply to the state legislature for a special bill dissolving their marriage. "Those who become disgusted," she said, "have only to engage a Lawyer, who steps forward, pleads the Cause, and the Legislature signs the necessary releases. A Single instance of an unsuccessful Application to authority, hath, I am told never yet been known—if the wedded Pair are unhappy it is enough."[39]

Judith exaggerated the ease and willingness with which Connecticut couples could end their marriages, but her views were clear. Propriety and duty demanded that marriage should be a lifelong commitment. She supported Julia Maria's refusal even to consider divorcing Adam Bingaman, although he abandoned her for years at a time. She never tired of praising the example of Mary, Queen of Scots, shaping her account of the unhappy monarch's life to serve as an object lesson on the virtues of a faithful wife. Mary's decision to wed Lord Darnley had been ill-advised, but even when she realized how unworthy her husband was, she refused to divorce him. As Murray told the story, Mary's faithfulness was rewarded when her tenderness and compassion led to Darnley's reformation.[40] A woman's virtue had triumphed over the weakness of a wastrel and a rake; Mary not only saved her marriage, she reformed her husband in the bargain.

Judith Sargent Murray's attitude toward marriage was both traditional and modern, conservative and radical. Although her pronouncements reveal a perspective that remained hopelessly contradictory, she always admitted that both current practice and even her own attitudes were largely the product of custom or habit. Thus it was custom that denied women economic independence, and custom that led them to believe that marriage was their only route to security and happiness. If she was correct to argue that women's position was culturally, not naturally determined, then the door was open for truly dramatic change. In the final analysis, nothing was sacrosanct. The future was limitless.

NOTES

[1] Judith Stevens to Winthrop Sargent, 8 May 1779, Judith Sargent Murray, Letterbook, 1:142, Mississippi Archives, Jackson, Miss.

[2] Judith Sargent Murray to Maria Sargent, 16 Nov. 1804, Letterbook, 10:966, 967.

[3] Judith Stevens to Maria Sargent, 15 Apr. 1788, Letterbook, 3:293, 294.

[4]Jan Lewis, "The Republican Wife: Virtue and Seduction in the Early Republic," *William and Mary Quarterly,* 3rd ser., 44 (1987): 689–721.

[5]Judith Sargent Murray to Major F_____, 10 Jan. 1798, Letterbook, 10:189.

[6]Judith Stevens to Winthrop Sargent, 13 Aug. 1787, Letterbook, 3:165.

[7]Judith Stevens to Maria Sargent, 16 Nov. 1804, Letterbook, 10:966, 967.

[8]Judith Stevens to Maria Sargent, 15 Apr. 1788, Letterbook, 3:294.

[9]Judith Stevens to Anna _____, 23 June 1782, ibid., 29; Judith Stevens to Miss Mary Parker, 8 Sept. 1784, ibid., 232.

[10]Judith Stevens to John Murray, 11 Nov. 1786, ibid., 178.

[11]Judith Stevens to Winthrop Sargent, 11 June 1788, Letterbook, 3:323.

[12]Judith Stevens to Maria Sargent, 15 Apr. 1788, ibid., 294.

[13]Judith Stevens to Anna _____, 3 July 178[2], Letterbook, 2:39, 40.

[14]Judith Sargent Murray, *The Gleaner: A Miscellaneous Production in Three Volumes* (Boston: L. Thomas and E. T. Andrews, 1798), 1:127.

[15]Judith Sargent Murray to Miss C_____ L_____, 1 Jan. 1797, Letterbook, 10:70.

[16]Murray, *The Gleaner,* 3:138, 140.

[17]Judith Sargent Murray to Winthrop Sargent, 24 Sept. 1804, Letterbook, 15:57.

[18]Judith Sargent Murray to Anna Sargent, 3 May 1813, Letterbook, 18:1.

[19]Judith Sargent Murray to Winthrop Sargent, 8 Sept. 1814, 12 October 1814, Letterbook, 19:[12], [16].

[20]Judith Sargent Murray to Winthrop Sargent, 27 Jan. 1816, Letterbook, 20:5.

[21]Judith Stevens to Mrs. Gardiner, 4 Apr. 1788, Letterbook, 3:292.

[22]Judith Stevens to John Murray, 10 June 1789, Letterbook, 4:45.

[23]Judith Stevens to Anna _____, 8 Oct. 1786, Letterbook, 3:160.

[24]Murray, *The Gleaner,* 1:136.

[25]Murray, *The Gleaner,* 3:30.

[26]Lewis, "The Republican Wife," 689–721.

[27]Abigail Adams to John Adams, 31 Mar. 1776, quoted in Edith B. Gelles, *Portia: The World of Abigail Adams* (Bloomington: Indiana University Press, 1992), 47.

[28]Judith Stevens to John Murray, 12 Aug. 1779, Letterbook, 1:199.

[29]Judith Sargent Murray to Epes Sargent, 5 July 1790, Letterbook, 4:156.

[30]Judith Sargent Murray to Winthrop Sargent, 8 Apr. 1816, Letterbook, 20:14.

[31]Murray, *The Gleaner,* 3:33, 77, 79.

[32]Judith Stevens to Winthrop Sargent, 8 May 1779, Letterbook, 1:181.

[33]Murray, *The Gleaner,* 1:18, 19.

[34]Ibid., 193.

[35]Judith Sargent Murray to Mrs. Barrell, 8 May 1789, Letterbook, 4:30.

[36]Murray, *The Gleaner* 1:167, 179.

[37]Ibid., 167.

[38]Ibid., 135.

[39]Judith Sargent Murray to Judith Sargent, 15 Sept. 1790, Letterbook, 4:233.

[40]Murray, *The Gleaner,* 2:246–49.

6

"The Maternal Character"

Just as eighteenth-century Americans had begun to reevaluate the relationship between husbands and wives, so, too, they reexamined the connection between parents, especially mothers, and their children. Increasingly, people viewed motherhood not merely as a biological given but as an experience laden with emotional overtones and moral values. They waxed eloquent over the "natural" virtues of women, all of which related directly to women's role as bearers and nurturers of children. But this approach had troubling implications. The more society defined women in terms of specific moral attributes, the easier it was to argue that men and women were qualitatively different. Judith Sargent Murray contended that the desire and the ability to be a wife were for the most part culturally shaped, but a woman's desire to bear children was instinctive. Although her understanding of the role of "wife" enabled her to demand equality for women, her view of motherhood led her to carve out a unique role for her sex. It apparently did not occur to her that such a role constricted women's sphere even though it claimed to elevate women's status.

Changes in the new nation's economic structure and the general acceptance of Lockean philosophy helped construct American views of motherhood in the eighteenth century. Judith Sargent Murray's religious views, her interpretation of the philosophy of the Scottish Enlightenment, and her own experience were crucial in shaping her understanding of the importance of mothers.

For Americans who lived in the countryside, economic life in the late eighteenth and early nineteenth centuries continued much as it always had. Farmers in the northeast may have become more enmeshed in a cash economy, but on the whole, rural families experienced few major changes in the structure of their lives in the years after the American Revolution. Even before the war, however, in port cities like Boston and Gloucester, market forces were pulling more and more men out of the home for longer periods of time. Almost by necessity, husbands began to delegate more domestic responsibilities to their wives. As a result, women came to regard the domestic arena as their own private sphere. What had begun as the unintended consequence of a practical division of labor was gradually transformed into a rigid ideology. Although this transformation did not reach its zenith until the second quarter of the nineteenth century, what historians have labeled the "cult of domesticity" had its roots in the new Republic.

The view of human nature associated with the English philosopher John Locke helped many Americans legitimate women's new found importance as mothers. At the end of the seventeenth century, Locke had argued that mothers were as capable as fathers where the task of parenting was concerned. By the end of the eighteenth century there were those who took Locke's position much further, arguing that women were uniquely qualified to raise their children. Such an argument flew in the face of popular wisdom. No one denied that only women could bear children and nurse them in infancy, but few seriously imagined that these tasks had much importance. What mattered was raising, training, and molding older male children, and this was a duty that traditionally fell to men. In New England, where the doctrine of original sin dominated religious discourse, everyone subscribed to the dictum of the Puritan minister John Robinson, who proclaimed that "there is in all children . . . a stubbornness and stoutness of mind, arising from natural pride, which must in the first place be broken and beaten down."[1] Women, it was assumed, were too weak, too irrational, too prone to kindness to exercise the discipline children needed.

Locke's environmentalist understanding of human nature seriously challenged older notions of innate depravity. For Locke, children were born neither evil nor good. They were malleable, impressionable "blank tablets." It was sense impressions or experience that "wrote" upon these tablets, forming individual character. Because mothers were especially close to their children during their earliest, most vulnerable years, they played a crucial role in laying the moral foundation upon which a child's future rested. Moreover, Locke argued that the carrot achieved better results than the stick. People learned by emulation and encouragement, not by coercion. Thus women were at least as able as men to guide their children.

In her insistence that experience created character, that humans were "plastic" and "made of mutable stuff," Judith Sargent Murray sounded like an unoriginal popularizer of John Locke's theories. But she was too religious to be an unthinking Lockean. Her views were more attuned to the Scottish Enlightenment than they were to Lockean materialism. In an unpublished essay written in 1781, she clarified her perspective. When she first read Locke, she said, she was aroused by a "daring spirit of opposition," for she could not accept any philosophy claiming that the human mind was once "vacant, and unimpressed." From the beginning, she insisted, the soul animated the mind. From the beginning, children knew some things instinctively. At the very least, they shared a social sense, an intuitive empathy for other human beings, and a moral sense, an innate knowledge of right and wrong.[2] The moral sense helped humans evaluate and respond to the various sense impressions upon which Locke put so much emphasis. The social sense, when properly nurtured, made civil society possible. Natural affinities based on instinct and emotion provided the foundations of individual rectitude and the basis of a moral republic.

The possession of the moral sense did not guarantee either an upright individual or a virtuous nation. Virtue had to be cultivated if it were to flourish, for the "latent seeds of vice" as well as virtue existed in every human.[3] Moreover, it was the *early* nurturing experience that molded a future adult's character. "Impressions," said Murray, were "generally made with success in the early part of life," when parents could "imprint on the opening mind, characters, ideas and criticisms" that would never be erased.[4]

Locke would have agreed with this characterization of the importance of early sense impressions, but Murray proceeded in a direction that was decidedly unLockean. A mother's ability to influence her children, she said, derived not from their character as empty vessels but from their innate "affection" for her, an affection that made them eager to please her and heed her instructions. The social instinct, according to the proponents of the Scottish Enlightenment, was strongest when it was directed toward objects closest to home, and it became weaker as the object of its affection moved further away. It was easier, then, to be attached to the family than to the national government. Family affinities were instinctive and easy to nourish. And habits of affection in one area might be transferred to another. It was in the family, then, that the child learned to "extend his regard from the little group which constitutes his *relative circle, to friends, to country, to the universe at large, until he commences a citizen of the domain of heaven.*"[5] Most important, it was the mother—naturally emotional and empathetic— who was uniquely qualified to nurture the social instinct that lay dormant in every child. It was she who awakened her children's innate sense of connectedness with the rest of God's creation, and it was her influence that provided the basis for an orderly and moral society. America's children, and thus America's future, were in the hands of the nation's mothers.

Judith Sargent Murray celebrated women's role as mothers long before she had a child of her own. Indeed, the longer she remained childless, the greater emphasis she accorded the moral and emotional significance of motherhood. Judith and John Stevens were childless, and despite Judith's attempts to transfer her affections to child substitutes, she admitted that the "situation of a childless wife" provided a "melancholy contrast" to the joys of motherhood.[6] While she was able to imagine a woman content without a husband, she found it almost unnatural to contemplate marriage without children. For her, motherhood was not just a biological fact, it was a woman's destiny. It gave meaning to her life and contributed to her lasting happiness.

Murray's view of motherhood represented a distinct departure from the matter-of-fact attitude of seventeenth-century women. Mothers of an earlier era loved their children, of course, but motherhood was only one of their many duties. They cooked meals, wove cloth, sewed clothing and linens, and kept the house in order. They gardened, made soap and candles, and on occasion worked in the fields or the shop. No one imagined that a mother's relationship to her children was fraught with special significance or that a mother bore children for sheer emotional fulfillment.

When Judith Sargent Murray contemplated the possibility of bearing children, however, she thought almost exclusively in terms of the pleasure motherhood promised to give her. Thus, in January of 1789, when she realized that she was pregnant, she was ecstatic. She had long since abandoned any hope of bearing a child. But if she was overjoyed, she was also frightened. While most eighteenth-century women survived childbirth, some did not, and enough women died to ensure that no one faced the ordeal without trepidation.

A first pregnancy was always difficult; a first pregnancy for a woman who was nearly forty promised to be especially hazardous. Judith's experienced friends did nothing to alleviate her misgivings, as they warned her to expect a painful and difficult delivery. In her darkest moments, Judith thought that it was "probable the angel of death may at the approaching period, receive a commission, to summon me to some aerial abode."[7] Even worse were her worries about the fate of the child growing inside her. Her own mother had experienced five successive miscarriages. What if her own child was born blind, or deaf, or dumb? And what, she feared even to ask, if it did not live?

As her "perilous hour" approached, Judith focused her attentions on preparations for the baby's birth. She left nothing to chance. She wrote to Boston for information about the latest styles for children's shirts and caps. She secured her aunt Maria Sargent's promise to raise the baby should her own worst fears be realized. She even began to fret about the cost of education, for the first time expressing true frustration at John's undisciplined approach to financial matters.

The Murrays also sought the services of a doctor to help Judith through what threatened to be a difficult delivery. The decision to forego the traditional services of a midwife for the less experienced but more "scientific" care offered by a physician was rare at the end of the eighteenth century. Most women, the vast majority of whom resided in rural areas, followed the example of their mothers and grandmothers before them, turning to midwives when the time for delivery arrived. Midwives seldom acted alone. Birthing was a communal experience and an exclusively female ritual, an occasion when friends and relatives—all women—filled the room to talk and laugh, eat and drink, distracting and comforting the expectant mother during her labor.[8]

Not all births ended happily, and when complications arose, midwives and friends comforted the bereaved, helped bury the dead, and submitted to God's will. Well into the eighteenth century, American women—especially in New England—viewed their world in providential terms. They worshipped a God who directed the most ordinary occurrences, who controlled storms and drought, war and peace, birth and death. For them, pain and suffering were part of the natural order. Even the death of an innocent child was God's will, and they did not blame themselves for an event they could not control.

By the time of Judith's first pregnancy, however, elite urban men and women had begun to rethink their old assumptions. They no longer believed that women should submit to unnecessary pain and suffering without protest, nor did their religious convictions force them to accept the death of newborns with equanimity. They wanted up-to-date scientific care. They thought that within limits, humans could influence their own destinies, and they were as likely to attribute death during childbirth to human error as to God's will. They began to call on male physicians to deliver babies. Although doctors lacked the experience of midwives, they claimed to possess expertise. They were also the exclusive owners of forceps and other instruments that cut short a painful labor, using them to wrench a reluctant baby from a mother's womb. Given her class background as well as her fears about the problems she faced because of her age, it is not surprising that Judith asked Dr. Samuel Plummer from neighboring Salem to deliver her baby. Although she dreaded the assault on her "delicacy" that a man's presence in her room implied, no sacrifice was too great if it meant that both she and her child would survive.[9]

Despite all her efforts to control nature, Judith's pregnancy ended in sadness. Years later, she would point to the ability of "the Enduring Sex" to withstand the pain of childbirth as evidence of women's strength and courage.[10] But at the beginning of August 1789, she was not comforted by thoughts of female superiority. For five days Dr. Plummer stood by as his patient suffered unremitting "agonies of a most tremendous kind." Finally he intervened. He had begun to doubt that the baby still lived and worried that Judith might follow her child to the grave. On August 5, he produced *"his instruments"* and delivered a baby boy who had died in his mother's womb a few hours earlier.[11]

Judith was devastated by her loss and unwilling to admit that the most skilled obstetrician could not have saved little George. She did not blame God or nature for her son's death. Instead, she lashed out at Dr. Plummer. "Had I been skillfully managed," she insisted, "my infant might have been preserved."[12] Human error had not only deprived her of her son, but made it likely that she would never bear another child. Perhaps, she thought, the old ways were better after all. Had the "Ignorant Butcher" simply bided his time, allowing nature to operate on its own schedule, the outcome might have been different.[13]

For three weeks Judith hovered near death. For five weeks she remained unable to sit up, her legs so swollen they were bigger than her father's thigh.[14] But it was her emotional rather than her physical pain that was most unbearable and most enduring. A year after her son's death she traveled with John to Philadelphia, where she hoped the novelties of an unfamiliar city would distract her, at least momentarily. Instead, she confronted constant reminders of her loss. When she visited Charles Willson Peale's Museum, one of Philadelphia's cultural attractions, her eyes were immediately drawn to a portrait of Mrs. Peale with a baby in her arms. "My eyes were wet," she wrote her parents. "Thus wrapped about by icy death, was my darling Babe, in the only view with which I was favoured of that form, for which I endured unutterable pangs—but enough of this."[15] On August 5, the Murrays were in New York City, where a packet of letters from home awaited them. Judith read with mixed emotions the news that her sister-in-law, Anna Sargent, had just given birth to a healthy baby girl. How ironic, she thought, that she should learn about Anna's good fortune on the anniversary of George's death. She would, she predicted, always be gloomy on this day.[16]

The birth, two years later, of Julia Maria hastened Judith's emotional recovery. Having finally achieved her most cherished desire, she plunged into motherhood with a sense of joy and dedication that would have bewildered her ancestors. She was determined to control every detail of her daughter's life. In some ways, at least for affluent women, a mother's duties were easier in the eighteenth century than they had been a century earlier. As they supplied more of their families' needs from the shops that increasingly lined urban streets, they had more time to devote to their offspring. But if their workload contracted in some ways, it expanded in others. Mothers like Judith Sargent Murray began to take their child-rearing duties more seriously, attaching special emotional significance to tasks they had formerly viewed as routine. Judith's Aunt Maria spent nearly all her waking hours with her children, attending to their every need with slavelike devotion. Had she lived a century earlier, she would undoubtedly have shared her duties with relatives or servants and would never have assumed that her children's welfare lay entirely in her own hands.

One task many women took to heart during this period was breast-feeding. New England women had never embraced the practice common to affluent European women, who, especially in the seventeenth century, had regularly handed their children over to a wet nurse. They nursed their own babies for practical reasons or because Puritan divines had argued that using wet nurses violated biblical precept. By the eighteenth century, however, women exalted breast-feeding, claiming to derive sensual or sentimental pleasure from the experience and maintaining that it would forge an emotional bond between themselves and their children. If a mother did not enjoy this "delightfully interesting employment," if she gave her child over to "mercenary hands," she was selfish, cruel, a monster. Only a woman who lacked sensibility, said Murray, would willingly deprive herself of the "raptures" that were "peculiar to the maternal character."[17] A woman who rejected the pleasures of motherhood was unnatural.

Breast-feeding had its drawbacks, of course. It limited a woman's freedom of movement, confining her physically to the home. Judith herself stopped traveling with her husband until Julia Maria was weaned.[18] There were, moreover, many women like Judith's niece Sarah, who could not breast-feed their own children and who suffered shame and anxiety as a result.[19] Sometimes breast-feeding was harmful to the mother. Julia Maria became ill when she tried to nurse her daughter Charlotte, who, said Judith, was "not easily satisfied."[20] She took it for granted that mothers who failed to breast-feed their children suffered physically and emotionally.

At some point, of course, the baby had to be weaned, a "heart affecting work" for both mother and child.[21] Most mothers began the process sometime between the ninth and twelfth months after a child was born, but Judith could not bear to wean her own daughter until she was nearly two years old. Julia Maria handled the transition with apparent ease. Judith, on the other hand, cried for days afterwards.[22]

Not only did eighteenth-century women spend more time with their children than had their mothers or grandmothers, they also worried more about the consequences of their efforts. They derived pleasure from their children, but at the same time, they were anxious, believing that even the tiniest mistake might do permanent damage at a time when their offspring were most vulnerable. Increasingly, women hesitated to rely on custom, common sense, or God's providence in raising their children. Instead, they scoured the growing body of child-care manuals looking for modern advice on a wide variety of subjects. At one time, authors had addressed those books to fathers, but by the mid-eighteenth century, mothers were their main audience. For Murray and her contemporaries, motherhood had become a vocation that required expertise, rationality, and constant effort.

The more mothers assumed that the physical and emotional fate of their children rested in their own hands, the more nervous they became. Childhood was fraught with danger in the eighteenth century, as disease and accidents regularly took their toll on the youngest members of society. A century earlier, just as they saw the death of babies during childbirth as God's providence, parents tried to accept the loss of their older children with stoicism, knowing that there was nothing they could do to alter divine will. By the time Julia Maria was born in 1791, however, mothers blamed themselves when they could not keep their children free from harm. A child's death incurred guilt as well as grief. Every stage in its life was crucial. The milestones of teething, walking, and talking were all potential crises mothers tried to handle with intelligence and sensitivity, tailoring their behavior to the needs of the child.

Murray worried endlessly about her daughter's physical welfare. Baby George's death had been traumatic. The death of her only living child would be devastating. Julia Maria had a delicate constitution, and Murray greeted her daughter's every sniffle with alarm. She kept the child in bed at the slightest provocation, sitting beside her day and night to make sure her condition did not worsen. She also watched Julia Maria's diet closely, refusing to allow her daughter to drink wine mixed with water, for instance, when she read that the practice, common in her day, was harmful.[23] After the family moved to Boston, mother and daughter spent every summer in Gloucester, where they were able to breathe the fresh sea air, free of the diseases that hovered over the capital city during the hottest months.

For Judith Sargent Murray, motherhood was a full-time job, and one that she professed to relish. Her every moment, she claimed, was devoted to her daughter's welfare. Her letters were filled with anecdotes describing Julia Maria's progress. Her poems sang praises to the joys of motherhood. If she had no time she could call her own, she did not complain. No sacrifice was too great. (See Document 10.)

Although Murray was equivocal in her opinion of wives who sacrificed their own interests for the sake of their husbands, she never wavered in her conviction that mothers should be prepared to give their all for their children. If she argued that most gender differences were culturally constructed, she was certain that women were endowed by nature and by God to be mothers. She was equally sure that no man was capable of learning to do what women did naturally. Men might, she conceded, assume responsibility for their older sons, but they could never do an adequate job of tending to young children or raising their daughters. When she contemplated her own death, she indicated that she preferred to leave Julia Maria in the hands of a woman rather than with her own husband. For, she told Winthrop, "It is seldom that an individual of your sex, however amiable he may be, is in every respect qualified to form the gentle female mind. Nature, although equal in her distributions is nevertheless various in her gifts, and her discriminating lines are perfectly obvious."[24]

Judith Sargent Murray's view of motherhood reveals a complicated understanding of gender roles, one she shared with many of her contemporaries. On the one hand, the elevation of the role of motherhood gave women a certain dignity and pride, even according them a tenuous and indirect connection to the well-being of the new nation. It strengthened a woman's ties to the family, even as it made her private life and decisions more important. A mother's influence, wrote Murray, affected not only her own offspring but "generations yet unborn."[25] As a result, she demanded equal education for women. On the other hand, the same perspective tended to circumscribe the sphere within which a woman operated, encouraging her to make her family, especially her children, the focus of her energies and ambitions. By defining woman "as mother," Murray seemed to be retreating from her belief that women's goals should know no boundaries. If, as she put it, nature was "equal in her distributions," nature was also "various in her gifts." The mind and soul may have been genderless, but there were, nevertheless, "perfectly obvious," and apparently innate and immutable, differences between men and women after all.

NOTES

[1]Quoted in John Demos, *A Little Commonwealth: Family Life in Plymouth Colony* (New York: Oxford University Press, 1970), 134, 135.

[2]Judith Sargent Murray, "Locke," 1781, Judith Sargent Murray, Repository, 281–83, Mississippi Archives, Jackson, Miss.

[3]Judith Stevens to John Murray, 21 Nov. [1781], Judith Sargent Murray, Letterbook, 1:369.

[4]Judith Sargent Murray, *The Gleaner: A Miscellaneous Production in Three Volumes* (Boston: L. Thomas and E. T. Andrews, 1798), 2:68.

[5]Murray, *The Gleaner,* 1:303; "Martesia," Repository, 134.

[6]Murray, "Cleora," 31 May 1777, Repository, 33, 34.

[7]Judith Sargent Murray to Maria Sargent, 15 July 1789, Judith Sargent Murray, Letterbook, 4:51, Mississippi Archives, Jackson, Miss.

[8]Catherine M. Scholten, *Childbearing in American Society: 1650–1850* (New York: New York University Press, 1985).

[9]Judith Sargent Murray to Maria Sargent, 15 July 1789, Letterbook, 4:51.

[10]Murray, *The Gleaner,* 3:197.

[11]John Murray to Colonel Paul Dudley Sargent, 1 Oct. 1789, transcript, Sargent House Museum, Gloucester, Mass.

[12]Judith Sargent Murray to Mrs. Lucy Sargent of Sullivan, 6 May 1790, Letterbook, 4:83.

[13]Judith Sargent Murray to Esther Ellery, 29 July 1790, ibid., 186.

[14]John Murray to Colonel Paul Dudley Sargent, 1 Oct. 1789, transcript, Sargent House Museum.

[15]Judith Sargent Murray to Winthrop and Judith Sargent, 17 July 1790, Letterbook, 4:174.

[16]Judith Sargent Murray to Maria Sargent, 5 Aug. 1790, ibid., 195.

[17]Judith Sargent Murray to Esther Ellery, 15 May 1797, Letterbook, 10:116.

[18]Judith Sargent Murray to Mrs. Barrell of York, 24 Dec. 1792, Letterbook, 8:87.

[19]Judith Sargent Murray to Esther Ellery, 29 Mar. 1797, Letterbook, 10:92, 93.

[20]Judith Sargent Murray to Maria Sargent, [?] Oct. [1814], Letterbook, 19:[22].

[21]Judith Sargent Murray to Anna Sargent, 17 Oct. 1800, Letterbook, 11:210.

[22]Judith Sargent Murray to Mrs. P_____ of Hampstead, England, 15 Nov. 1794, Letterbook, 8:243.

[23]Judith Sargent Murray to Winthrop Sargent, 7 Mar. 1796, Letterbook, 9:543.

[24]Judith Sargent Murray to Winthrop Sargent, 1 Nov. 1796, ibid., 598.

[25]Judith Sargent Murray to Anna Sargent, 28 Feb. 1799, Letterbook, 10:361.

7

A "Most Extensive Education"

Judith Sargent Murray never tired of complaining that she had been "robbed of the aids of education."[1] Her insatiable appetite for learning drove her desire to transcend what she viewed as the artificial limits to her ambitions. In this respect as well, she was in agreement with many middle- and upper-class women of her time. Both Abigail Adams and Mercy Otis Warren lamented their own inferior educations and called for an expansion of opportunities for future generations of women. They had a legitimate grievance. By any objective standard, women's education before the Revolution was quantitatively and qualitatively deficient. Although conditions improved slightly in the postwar era, over the next century women would view their lack of educational opportunities with despair.

Even in Puritan New England, which put a high premium on literacy, women's education had traditionally lagged behind that of men. Because the Bible was central to their religion, the Puritans wanted everyone, even women, to be able to read. But John Winthrop, the Massachusetts Governor, was not alone in arguing that women were more emotional, less rational, and less educable than men, and that too much learning might be harmful. Even those who agreed that women should know how to read did not believe they *needed* to know how to write. Merchants, lawyers, doctors, and farmers had to be literate to engage in the everyday business of an increasingly complex economy. Most women, however, could do their jobs effectively without being able to sign their own name.

By the end of the seventeenth century, attitudes toward women's education gradually began to change. In the northeast, families at the top of the social hierarchy wanted their daughters to be "accomplished," genteel, and refined. Thus, girls like Judith Sargent learned to read and write, and often obtained a rudimentary knowledge of French. But even at mid century no one seriously argued that women required an education to do what their mothers had done very well without formal schooling. Women had always been able to acquire and pass on their skills orally and informally, through face-to-face interaction, and everyone assumed that they would continue to do so. The city of Boston offered no free education to girls until 1789. Gloucester did not admit girls to public school until shortly before the Revolution, and then their education consisted of only the most cursory writing lessons, which occupied, at most, two hours a day.

By the end of the eighteenth century, most Americans agreed that women were *capable* of being educated, and many even argued that they *should* be educated. But what did women need to know, and why did they need to know it? What areas of intellectual endeavor should be opened to them, and what areas should remain off-limits? Despite differences of opinion on specific issues, the general trend was obvious. John Locke's emphasis on the malleability of human nature had undermined the notion that female intellectual inferiority was immutable. The enlightenment faith in human potential, the American Revolution's emphasis on equality and individual rights, and the Republic's desire to create a wise and virtuous citizenry led some Americans to mount a concerted campaign for improvements in women's education. Judith Sargent Murray eagerly positioned herself at the center of the discussion, arguing that women should have access to the same opportunities that men did. Unlike many of her contemporaries, she also insisted that women needed education not only to make them better wives and mothers, but to improve their own lives.

In many ways, Murray's views were simply a reflection of the potpourri of values, hopes, and fears that characterized postrevolutionary America. She wanted women to share in the promise of liberty, equality, and individual opportunity that lay at the core of the nation's struggle for independence. She hoped that America would achieve cultural as well as political independence from Europe and that independence would lead to a new citizenry—literate, public-spirited, and worthy of the role it would play in a society where the people were sovereign. She wanted women to have a vital part in the movement for cultural autonomy. Like many of her fellow Federalists, however, she worried that America might not be able to achieve a cultural revolution to match its military victory. As they witnessed the "atheistic" rampages of the French Revolution and the rise of Thomas Jefferson's Democratic Republicans, many Americans feared that their experiment with independence had been a ghastly mistake. In this context, the training of the next generation was crucial.

Those who argued for improvements in women's education assumed that women were intellectually equal to men, but Murray knew that many of her contemporaries were not yet convinced of women's innate abilities. She launched her own defense of women's education to discredit all lingering notions of female inadequacy. While she freely admitted that women and men had unique physical attributes, she insisted that "the distinction male and female, does not exist in *Mind*."[2] If women generally failed to measure up to the standards set by their male counterparts, their poor education, not their "radical inferiority," was to blame.[3] In public and private, Murray echoed the same refrain, making copious lists of intelligent and accomplished women throughout history to prove that "considered in the aggregate," the "minds of women [are] *naturally* as susceptible of every improvement as those of men."[4]

In arguing that women and men were intellectual equals, Murray relied heavily on Lockean philosophy, as she tried to account for that "affected ignorance, and childish imbecility which is supposed the characteristic of the female world."[5] If both women and men were "made of mutable stuff," then, she insisted, they could both be shaped for good or evil.[6] Thus, she airily dismissed evidence suggesting that women were intellectually weak, maintaining that a male-dominated power structure systematically denied women the opportunities routinely offered to men. To prove her point, she noted that at the age of one or two, boys and girls were clearly equal in ability. It was only when they grew older, as boys were taught to "aspire" while girls were "constantly confined and limited," that gender-based intellectual differences began to appear.[7] Women, she maintained, would have made many important contributions to society had not "ignorant or interested men, after clipping their wings, contrived to erect around them almost insurmountable barriers."[8]

It was not only poor education that created a hostile intellectual environment for women. Custom, too, constrained them. Indeed, it was a measure of their innate ability that women were able to withstand as well as they did a socialization process designed to render them weak and ineffectual. In particular, women's preoccupation with traditional domestic duties inhibited their intellectual progress. While at times Murray claimed to relish the tasks associated with housewifery, more often she complained of the drudgery, the mind-numbing repetitiveness, and the time-consuming nature of housework. However important domestic tasks were, they left virtually no time for the edifying life of the mind. It was necessary, she thought, for the world to accept the fact that "females possess talents, capable of extending their utility beyond the kitchen, or the parlour."[9]

Proving that women had the capacity to be educated was easy compared to showing that women *should* be educated. Not every American agreed with the more liberal-minded Dr. Benjamin Rush and the lexicographer Noah Webster that it was *not* a waste of time to teach girls more than how to read, do simple arithmetic, and perhaps to write. Some feared that educated women would become dissatisfied with their traditional duties and "unsexed" by their intellectual achievements. Too many others believed that a learned woman was a threat to order and stability.

Although Judith Sargent Murray had no wish for a world where distinctions between men and women ceased to exist, she argued that education did not destroy a woman's femininity, and that even the most well-educated matrons cheerfully relinquished their pens for their pots and pans when duty demanded it. The domestic arts were easy to learn, and once learned they required no further mental ability. It did not, she noted with acerbity, require a genius to make a cake or sew a seam in a garment.[10] A woman could easily ply the needle while her mind roamed freely over a wide range of literary or political topics. The story of Margaretta was designed in part to prove just this point. (See Document 11.) Despite her excellent education, Margaretta "was not unfitted for her proper sphere." She whipped up delicious puddings, ironed linens, and was the "complete housewife." Her education, moreover, led her to disdain the frivolous world of fashion and to devote her time to reading or charitable activity instead of wasting hours visiting, playing cards, or dancing. Far from "unsexing" her, education gave her the ability to live the simple and useful existence that formed the heart of the republican ideal.[11]

Indeed, Murray insisted, a good education actually prepared a woman to assume the role nature and custom had assigned her. She agreed with her compatriots who argued that women wielded considerable influence over the morals and manners of adult men. No man, said one observer, would risk the disapproval of an admirable woman. "Wherever ladies are highly improved by a well-directed and refined education, there the gentleman will soon become so," for "the fair part of creation rule the world."[12] If men strove to earn the praise of women, then it was essential that women be educated in the principles of liberty and virtue in order to guide their husbands, brothers, and friends. Women might not be able to vote or hold office, but they still exercised considerable indirect political influence.

Even more important than her desire to turn women into good wives was Murray's determination to encourage society to educate mothers. Winning independence and ratifying a new constitution were no assurance of a stable and lasting union. A king had no need of an educated and public-spirited rank and file, but a Republic would perish without it. America's fate depended on the ability of its citizens to educate themselves, and more to the point, on the intellectual attainments of its women. In this sense, Murray agreed with leading advocates of women's education like Benjamin Rush, who maintained that since women bore the primary responsibility for raising children—especially sons—the future of the Republic was in their hands.

Simeon Doggett, a Unitarian minister, argued that because children were "in the arms of their mothers" during their infancy, women formed their character.[13] Murray agreed. Early childhood, she said, was the "seedtime." A baby was an unformed "child of expectation" upon whom mothers could exert their influence with ease.[14] "A mother," she explained, "is certainly the most proper preceptress for her children, and it [is] for this reason that I would educate a daughter upon the most liberal plan." It was the mother, who was "more or less employed in teaching the young idea how to shoot."[15]

Murray became more convinced of the need for women's education after 1801 when her brother Winthrop gave her responsibility for shaping the education of his sons, stepsons, and stepdaughter. For the most part, her experience was an unhappy one. (See Document 12.) Two of her young charges were dismissed from Harvard. Another failed to complete his studies at Phillips Exeter Academy. Winthrop removed a fourth son from her care before she had a chance to see if her methods might work with him. Murray explained her failures in gendered terms. "Among the weeds which infest the garden of science," she said, "a contempt for the female world is of a growth astonishingly rampant, and a Woman, especially an *old Woman* is considered the most inefficient and insignificant being in the human family."[16] Her methods were sound, she insisted. The problems she encountered as her nephews grew older and began to defy her, were a measure of women's inferior status. Men, she said repeatedly, refused to accept "petticoat government."[17]

Still, Murray admitted that while male contempt for women was the product of prejudice, it was in some respects justified. Their inadequate education, she complained, had rendered women "impotent," making them poor mothers and worse teachers.[18] Her own failures occurred because society undervalued women and did not provide the education they needed to raise their children. If the home was the best place to prepare young boys as moral and virtuous citizens, her own experience—writ large—portended a national tragedy.

In her belief that education would produce a virtuous nation, Murray echoed the refrain of many men and women in the years after the Revolution. Everyone assumed that a woman should use her education to serve her husband, her children, and through them, her country, and that she should study to be "honored and beloved at home" rather than admired abroad.[19] So long as education merely preserved domestic tranquillity and strengthened the position of mothers, it did not threaten conventional gender roles. But Murray's case for the value of women's education went further. She believed that it could help women secure a better quality of life for themselves.

Education, Murray argued, made women happier wives. An educated woman would choose a husband with great discernment. Once married, she would accept her wifely status with grace, and would not be filled with the false expectations she gleaned from silly novels. Because she understood human nature, she would not expect her husband to be perfect. She would be intelligent, serious, and modest, eschewing the frivolity and idleness associated with the degenerate aristocracy of the Old World in favor of the simplicity and usefulness of Republican America. Most important, she would be an equal companion to her husband. She would have no reason to complain that her inferior education made her unfit to discuss weighty subjects such as science and politics. "By strengthening the body and exercising the mental capacities," explained Murray, "we shall be rendered more capable of managing our families, of systematizing morality, and of becoming the friends of our husbands."[20] Education was the foundation for companionate marriage.

Education not only made women happier wives, but it provided single women the practical means to enjoy true independence. Murray knew from experience what many observers knew only abstractly: Women could not always rely on family, friends, or husbands for their own financial welfare. She had faced poverty on occasion and she was always terrified that John Murray's death would force her and her daughter to depend on the charity of her siblings. Worse, she feared that Julia Maria would feel compelled to marry an unworthy suitor simply because marriage represented her only opportunity for economic security. "THE SEX," she lectured, "should be taught to depend on their own efforts."[21] If the new nation placed a premium on independence for its male inhabitants, women, too, should be educated to take care of themselves.

When Americans argued that women could and should be educated, they disagreed about what middle- and upper-class girls should learn. They had to know how to read, do simple figures, and write with a clear hand. A knowledge of history, geography, astronomy, and natural philosophy was also important. They should be acquainted with the needle and the loom. And most people thought that dancing was good exercise and a better use of spare time than card playing or gossip. Beyond that, some added a knowledge of French or talked favorably of painting, draw-ing, and music. Others criticized these accomplishments as frivolous.

In theory, if not always in practice, Judith Sargent Murray's view of an ideal curriculum for women was broad and ambitious. Long before she became a mother, she had developed a theory of education based on her own understanding of human nature. Murray conceded, however, the vast difference between "speculative opinion" and "embodying such opin-ion, by a regular series of action."[22] If she was unsure about some details, on one point she never wavered. Girls should be accorded "the most extensive education" that the human mind could devise.[23] Any endeavor that "could by the most remote construction be deemed feminine" should be open to women.[24] (See Document 11.) Women, she argued, should even learn Latin and Greek.

A few "exceptional" women in England and America knew something of the dead languages, but such study was traditionally a male preserve. Admission to Harvard and Yale required a knowledge of Latin and Greek. Any man who aspired to professional status, especially the ministry or the law, or wished to lay claim to gentility studied the classics. Educators did not consider Latin and Greek essential for women, and many argued that the "pagan" message and risqué images of the ancients were harm-ful to the delicate female mind. Latin and Greek were also part of the rhetorical tradition, and because women seldom spoke in public, there seemed to be little point in teaching them what would clearly be irrele-vant to their needs.

Judith Sargent Murray's resentment of her parents for refusing to allow her a classical education sharpened in the 1770s, when her youngest brother, Fitz William, began what for him was the hopeless task of learning Latin. As she observed his tear-stained face, she wondered why she had been so arbitrarily excluded from an endeavor her brother despised. This kind of exclusion came to symbolize the artificiality of most gender distinctions. If studying the ancients was essential to the good character of young men, why would it not be equally essential to young women? She had no doubt that women were intellectually capable of learning Latin and Greek. The pages of *The Gleaner* were replete with examples of women who were steeped in the classics yet did not betray a lack of femininity.

Murray's ignorance of Latin and Greek was a humiliating reminder of her powerlessness. When Winthrop's sons came to Boston, she found that she soon lost their respect because she could not help them with their studies. Her deficiencies were so obvious, the boys simply refused to obey her. It seemed unnatural for a grown woman to admit her inferiority to a boy, yet this was what the antiquated customs of eighteenth-century society guaranteed.

Judith put her educational philosophy into practice whenever she had the chance. Her letters to the young Fitz William were so full of advice, the hapless boy finally begged her to stop writing altogether. The project that was dearest to her heart, however, was the education of her daughter. From the moment of Julia Maria's birth, Judith had "one grand object in view": to give her daughter "such an education as may, if her mind be tolerably ingenious, furnish her in whatever situation she may be placed, with sources of profit and amusement—with an antidote against that ennui of which females are *especially* too often found complaining."[25] In short, she wanted Julia Maria to have the education that she herself had never enjoyed, and she was willing to do anything, make any financial or personal sacrifice, to achieve it.

Judith preferred to teach her daughter herself. By the time she was five, Julia Maria could read, spell, and do plain sewing. But Judith knew that her daughter would soon advance beyond her own ability to teach her, and she reluctantly turned to the experts for help. In 1798, Julia Maria enrolled in Mr. Payne's Federal Street Academy. Judith accepted the move with mixed emotions. Although she was delighted to be able to afford an excellent education for her daughter, she admitted to more than a few misgivings as she watched Julia Maria leave her care for the first time. She never trusted strangers, no matter how competent, to take the interest in her daughter's education that she herself did. (See Document 12.)

In fact, Judith did not leave Julia Maria's education in the hands of the instructors at Mr. Payne's establishment. The girl never spent more than four hours a day at the Academy, and even then, Judith meticulously—some would say obsessively—monitored her progress. "The familiar picture of the hen with one chick is often present to my view," she admitted.[26] She heard her daughter's lessons, tutored her when she could, and sent a steady stream of notes to Mr. Payne complaining about the quality of Julia Maria's instruction: The preceptors allowed her daughter to be too careless; they did not give her the attention she deserved; they did not correct her when she formed her letters improperly; they accepted an imperfect lesson as easily as a perfect one. At one point, Julia Maria's writing teacher grew so frustrated, she abandoned her little pupil altogether, declaring that she could never satisfy the exacting requirements of the child's doting mother. Only Judith's abject apologies persuaded her to resume her duties.

Murray was delighted when Anna Williams, Winthrop's stepdaughter, came with her brothers James and David to live with the Murrays.

She had always wanted a sister for Julia Maria, fearing that lack of female companionship would stunt her social and mental growth. She believed children learned more when they engaged in friendly competition and had someone their own age to emulate. Unlike her brothers, Anna fit easily into the household routine. She attended Mr. Payne's school with her cousin. The two girls learned to play the piano and had lessons in painting, voice, and dancing. In 1801, the Murrays hired a French tutor for Anna and Julia Maria, and in the fall of 1806, Judith realized one of her most cherished dreams when she engaged a Latin tutor for the girls.

Judith was pleased with her efforts to educate her niece and daughter, and despite a nagging sense of her own inferiority, she pronounced her methods a success. Winthrop, always more traditional, disagreed. He was stunned when Anna returned home and seemed to know very little of the culinary arts. While Judith was hurt by her brother's criticism, she spiritedly defended her priorities. It would have been an unpardonable waste of her niece's time and Winthrop's money, she insisted, to distract the girls from their lessons by teaching them how to roast a joint of beef or scrub a floor. Of course, even the wealthiest woman should be able to occupy "that useful domestic sphere, in which custom, and perhaps nature has designed they should move," but "the knowledge of every thing in the domestic line . . . may be learned in six months, as well as in six years." Her brother's criticism, she said, was completely unfair.[27]

Winthrop clearly thought Judith's educational plan unsuitable and altogether too revolutionary. In fact, despite her grandiose rhetoric, Judith's methods, and the course of study she devised, reveal a traditional bias. Julia Maria and Anna were "accomplished," to be sure, but they were hardly prepared for a wide variety of occupations. Even the Latin lessons of which Judith was so proud lasted less than a year. It is fair to wonder why she wanted the girls to study Latin at all. She surely did not imagine that a familiarity with the classics would lead to a legal or political career. The Murrays would not even allow their daughter to display her talents as a public speaker. As Murray wrote Mr. Payne, "a modest adherence to the rules prescribed to her sex, will not allow a *personal* solicitation of public attention."[28] What, then, would Julia Maria do with a knowledge of Latin? At most, it might give her some pleasure and make her a better mother. At the least, it was simply another accomplishment.

Murray believed women "capable of the most arduous achievements."[29] She hoped her daughter's future would include more than the "drudgery" of needlework.[30] Yet her vision was limited. She wanted Julia Maria to be a good Republican mother. Beyond that, she vaguely imagined that education would prepare her daughter to give voice lessons or to be a teacher, should she be thrown on her own resources, occupations that would "consist with the female character."[31]

Despite her parents' financial sacrifices on her behalf, Julia Maria never used her education in any practical way. Her marriage to Adam Bingaman made it unnecessary. She may have been a fine mother to little Charlotte, but for much of her adult life she made little use of her accomplishments. Abandoned for years by her husband, she refused to attend the theater, appear in a ballroom, or accept a party invitation. On occasion she had tea with close relatives, but for the most part she remained in seclusion, waiting for Adam to return to Boston or transport her to Natchez. If her education was intended to prepare her for "independence" and encourage her to "reverence herself," it did not deliver her from a more traditional, sheltered existence than that experienced by her less-educated mother.

NOTES

[1] Judith Sargent Murray to Winthrop Sargent, [Fall 1803], Judith Sargent Murray, Letterbook, 12:878, Mississippi Archives, Jackson, Miss.

[2] Judith Sargent Murray to Mr. Redding of Falmouth, England, 7 May 1801, Letterbook, 11:287.

[3] Judith Stevens to Winthrop Sargent, 3 July 1778, Letterbook, 1:122.

[4] Judith Sargent Murray, *The Gleaner: A Miscellaneous Production in Three Volumes* (Boston: L. Thomas and E. T. Andrews, 1798), 1:193; 3:197, 198.

[5] Judith Sargent Murray to Mrs. Barrell of York, 25 Nov. 1800, Letterbook, 11:229.

[6] Judith Sargent Murray to Winthrop Sargent, 22 Feb. 1796, Letterbook, 9:538.

[7] Judith Sargent Murray, "The Sexes," Judith Sargent Murray, Repository, 226, 227, Mississippi Archives, Jackson, Miss.

[8] Murray, *The Gleaner*, 3:197.

[9] Judith Stevens to Mrs. Pilgrim of London, Old England, 2 Sept. 1786, Letterbook, 3:140.

[10] Judith Sargent Murray, "The Sexes," Repository, 227, 228.

[11] Murray, *The Gleaner*, 1:71–73.

[12] Simeon Doggett, "A Discourse on Education," 1797, in *Essays on Education in the Early Republic*, ed. Frederick Rudolph (Cambridge: Harvard University Press, 1965).

[13] Ibid., 158.

[14] Judith Sargent Murray to Miss Mary Allen, 9 June 1788, Letterbook 3: 119; Judith Stevens to Anna _____, 23 June 1785, Letterbook, 2:340; Judith Stevens to Miss Gardiner, 8 Sept. 1785, Letterbook, 3:11.

[15] Judith Sargent Murray to Winthrop Sargent, [September 1803], Letterbook, 12:878.

[16] Judith Sargent Murray to Winthrop Sargent, 27 Nov. 1814, Letterbook, 19:29.

[17] Judith Sargent Murray to Winthrop Sargent, 5 June 1815, Letterbook, 10:109.

[18] Judith Sargent Murray to Winthrop Sargent, 8 Aug. 1815, Letterbook, 19:142.

[19] Benjamin Rush, "Thoughts Upon Female Education, Accomodated to the Present State of Society, Manners and Government in the United States of America," 1787, in Rudolph, ed., *Essays on Education,* 28–38.

[20] Judith Sargent Murray to Mrs. K_____, 21 Apr. 1802, Letterbook, 11:350.

[21] Judith Sargent Murray to Maria Sargent, 16 Mar. 1793, Letterbook, 8:103.

[22] Judith Sargent Murray to Mrs. Barrell of York, 29 Jan. 1795, ibid., 258.

[23] Ibid., 259.

[24] Murray, *The Gleaner,* 1:70.

[25] Judith Sargent Murray to Maria Sargent, 6 May 1792, Letterbook, 8:38.

[26] Judith Sargent Murray to Mr. Sargent of Hampstead, 21 Oct. 1799, Letterbook, 11:75.

[27] Judith Sargent Murray to Winthrop Sargent, 17 Dec. 1808, Letterbook, 15:77; Judith Sargent Murray to Winthrop Sargent, 7 Oct. 1811, Letterbook, 17:20, 21.

[28] Judith Sargent Murray to Mr. Payne, 11 Nov. 1803, Letterbook, 11:888.

[29] Judith Sargent Murray to Mrs. Barrell of York, 25 Nov. 1800, ibid., 229.

[30] Murray, *The Gleaner,* 1:69.

[31] Judith Sargent Murray to Esther Ellery, 24 Mar. 1800, Letterbook, 11:153.

8

A "Mania" for Literary Fame

Judith Sargent Murray was always something of a "scribbler." Before she was nine, she had already written what she called simply "a history." Even after someone stole her "imbecile effusion," she continued to devote at least an hour each day to a task that she found both soothing and gratifying.[1] At first she wrote purely for her own pleasure, but gradually she began to share her work with her relatives and close friends. By the time of the American Revolution, she harbored a not-so-secret desire for literary fame but needed considerable courage to expose her work to the eyes of an invisible, impersonal public. It took even longer to imagine that she might earn fortune as well as fame with her talent.

An avid reader, Judith was aware that there were any number of women in Europe and America who wrote for the public. These writers served as role models for countless young women, who were convinced that they too could gain public attention through their writing. Most women were content to influence public affairs indirectly as sisters, wives, and mothers, but a few—Judith Sargent Murray among them—sought a direct and immediate impact.

In the beginning, Judith's pleasure in writing was manifested in her letters. Letter writing served simply as "an admirable substitute for the privilege of conversation."[2] Her view was not unusual. As people left worn-out farms and villages in search of better opportunities, letters maintained ties of kinship and affection. The task of keeping families and friendships intact often fell to women, who could write down their thoughts at odd moments throughout the day, in between household chores. Women wrote letters to parents, siblings, and acquaintances to recount ordinary experiences and cares, births and deaths, joys and sorrows. Letter writing was a form of talking and thus one of the most important links with the outside world that women were able to forge.

But it was more than that. The eighteenth century was "the great age of the personal letter."[3] More and more homes boasted special writing desks, an indication that letter writing had become not just an elite woman's accomplishment but a popular art form many Americans took very seriously. Proper letter writing entailed its own rules. Each letter was a self-revealing "performance" by which a reader could judge the author's character, grace, and accomplishments. (See Document 13.)

Murray understood the literary value of her letters. In the 1770s, she began copying her correspondence into bound letterbooks she enjoyed reading on occasion, proudly observing her improvement in expressing her thoughts and reliving past experiences. It was a way, she said, "of comparing *myself* with *myself*."[4] It was also a little like keeping a diary, and she hoped that one day Julia Maria would find as much pleasure in these letters as she did. They were, in their own way, a bid for earthly immortality.

Whether women wrote formal missives to men or casual acquaintances, or more spontaneous outpourings to close friends and relatives, letter writing introduced them to a broader audience. Good letters were often good stories. Correspondents experimented with dialogue and description. They recorded their feelings and their impressions of people, places, and events. Sometimes they organized a letter around a particular theme. Most letters were semipublic documents—read aloud and shared among family and friends—so that, from the beginning, their audience was somewhat broad and undefined. Then, too, the eighteenth century was the heyday of the "epistolary novel," in which the story unfolded through a series of letters. Epistolary novels were relatively formless, often had a chatty quality, and allowed their authors to commit occasional grammatical errors in the name of "realism." Because they were accustomed to writing letters, women often saw the epistolary novel as a tempting, almost natural model.

Murray enjoyed writing letters and employed the epistolary technique in her *Gleaner* essays. There is no doubt that her personal letters were an essential stage in her development as a writer. During the American Revolution, her brother Winthrop and John Murray insisted on sharing her letters with fellow officers. She immediately grasped the difference between writing for friends and writing for strangers. "Efforts acceptable to the bosom of friendship," she noted, "the cool eyes of a stranger will methodically examine."[5] Still, she was pleased by the praise she received from these potential critics. Her letters often served as dress rehearsals for her published essays. On countless occasions, she expressed thoughts to close friends before writing them out for public consumption.

Murray was also proud of her ability as a poet. "She wrote poetry by the acre," laughed her cousin, Lucius Manlius Sargent. "This was her stumbling block."[6] Like many educated women of her class, she sent little verses to friends along with gifts of aprons or needlebooks. Every occasion prompted a few lines. Notwithstanding her cousin's unkind remarks, Murray's verses were no worse than most of the poetry of the age. They were didactic, highly stylized, and intensely patriotic. American poets were concerned above all with inculcating moral truths. Many poems were almost essays in verse form, their utilitarian purpose never far below the surface. If these poems seem stilted and contrived today, they were admired in their own day. The neoclassical couplets of Alexander Pope were a standard model. Anxious beginners, careful to get everything right, turned out formulaic poems, with proper rhythm, cadence, and rhyme. There was no attempt to match mood or purpose to a particular form, since form did not follow function. Poets repeated or multiplied images and saturated their lines with exclamations, interrogatives, and underlined words.

Murray loved writing poetry. She could easily compose a few verses in a single sitting. Her longer poems, some of which went on for pages, took days to write. After she began publishing her work, she sent reams of her efforts to various New England magazines. She also wrote patriotic poems for her cousins and nephews to recite on special occasions, and she introduced every essay in *The Gleaner* with one of her own verses.

If Murray saw herself as a poet, scholars today remember her primarily as an essayist. Once she agreed to publish her Universalist catechism, she found it impossible to resist the temptation to publish again. In 1784, two years after the catechism appeared, she wrote an essay for the *Gentleman's and Lady's Town and Country Magazine*. The essay, "Desultory Thoughts Upon the Utility of Encouraging a Degree of Self-Complacency Especially in Female Bosoms," outlined her belief in women's intellectual ability, a view which formed the core of her writing for the rest of her life. Following common practice, she adopted a pseudonym, writing under the name "Constantia." In 1790, as "Constantia," she began publishing her work in the *Massachusetts Magazine*. "On the Equality of the Sexes," a two-part essay, appeared in March and April, and "On the Domestic Education of Children" in May. In 1792, Murray began submitting essays to the *Massachusetts Magazine* in two series. Her first "Gleaner" essay appeared in February, the first "Repository" essay in September. Both series continued until 1794. When Murray wrote for the "Repository," she called herself "Constantia," but for "The Gleaner" series she adopted a male persona. As a man, the Gleaner could freely wander through public spaces, talking to strangers, and listening and commenting on everything with the confidence that his views would be taken seriously. Murray's choice of subjects reflected her belief that the mind was genderless. She was determined to write authoritatively on every subject, not just "women's issues," to demonstrate that women had the ability and the right to influence public affairs in a public forum.

By publishing her essays, Murray joined contemporaries on both sides of the Atlantic in challenging traditional gender definitions and crossing customary gender boundaries. She wrote at a time when intellectual debate influenced public life, when writers believed they were engaged in an important business and, like clergymen, were taken seriously. Not interested in art-for-art's sake, they were determined to use their talents to shape their world. To write for publication was surely less radical than attempting to vote or hold public office. Still, as the Gleaner "himself" put it, to write for publication was to open locked gates and scale hitherto unbreachable walls.[7]

Women who entered the once-forbidden public arena used their talent to probe, even to renegotiate, the boundaries that divided male and female. They remained at home, in the private sphere, yet at the same time they participated in the vigorous public dialogue that dominated the nation's intellectual and political life, thus claiming some rights of citizenship for themselves. Writing provided a way, in Murray's words, "to travel from one quarter of the globe to another" while remaining "stationary."[8] It allowed women to exert direct influence on the world of affairs without asking their husbands or sons to speak for them. To publish was not simply to seek fame but to seek power.

Murray was conscious of the potential importance of her work. In her "Gleaner" essays she created a number of fictional characters who served as examples to prove that private writing could influence public life. Margaretta was reunited with her real father, for instance, when he happened to read the Gleaner's account of his daughter's experiences in an old edition of the *Massachusetts Magazine*.[9] A "Sea Commander" wrote begging "him" to continue the story of Margaretta because of its salutary effect on his daughter. A "Bellamour" promised to reform his spendthrift ways if Margaretta would marry him. "Rebecca Aimwell" valued the Gleaner's hints on the education of young girls.[10] A writer's influence, Murray believed, extended well beyond the little closet where she plied her pen.

Because women writers challenged the status quo, they were subject to disapproval. Sometimes critics simply refused to believe women capable of writing anything that could be considered logical or significant. The philosopher Jean-Jacques Rousseau claimed that "whenever a female draws the pen, it is well known that some Man of letters sits behind the curtain to guide her hand."[11] Indeed, it was partly for this reason that Murray assumed a male persona in the "Gleaner" essays. When she finally proclaimed her "real" identity in "The Gleaner Unmasked," admitting that she was that "identical *Constantia*" her readers might remember from her earlier publications, she explained her strategy. She had observed "the indifference, not to say contempt, with which female productions are regarded." People generally greeted women's work with a *"significant shrug,"* refusing to take it seriously. Because she wanted her readers to judge her work objectively, she chose not only to remain anonymous, but to take on a more socially acceptable "borrowed character."[12]

Murray never doubted the worth of her own opinions, and she did not shrink from expressing her views on politics and other public matters. But she was obsessed by her fear that people would question her ability as a writer. As usual, her inadequate education haunted her. She rewrote every poem and every essay before sending them off. When careless printers "mutilated" her efforts, removing paragraphs or omitting a single comma or semicolon, she demanded an errata page. "I confess," she said, "I am tenacious of a word."[13]

She should have been comforted to know that even well-educated women shared her sense of inadequacy, especially as the conventions of spelling and grammar became increasingly exact throughout the eighteenth century. Most perplexing of all was the tricky business of punctuation. When Murray's printer objected to her dashes, she was thrown into a "fit of horrors," seemingly unaware that all women, even the redoubtable Mary Wollstonecraft, preferred the dash to the comma.[14] "Proper" punctuation—the use of the period, comma, semicolon, and colon—originated in the emphasis on rhetoric, or public speaking, that dominated male education. Each punctuation mark was a signal telling orators how long to pause between phrases. The dash, which indicated a more private and informal purpose, moved with women from private to public writing. No wonder they were often nonplussed.

When she was not apologizing for her own defects, Murray defended women writers in general from undue criticism. She admitted that women had been "unfashioned by the cultivating hand," that their efforts might be neither "elegant nor correct." Still, she argued, although women might be guilty of "the heinous crime of mistaking a colon for a full stop," grammatical rules "originated in convenience." They were hardly God-given commandments. Moreover, although women committed superficial errors, they remained capable of "brilliant efforts," all the more remarkable because they came from the pen of untutored genius.[15]

Judith Sargent Murray's "Gleaner" essays were probably most popular not for her pronouncements on education or politics but for her serialized story "Margaretta." The title character was a young orphan who was adopted by the childless Mr. Vigillius and his wife, Mary. Murray described Margaretta's education, her courtship, and her marriage with an eye to presenting parents an object lesson in proper childrearing techniques while giving young women advice on choosing a husband and being a good wife and mother. Many readers, however, were surely more interested in Margaretta's near-disastrous attachment to the conniving Sinisterius Courtland or in the economic and emotional calamities she faced in her marriage to the virtuous Edward Hamilton than in the moral lessons Murray proffered.

Murray was at best ambivalent about the growing popularity of romantic fiction, especially among impressionable young girls. She refused even to entertain the notion that the story of Margaretta was little more than a thinly disguised novel. Like many novelists, she implied that hers was a true story, not a work of fiction. The heroine, an orphan, was a stock character, and her near seduction, a fate she escaped only as a result of her rational virtue and her willingness to heed the advice of her loving parents, was also a standard ploy. Even the villainous Courtland, a reprobate, was ultimately redeemed by the love of a good woman—eighteenth-century writers always valued a "reformed rake." And Murray's pages were replete with the usual misunderstandings, long-lost relatives, and cases of mistaken identity typical of the genre.

Murray quickly felt at home in her role as a published poet and essayist. She knew of too many respectable women who were similarly engaged to feel awkward about succumbing to her own desire to win adulation. Admittedly, her unabashed "mania" for fame was somewhat unusual.[16] Still, Mercy Otis Warren published plays and poems, and even wrote a history of the American Revolution that she signed with her own name. Sarah Wentworth Morton's poetry, written under the pen name "Philenia," won her the sobriquet "The American Sappho." Judith's friend Sally Barrell was a novelist, as was Susanna Rowson.

If she could justify her quest for fame, Judith found it more difficult to legitimize her pursuit of material profit. A married woman with pretensions to respectability found it somewhat risky to enter the marketplace of ideas, but to thrust herself into the commercial marketplace, to compete not only for honor but for money, put her in a far more delicate position. Sometime before the spring of 1795, however, Murray began to write with an eye to earning fortune. She justified her change of heart in a manner that echoed her earlier efforts to defend her Universalist catechism: She needed money, she said, not for herself, not to improve her standard of living, surely not due to an avaricious desire for luxury, but to pay for Julia Maria's education. She entered the marketplace with real reluctance, she claimed, contending that it was a sacrifice only a loving mother could appreciate. But enter it she did, not as a poet or an essayist, but as a playwright.

As long as she could remember, Judith Sargent Murray had possessed a "romantic" fascination for the theater. She had longed to see a play, to lose herself for an hour or so in its "variety of wonders."[17] In America, however, and especially in her native New England, many people disapproved of the dramatic arts. The Puritans had left their mark on Massachusetts, and generations of their descendants continued to believe that plays, like novels, were sinful. Nor did the legacy of the American Revolution do much to disarm the theater's critics. George Washington may have welcomed the diversion provided by amateur dramatics during the long, cold nights at Valley Forge, but most patriots saw plays as part of the effete aristocratic heritage of Europe and were determined that their influence would not corrupt the still-innocent republic. Murray had her first taste of the forbidden fruit when she visited the relatively cosmopolitan city of Providence, Rhode Island, in 1788. There she was transported by the "beautifully sublime language" of Hannah More's *David and Goliath*. She was also struck by the "universal applause" that a woman playwright's efforts had garnered.[18]

In the winter of 1790, Judith tried her hand at amateur theatrics for the first time when a few audacious Gloucester gentlemen decided to produce their version of George Farquhar's *The Recruiting Officer* on a winter evening when the town was virtually shut off from the rest of the world. Murray's reputation as a published poet made her a likely candidate to write an epilogue for the play. The production was a huge success with at least one member of the audience: Murray rushed home as soon as the curtain fell to write to her Aunt Maria about the glorious event. The audience, she said, "laughed, admired and applauded," and everyone was "rendered almost giddy by clapping of hands." "Strange to tell," she continued with unconcealed pride, even the epilogue was well-received.[19] For the next two years, she eagerly accepted other invitations to write prologues and epilogues for Gloucester's thespians.

Although she later made light of her first dramatic efforts, Murray clearly relished the praise. The theater was uniquely suited to satisfy her hunger for recognition. The reward was both immediate and public, and she basked in the praise of her friends, taking each sound of laughter and murmur of approval to heart.

In the years after the Revolution, Massachusetts steadfastly refused to legalize theatrical productions, despite the determined efforts of some

Bostonians, who in the 1790s mounted a campaign to remove the legislature's strictures against the licensing of theaters. Eventually, they ignored the law, opening the Federal Street Theater in 1794 under the management of an Englishman, Charles Powell. Two years later, Powell laid plans to open the rival Haymarket Theater. Neither establishment operated legally until 1797, when the legislature finally agreed to license plays in Boston but continued to ban them elsewhere in the state.

Almost as soon as the Federal Street Theater opened, Judith began to consider writing a play. Her prologues and epilogues had been good enough to convince the *Massachusetts Magazine* to reprint them without her permission. She was as familiar with the rules of playwriting as anyone, and her personal letters often exhibited a dramatic quality. By 1794, the Murrays were in Boston and needed money. Judith could not resist the temptation.

On March 2, 1795, the Federal Street Theater presented *The Medium,* a five-act comedy "written by a citizen of the United States."[20] Unfortunately, the play "made its appearance under great disadvantage." Two of the actresses became ill, but Powell went ahead with the production. Neither of the replacement actresses had much time to rehearse, and during the second act, one forgot her lines. The rest of the cast "hobbled through," but the play was surely damaged.[21]

Such dismal performances were not unusual in the early days of American theater, and in fact the play had its defenders. But Murray considered the entire affair a fiasco. Robert Treat Paine's magazine, the *Federal Orrery,* stated that *The Medium* was the joint effort of Mr. and Mrs. Murray, embarrassing John and forcing him to deny publicly that he had seen a "single sentence, line, or even word of the comedy" until he watched the play being performed.[22] While Paine did not attack the play, others did. One critic claimed that it was little more than a "string of tedious, insipid, unconnected dialogues."[23] Desolate, Murray refused Powell's offer to give her play a second performance.

Although she was disappointed by the reception of her play, Judith persevered. She tried to persuade the manager of the Chestnut Street Theater in Philadelphia to produce *The Medium.* Failing that, she considered publishing and selling it under a new title, *Virtue Triumphant.* She also wrote a second comedy, *The Traveller Returned,* which appeared in March of 1796.

This time, the actors remembered their lines and the play ran for two consecutive nights. It was greeted with "unbounded applause."[24] Had it been accorded a third performance, Judith would have received a portion of the profits. Unfortunately, the *Massachusetts Mercury* proclaimed the play a success, but the *Orrery* damned it with faint praise. Paine thought the acting good and admitted that its author had some "dramatic talent," but he added that the play was still in need of considerable improvement.[25]

Paine was not known for his kindness either to plays or to actors, and Murray should have been satisfied with the positive comments he threw her way. Instead, she defended the play in a private letter to her critic. Paine promptly published the letter along with his own vicious rejoinder. He had been much "too lenient" in his first review, he claimed. In fact, the public had "universally condemned" the play. It had no "interest, plot, sentiment, or humor." It was dull, moralistic, and clotted with "turgid phrases," "forced conceits," and "filched ribaldry."[26] Mortified, Murray withdrew *The Traveller* from production. Her plays had brought her considerable pain, and she had gained nothing from her efforts but a private box at the Federal Street Theater.

It was not until 1804 that Judith wrote a third play, *The African*. It took her four years to persuade the manager of the Federal Street Theater to produce it. Again, she kept her authorship a secret, convinced that prejudice against her husband's religious beliefs would guarantee unfavorable reviews and a hostile audience. When she was once more the victim of a poor performance—this time it was the male actors who forgot their lines—she demanded the immediate return of all existing copies of the manuscript. "My literary hopes are prostrate," she said. Her career as a playwright was over.[27]

Judith Sargent Murray's brief stint as a dramatist brought her no fortune in her own time and less fame in the decades to come. The same cannot be said of the three-volume work she called *The Gleaner*. Shortly after the disappointing reception of *The Traveller Returned,* Judith began turning her "Gleaner" essays into a "miscellaneous work." The first volume was composed primarily of her old "Gleaner" essays. The other two volumes contained previously unpublished essays and poems, as well as new material, including a continuation of the story of Margaretta, written specifically for the book. Volume three also included her plays and a few letters from the Boston papers attacking and defending them.[28]

Truly a "miscellany," *The Gleaner* covered a wide variety of subjects, from paeans to virtue and philanthropy to a defense of the Federalist party, from essays on economy to her now famous "Observations" on women's ability. "It is written with care," she told an acquaintance, "and in the highest style of elegance, propriety of diction, and chastity of sentiment, which I could command."[29]

Unlike many women, Murray assumed full responsibility for the difficult process of preparing *The Gleaner* for publication. The American public was more literate than it had been a century earlier, but the audience for books remained small. Moreover, the cost of paper and printing rose steadily throughout the 1790s, making it hard to sell books at a reasonable price. Aspiring authors had to round up a sufficient number of subscribers before a printer would set a single line of type and eventually secure payment from all their patrons. If they did not collect enough money to cover printing costs, they suffered the loss.

Given her ambivalence about the propriety of writing for money, Murray's foray into the marketplace must have been a challenge. Still, she was relentless in her efforts to control every detail of her venture. She sent subscription lists to friends, relatives, and total strangers. When she secured the signatures of George Washington and John Adams, she shamelessly used their implied endorsement to stir the patriotic sentiments of potential customers. She also appealed to sheer vanity, promising to print the names of all subscribers at the end of the last volume. Even as she begged for support, she found herself apologizing. Admitting that she hoped her book would bring praise and profits, she insisted that she aimed primarily at *"instructing in some small degree"* the young persons she hoped would read *The Gleaner.* If she could persuade others—and perhaps herself—that she acted as a moral mother, not as a commercial animal, she might be able to deflect the criticism she was sure would come her way.[30]

In February of 1798, *The Gleaner* was ready for distribution. Although Judith rejoiced at seeing her book in print, her most arduous task remained. It was relatively easy to distribute the books but more difficult to secure payment. Often she had to beg for reimbursement six or seven times before customers complied. Even more worrisome were her concerns about the critical reception the work would receive. She claimed not to expect "universal approbation" but said she would suffer "extreme mortification" if any subscriber felt cheated by the quality of the book.[31] In fact, *The Gleaner* was "both lavishly praised, and severely censured."[32] Her friends and relatives loved it. Even President Adams, to whom it was dedicated, praised the finished volumes. Of those who sneered at her efforts, her most outspoken detractors were either Jeffersonian Republicans or enemies of the Universalist religion.[33] They may not, as Judith insisted, have had a "systematic plan" to prejudice the public against her work, but they clearly had an axe to grind.[34]

At the very least, *The Gleaner* was a qualified financial success. Although Murray never sold all her copies, and in later years was reduced to giving them away to new acquaintances, she sold enough to pay the mortgage on the Franklin Place house. She was surely pleased that through her efforts, the family now enjoyed a measure of financial security.

Although she submitted an occasional essay or poem to the *Boston Weekly Magazine* and its successor, the *Boston Magazine,* and made one more attempt as a playwright with *The African,* Murray's interest in publishing almost died with *The Gleaner.* There were a number of reasons. It is probably no accident that gender divisions appeared to be hardening and women seemed less optimistic about their future place in the Republic. Moreover, Murray was more deeply hurt by the criticism from some quarters than she cared to admit and discouraged by her failure to arrange a second edition. She had harbored unrealistically high hopes, and when the book failed to have the desired impact, she found it difficult to contemplate another major project.

Then, too, these were busy years. Her attentions were focused on Julia Maria as well as her brother's children. She cared for her husband after his stroke and helped him finish his autobiography and prepare an edition of his correspondence for publication. The passage of time also took its toll on her own health. She was often ill, and her eyesight became so poor that she could no longer write in the soft light of the early morning or evening, the times she had always reserved for a pastime that had once been the source of her greatest happiness.

There were other, more unsettling reasons for Murray's reluctance to continue writing. In March of 1799, her brother Fitz William's son asked her to write a poem to be read at Billerica Academy's celebration honoring American independence. She gladly complied with her nephew's request, but something went terribly wrong. The details of the incident remain unclear, but it is obvious that in some way, the younger Fitz William used the poem to humiliate his aunt. It was, she said, "an instance of ingratitude, partaking much of cruelty," and she doubted that she would ever "wholly surmount its effects."[35]

Even more distressing was her quarrel with her Aunt Maria's son, Lucius Manlius Sargent, in the summer of 1806. He had once been Judith's favorite cousin. Highly talented, he was also spirited and mischievous, given to rash actions with little thought for their consequences. In August, the *Repertory* printed his "unsuitable imitation" of Judith's poetry, filled, she said, with "smut and ribaldry" and obviously designed to mock her claims to talent. At the same time, he sent a forged letter to the *Columbian Centinel* in which Judith purportedly sang her own praises. Not finished, he cut up a copy of *The Gleaner,* filled it with "insulting remarks," and left it on her doorstep.[36] Judith was bewildered by his cruelty. Thereafter, she grew increasingly depressed and reclusive. As late as November she refused to attend a "gala" at Maria's home, fearing that Lucius Manlius would seize upon the occasion to ridicule her once more.[37]

In 1808, Judith rejected a suggestion by a "young friend"—perhaps Lucius Manlius—that she write a biography of another nephew, Winthrop Sargent. Due, she explained, to the "repeated mortifications, and rebuffs, which I have encountered in my literary career," I will never again "venture upon so fluctuating an ocean as public opinion, except my invitation to embark, should be both public and unequivocal." At least some of her manuscripts would survive her death, she said. It was up to her survivors to decide whether her unpublished work would be printed or "consigned to oblivion."[38] She, herself, would do nothing more to secure literary immortality.

NOTES

[1]Judith Sargent Murray to the Rev. William Emerson, 21 Nov. 1805, Judith Sargent Murray, Letterbook, 13:76, Mississippi Archives, Jackson, Miss.

[2]Judith Sargent Murray to Winthrop Sargent, 30 Nov. 1795, Letterbook, 9:520.

[3]The phrase comes from Howard Anderson and Philip Irvin Ehrenpris, "The Familiar Letter in the Eighteenth Century: Some Generalizations," in Anderson et al., *The Familiar Letter in the Eighteenth Century* (Lawrence: University Press of Kansas, 1966), 269.

[4]Judith Sargent Murray, Introduction, Letterbook, 1:n.p.

[5]Judith Stevens to Maria Sargent, 5 Dec. 1781, Letterbook, 1:372.

[6]John H. Shephard, *Reminiscences of Lucius Manlius Sargent* (Boston: David Clapp and Sons, 1871), 30.

[7]Judith Sargent Murray, *The Gleaner: A Miscellaneous Production in Three Volumes* (Boston: L. Thomas and E. T. Andrews, 1798), 1:152, 153.

[8]Judith Sargent Murray to Mr. Holderness of Wexford, Ireland, 11 Aug. 1798, Letterbook, 10:265.

[9]Murray, *The Gleaner,* 1:289–300.

[10]Ibid., 63, 64.

[11]Judith Sargent Murray to Mr. Paine of the *Federal Orrery,* 11 Nov. 1794, Letterbook, 8:241.

[12]Murray, *The Gleaner,* 3:313, 314.

[13]Judith Sargent Murray to the Editors of the Massachusetts Magazine, 8 Feb. 1790, Letterbook, 4:76; Judith Sargent Murray to Mrs. Mackie of Philadelphia, 22 Dec. 1790, Letterbook, 6:399.

[14]Judith Sargent Murray to Epes Sargent of Hampstead, 6 Nov. 1797, Letterbook, 10:173.

[15]Murray, *The Gleaner,* 2:275, 277.

[16]Murray, *The Gleaner,* 1:vii.

[17]Judith Stevens to Winthrop Sargent, 15 May 1786, Letterbook, 3:356.

[18]Judith Stevens to Anna _____, 7 Nov. 1788, ibid., 356.

[19]Judith Sargent Murray to Maria Sargent, 19 Jan. 1790, Letterbook, 4:68.

[20]*Federal Orrery,* Feb. 26, 1795.

[21]Judith Sargent Murray to Mr. Sargent, 4 May 1795, Letterbook, 8:301; Judith Sargent Murray to Mrs. Bache of Philadelphia, 19 June 1795, ibid., 312.

[22]*Federal Orrery,* Mar. 2, Mar. 5, 1795.

[23]Murray, *The Gleaner,* 3:14.

[24]Judith Sargent Murray to Esther Ellery, Letterbook, 10:16.

[25]*Federal Orrery,* Mar. 14, 1796.

[26]Ibid., Mar. 21 1796.

[27]Judith Sargent Murray to Alexis Eusteaphieve Esq., Russian Counsel, 20 Jan. 1817, Letterbook, 20:42.

[28]Judith Sargent Murray to Mr. Sargent of Hampstead, 30 Sept. 1797, Letterbook, 10:155.

[29]Judith Sargent Murray to the Reverend Robert Redding, Truro, England, 14 Dec. 179[6], ibid., 68.

[30]Judith Sargent Murray to Mr. S_____ B_____ Esquire, 6 Mar. 1797, ibid., 85.

[31]Judith Sargent Murray to Mrs. S_____ of G_____, 14 May 1798, ibid., 217, 218.

[32]Judith Sargent Murray to Mr. Carpenter, 4 Oct. 1806, Letterbook, 14:24.

[33]Judith Sargent Murray to Mr. C_____ of Richmond, Virginia, 18 May 1798, Letterbook, 10:223; "American Literature Reviewed," *The Monthly Register, Magazine and Review of the United States,* 1806, 21–27.

[34]Judith Sargent Murray to Mr. Carpenter, 4 Oct. 1806, Letterbook, 14:24.

[35]Judith Sargent Murray to Mr. Sargent of Hampstead, 31 July 1799, 26 Dec. 1799, Letterbook, 11:40, 112.

[36]Judith Sargent Murray to [?], 28, 29 Aug. 1806, Letterbook, 14:4–6.

[37]Judith Sargent Murray to Maria Sargent, 10 Nov. 1806, ibid., 37, 38.

[38]Judith Sargent Murray to [?], 6 Oct. 1808, Letterbook, 15:61.

9

Conclusion:
"God Doth Equally His Gifts Impart"

In her private life as in her public observations, Judith Sargent Murray was devoted to her belief in the intellectual equality of men and women. Wherever she went, she wanted to discuss issues of interest to "the Sex." Almost all historians would agree that hers was a major voice in the new nation's discussion of gender roles. They describe her variously as an "advanced thinker," one of the "central architects of the new female ideology," or the "chief theorist of republican womanhood."[1] Her essays, poems, and private letters all attest to her determination to expand opportunities for women and to challenge conventional definitions of masculinity and femininity.

Abigail Adams's injunction to her husband, John, to "remember the ladies," is famous, but it was Murray who cared more deeply about relations between men and women, who systematically analyzed and questioned her society's conception of women's nature. She accepted some of the limits that circumscribed even the most educated and capable women of her era, even as she examined and probed those limits, pushing them as far as any American woman dared to do in the years after the Revolution. While she agreed that men and women were different in many significant ways, she sought whenever possible to emphasize their similarities, their common humanity. Moreover, unlike most of her contemporaries, she was not content merely to advocate reforms in the domestic sphere. She demanded equality in the private relationships between men and women, but she also tried to carve out a place for women in the public arena. She argued that wives and mothers played an important civic role when they used their influence to educate their husbands and sons in the ways of virtue. As a writer, she was one of a handful of American women who intruded directly upon the public domain, daring to discuss political and military affairs as well as domestic matters. When she urged girls to learn to support themselves, her advice was more daring than it now seems. In a society that equated independence with citizenship, Murray's determination to give women tools that would help them achieve economic autonomy had significant political implications. Above all, she wanted women to make choices about their own lives, to be self-actuating beings who determined their own futures.

It is tempting for modern readers to give Murray's views a more radical interpretation than they deserve. Although she may have been an advanced thinker for her age, she remained an eighteenth-century woman who operated within the ideological and social constraints of her day. If she envisioned a political role for women, she was no suffragist, nor did she especially care about practical economic issues such as equal pay for equal work. If she argued that men and women were equal in "mind" or "spirit," she also concurred with the increasingly prevalent notion of "separate spheres." She grew impatient with ennervating domestic duties, but she assumed that women were responsible for a well-run home. She was as traditional as she was modern.

Murray was a creature of the eighteenth century, yet her perspective also reflected the social views of New England Federalism, which she embraced and defended with as much conviction as she did her belief in gender equality. Like most members of Massachusetts's merchant class, she was disturbed by the "democratical excesses" that seemed to have engulfed the new nation in the wake of the Revolution. The urban centers, in particular, were becoming increasingly disorderly, as European immigrants and people from America's own hinterland—women as well as men—flocked to the cities in search of opportunity. Some members of this rootless population succeeded. Many more did not. They became beggars, thieves, and prostitutes, wandering the streets and struggling simply to stay alive in a society that was hostile to their very existence. Worse, these men and women were highly visible. They strolled in the parks, met in taverns, and caroused and rioted in the streets, defying the rudimentary rules of civilized society.

Anarchy seemed to reign, and upper-class Americans felt helpless. Elite women found themselves in a particularly anomalous position. Politically, their society cast all women as the "other." Like children, servants, and slaves they were dependents who had no direct connection to the government. Socially, however, these women saw themselves as not only different from but also superior to the poor, the emigrant, the African American, and they sought to distance themselves from the lower orders. They regarded themselves as more akin to rational, orderly, elite men than to the servant women and prostitutes who pervaded the urban subculture. By identifying with the men of their own class, women like Judith Sargent Murray denied any connection to the vulgar and blatantly sexual women beneath them. To claim their own rationality, purity, and spirituality, they denied the importance of their own female bodies and reasserted their genteel identity, thus winning back the cultural authority the new order threatened. It is in this context that Murray's view—class divisions were real while gender divisions were artificial—begins to make sense. If it was mind, not body, that defined human nature, then rational women were more like their male counterparts than like the animalistic, sensual, promiscuous women who had taken over the streets. In essence, they were claiming that class, not sex, determined their identity.[2]

Murray spoke the language of liberalism when she dreamed of a new nation that would reward people on the basis of their merits, not their sex. She attacked what she saw as artificial barriers erected by ignorant, small-minded men and maintained by unthinking, tyrannical custom. Margaretta Hamilton, Murray's depiction of an ideal woman, was fully aware of the "laws of custom," yet she never blindly obeyed them. Her "humanity," even her "convenience," mattered more to her than ill-conceived and arbitrary precepts.[3] Although Murray agreed that custom gave order to society, she maintained that many of its dictates, especially where women were concerned, were "injurious to the well-being of society."[4]

Murray despised all conventions that prescribed acceptable behavior for women, circumscribing their actions in the physical as well as the mental world. She complained, for instance, that unlike her father, her brothers, and both her husbands, she was rarely able to travel freely. "I regret the shackles of my sex," she wrote from Gloucester, "which chain me to this remote spot—It would be my choice to traverse every part of the habitable globe."[5] In 1812, when she gave Julia Maria permission to go alone to Cambridge to watch Adam Bingaman's end-of-the-year Harvard orations, she urged her daughter to be mindful of her reputation. "A young Lady in a crowd, without a Parent, or some other guardian Matron," she warned, "seems not to be moving in her appropriate sphere."[6] As a young woman, during her first marriage, she had hesitated to attend a simple country dance without her husband, although she described the affair as a scene of "rural Innocence" attended by "many respectable females."[7] One of the unexpected benefits of old age had been Murray's discovery that society excused in mature women what it did not tolerate in girls. Only when she was a grandmother was she able to travel as far as her health and pocketbook allowed.

The tradition dictating that American women abandon their own names when they married also drew Murray's fire. After she wed John Murray, she always signed her name, "Judith Sargent Murray," in part, as we have seen, because she was genuinely proud of her family name. But she also liked the practice, because it helped women retain something of their own identity. In France, she wrote approvingly, "a female never relinquishes her name, but adds thereto that of the person with whom she is connected in wedlock: It is," she added wryly, "the present rage to copy the French, and I do not object to accepting this regulation as a precedent."[8] For someone who questioned the American alliance with the French during the War of Independence, and who, like all Federalists, deplored the French Revolution, this was no small concession.

Judith Sargent Murray's vision of a meritocratic society was particularly obvious when she discussed literary opportunities for women. Writing as "the Gleaner," she hoped that in America, "to every member of the mental Commonwealth, the road to literary honours may be alike open," so that "the meritorious of every age, sex and description" would be welcome. Surely no democrat, Murray knew that individuals were unequally endowed with intelligence and talent. Some people were driven by intellectual passion, while others were "stupidly dull." Such distinctions, however, were not gender-based. Women as a group did not have a "weak, a servile, a degenerate soul," nor were all men possessed of "Greatness of Mind." The historical record was replete with instances of male stupidity, yet "mighty Man" unjustly claimed power and virtue for himself solely because of his male identity. "God," she insisted, "doth equally his gifts impart."[9]

Murray believed that society as well as the individual would benefit from the public acknowledgment of women's intellectual merit. People naturally sought recognition for their achievements. Just as children hoped for a toy, a sugarplum, or a mother's smile as a reward for obedience, authors desired a "splendid name" and strove for excellence. If potential geniuses knew their efforts would be denigrated or ignored, they would cease to write and everyone would suffer. Every country should institute a program that accorded public recognition to the literary talent of both men and women.[10]

Murray's view of women's intellectual equality was a logical development of her religious and philosophical beliefs. The "imposing authorities of nature, reason, and scripture" all agree that "the distinction male, and female, does not exist in *Mind*." Those differences that existed were "accidental," not essential. It was for this reason that she believed in the possibility of a genderless meritocracy. "I only contend," she said, "for the *practicability* of [women] attaining, as far as it depends upon mind, the loftiest heights." The same metaphors appear and reappear in her work. She talked of "insurmountable barriers" and "ignorant or interested men" who clipped the wings of women trying to soar to the "loftiest heights." She did not mind distinctions based on ability and class. It was artificial distinctions such as gender that she could not accept.[11]

Murray's assumption that men and women were mental equals and her demand for equal educational opportunities echoed the thoughts of many, though surely not most, genteel women of her era. She was more willing than most of her contemporaries, however, to contemplate, if not openly advocate, an active political role for women. After the American Revolution, attitudes toward citizenship were subject to question. Men without property seized new opportunities to demand political rights for themselves and redefine their relationship to the state, but most women, even those who discussed political issues without apology, like Abigail Adams and Mercy Otis Warren, did not attempt to forge a new relationship between themselves and the nation.

Judith Sargent Murray, while no Susan B. Anthony, was an exception. Yet to be sure, when she complained that women's customary roles were irrational and confining, she never envisioned herself in the statehouse. Women's work was stultifying because it destroyed the spirit and did not "elevate the mind," not because it kept women away from politics.[12] Moreover, when she praised the American system of government as a career "open to all," in which anyone could "pursue the splendid prize," she did not seem to notice that only men could compete for public office.[13] And when she pounced on every failure to recognize the talents of women writers, she was often oblivious to the political discrimination women endured.

Still, Murray did not ignore political issues. According to conventional wisdom, true citizens were linked to their government by their public-spiritedness, especially their willingness to risk their life on the battlefield. In such a civic climate, politics was a gendered concept. Women, even property-owning women, were by definition weak, dependent, capricious, and self-indulgent, and thus naturally incapable of acquiring the "manly" attributes associated with citizenship. Murray's "Observations on Female Abilities," with numerous examples of women who were heroic and strong, brave and patriotic, attempted to refute the sex-based assumptions that informed the way most Americans viewed the political world. (See Document 15.) As a group, she argued, women were "as capable of supporting with honour the toils of government" as men.[14] If military sacrifice was essential to citizenship, women were equal to the task, for history provided many examples of women who exhibited "incredible bravery" and performed extraordinary acts of heroism.[15] Throughout *The Gleaner,* Murray scattered stories of capable and energetic queens who ruled their subjects wisely and even led them into battle with as much courage as any man. In her own time, she believed that Abigail Adams was her husband's most "valuable auxiliary," and that John Adams "submitted *every transaction* of his administration" to her before making a decision. There were, she asserted, many men in Boston who declared that "was the President called out of time, they should rather see Mrs. Adams in the Presidential chair, than any other character now existing in America."[16] Murray considered political and military women exceptional, but their existence proved that women had the ability to perform their part on the public stage without fear of failure. America, she asserted, might not yet have produced a "female Washington," but she refused to rule out the possibility.[17]

Generally, Murray advocated a quiet political role for women. She was more likely to petition the president on behalf of her relatives, using the flowery language of supplication, than to demand the right to vote or hold office. She praised women who used their traditional influence as wives and mothers to mold the new nation's citizens. Her description of Margaretta Hamilton's impact on public affairs is revealing. Each day, Margaretta strolled through her enclosed garden with her children. Every villager enjoyed access to this earthly haven, and petitioners often came to her seeking assistance. She listened judiciously to their pleas, advising the worthy and gently rejecting the spurious. Her acts of benevolence became widely known, affording her the adulation she deserved. Her deeds had the added benefit of providing an object lesson in benevolence to her children. Thus Margaretta could perform her duties as mother, affect the world beyond the home, and earn renown without ever leaving her garden.[18]

When Murray stepped "out of her sphere" to express her political opinions, she legitimated her actions by linking her public concerns with her private role. Women cared about politics, Murray said, "as wives, as Mothers and as friends." Their own fate was tied to their fathers, husbands, and brothers. It was only natural for them to care about the future of the nation.[19] Indeed, Murray's political interests were often sparked by personal concerns. She wrote a long poem defending the much-maligned Society of Cincinnati for instance, because her brother Winthrop was an ardent supporter. In 1796, as Winthrop struggled vainly to secure a congressional sinecure, Murray commiserated, "Say not that this matter is uninteresting to me! Am I not interested, deeply interested, as a sister, in whatever can affect you, and am I not likewise most essentially interested as a daughter of Columbia? Yes, indeed, I am truly interested, for in the fate of my Country, in the Virtue of her Legislature, my most important wishes are involved."[20]

Occasionally Murray implied that all women, as "daughters of Columbia," had political views, rights, and responsibilities that adhered to them directly, and that women's unique qualities made some sorts of public activity essential to the preservation of their rights. In a letter to her sister, Esther, she claimed that a woman could never obtain a fair trial in America because only men sat on juries. "Men," she said, "are not our peers." Thus "are our privileges in this, as in many other respects, tyrannically abridged."[21]

Murray maintained that women had both the ability and the need to analyze the political questions of the day. "Reason allows," she maintained, "a measure of patriotism, even to the female bosom."[22] While she agreed that women should not be *"ostentatious,* or *intrusive"* in displaying their knowledge, neither did she think they should lapse into "childish imbecility." Indeed, would women not fail in their duty, if they allowed the country to sink into corruption? What, after all, was politics "but a capability of distinguishing that which will probably advance the real interest of a Community?" If politics, like war, was at bottom a moral issue, who was more qualified than women to enter any public debate? Echoing Shylock's speech in Shakespeare's play *The Merchant of Venice,* she applied his defense of his own humanity to women. They, too, were human. They had eyes and hands. They could be destroyed by tyranny. They were hurt by the same weapons and suffered from the same diseases. Thus, they were "equally concerned with men in the public weal."[23]

When Murray spoke the language of liberalism to demand a political voice, she was on fairly solid ground. The language of republicanism was more problematic, for the republican emphasis on independence, public spirit, and bravery was not conducive to the traditionally accepted definition of femininity. Still, she found room to maneuver. Women were the most selfless creatures in America. If citizenship demanded sacrifice, then women were surely ready to accept the statesman's laurels. They willingly relinquished their own name and identity, their desire for advancement and recognition, for the good of their family and country.

If Murray hoped to define a political identity for women, she was even more intent on proving that women had practical business ability. Custom, law, and education combined, she argued, to deny women the chance to reach their level of competence. In *Virtue Triumphant* Murray offered a fictional case in point when she contrasted the character and capability of the formidable Matronia with that of the widower Ralph Maitland. Matronia, who had never married, was intelligent, businesslike, and more than able to look after her own affairs. Maitland was foppish, vain, and inflexible. Yet when Matronia approached Maitland for a loan, she admitted that she engaged in "negociations which custom hath in some sort interdicted my sex." Worse, she had to endure Maitland's foolish comments and ward off his clumsy attempts at romance before he took her seriously. Clearly, she was his superior, yet she was at his mercy in an arena that custom designated as male.[24]

Murray was not alone in arguing that, in intellectual endeavors, women should be allowed to rise as far as their natural abilities would take them, but few of her contemporaries were concerned with economic opportunities for women. In her zeal to teach women to *"reverence themselves,"* to put "independence . . . within their grasp," Murray was unusual, if not singular.[25] Her characterizations of "farmeresses" and "she-merchants" implied that women were well able to take care of themselves if they had to, even if they would not do so under normal circumstances. Her "Gleaner" account of a young Massachusetts woman whose early upbringing made her stronger and taller than normal implied that even physical differences between men and women, often used to justify male superiority, were as much the product of environment as of nature.[26] "With proper attention to their education, and subsequent habits," she maintained, women "might easily attain that independence, for which a Wollstonecraft hath so energetically contended."[27]

Murray's words sound reassuringly modern, but her vision was always limited. Margaretta's highest aspiration, despite her education, was a "matrimonial career."[28] God and nature, not society alone, demanded that the duties of wife, and especially of mother, supersede all others. Murray raised her daughter and niece to be "accomplished," to be good wives and mothers, not to enter the world of business, law, or the ministry. When she mentioned the remunerative work of her friends and relatives, she was describing women who were seamstresses, teachers, or governesses.

In particular circumstances, Murray conceded that women's traditional skills were insufficient to earn them an "independency." When Reverend Sewall of Portsmouth, New Hampshire, fell ill, his daughters' proficiency as "needle women" did not earn enough to keep the family afloat. Murray's prescription for their woes is revealing. She did not use the occasion to demand expanded employment opportunities, nor did she encourage her friends to forsake the needle in favor of a shovel or a law book. Instead, she looked to the government to guarantee "pensions adequate to their wants" to its worthy but unfortunate female citizens, thus envisioning an institutional guarantee of a comfortable dependence.[29]

Murray may have believed that men and women were intellectual equals, but she never denied that they were also different. "Nature," she explained, "although equal in her distributions is nevertheless various in her gifts, and her discriminating lines are perfectly obvious."[30] In fact, she bristled when people denigrated women as nosy, capricious, vain, or frivolous. Sometimes she excused such vices as yet another result of inadequate education and low expectations. Just as often she argued that women had no monopoly on vice. She knew as many coxcombs as coquettes: "I would only inquire whether *Vanity* doth not as often predominate in a male as in a female bosom?" By the same token, she believed that there were "to be found in both sexes — *Rational Beings.*"[31] She even took advantage of social prejudice, relying upon what she called the "artillery of my sex"—"argument, entreaty, prayers, and if need be tears"—to achieve her ends.[32]

Murray was just as likely to claim some virtues — if not many vices — as particular attributes of women. (See Document 14.) "Sympathy" was "one of the most endearing features in the female mind"[33] and women's "feelings were more exquisite" than men's.[34] Curiosity, chastity, and tenderness were also qualities that women possessed in abundance.[35] Murray did not deny that men could cultivate these virtues. She admired a manly tear and masculine tenderness as much as anyone. Her ideal man was as compassionate as he was brave, as chaste as he was strong. She had once urged Winthrop not to be corrupted by military life, to exhibit the "tender passions" and the "gentler Virtues" that women naturally possessed. And she begged Fitz William to abandon his quest for prosperity in favor of the "tender, social, and domestic" side of his character.[36] She was convinced, however, that while men could embrace the feminine virtues, it was more difficult for them to do so. "These men," she wrote her sister, were, "a very few excepted — so wholly absorbed in the grand pursuit" of profit that it took all their energy.[37]

Murray's contradictory views reflected her society, whose attitudes toward gender were unstable. The very notion of "virtue" was changing, from a public, military, and hence, masculine attribute, to a private, domestic, and hence, feminine one.[38] Men were increasingly caught up in an individualistic, competitive ethic that devalued old notions of self-sacrifice and disinterestedness; women were increasingly identified with piety, chastity, and self-sacrifice. Americans were moving toward a binary world: Men were rational, women emotional. Men were individualistic and competitive, while women valued relationships and cooperation. Society praised women as mothers and wives but confined them to a separate private sphere that was important but not equal.

In some ways Murray resisted a future that embraced gender differences, arguing that women were defined more by their humanity than by their sex. In other ways she welcomed a society that separated women from the corruption and degradation of the public world, and that accorded them an elevated position on a very small pedestal. Murray's defense of Mary Wollstonecraft reflects her ambivalence. Wollstonecraft's *A Vindication of the Rights of Woman* was published in Philadelphia in 1794, although portions of it had appeared in various periodicals before that date.

When she read the *Vindication,* Murray felt she had found a soul mate. Indeed, many praised the book when it was first published. In 1799, however, William Godwin's *Memoirs of Mary Wollstonecraft Godwin* appeared in America. Godwin had written the book after his wife's death in a misguided effort to win sympathy for her and for her beliefs. Its effect was devastating. Godwin portrayed Wollstonecraft as a passionate, sexual being whose three-year affair with the American poet Gilbert Imlay produced an illegitimate daughter. When Imlay spurned her for another woman, Wollstonecraft twice tried to end her life. She formed a second illicit relationship, this time with Godwin, and again became pregnant. Only then did the two marry. She died in childbirth a few months later.

The *Memoirs* destroyed Mary Wollstonecraft's reputation. Worse, it provided ammunition to those critics who had never supported women's rights and caused even sympathetic observers to reexamine their views. Murray continued to support Wollstonecraft, but she did so in a way that scarcely distinguished her from the English feminist's detractors.

In April of 1802, Murray wrote to a friend, a woman who had condemned Mary Wollstonecraft. "Your ideas," she sniffed, "are perfectly in unison with the *public mind."* It has become "fashionable to condemn that unfortunate woman." Always quick to chastise those whose ignorance destroyed their better judgment, and mindful that as a Universalist she had endured her share of prejudice, Murray attributed the attacks on Wollstonecraft to the human tendency to believe the worst. She herself intended to give the English woman the benefit of the doubt.[39]

Murray had also read Godwin's *Memoirs.* She was familiar with the claims that Wollstonecraft was an atheist, an opponent of the institution of marriage, and a leveler whose ideas would undermine all order. Significantly, she did not defend any of the opinions attributed to Wollstonecraft. Instead, she reinterpreted Wollstonecraft's message, framing it in conventional terms.

She began with the charge that Wollstonecraft was an atheist. To the contrary, Murray asserted, her work breathed a "deep sense of religion." True, she had claimed that the biblical account of creation, especially the description of Eve's genesis from Adam's rib, was a "poetical story," but many Christians believed that the first five books of the Bible were mere allegory. Those arguments, Murray said cautiously, had "some weight." More important, Wollstonecraft quoted the scriptures with obvious approval, praising God as perfect, as the creator, as the author of all order. She believed in the soul's immortality, and only demanded that women, who were equal before God, should have equal rights before man. Is this, Murray asked, the work of an atheist?[40]

Murray was especially creative in her defense of Wollstonecraft's view of marriage. In her skilled hands, the English writer became the supreme advocate of the institution. She admitted that some charged Wollstonecraft with trying to "disseminate principles the most licentious, demoralizing, and consequently detestable," and that she was the "most profligate and abandoned of women." Her own words, however, gave the lie to such accusations. Far from seeking to destroy marriage, Wollstonecraft saw it as the basis of social virtue. She wanted only to secure a more equal place for women within an institution that embodied patriarchal injustice so that she could "render females more respectable as daughters, wives, mothers and members of society." Wollstonecraft thought that husbands and wives should work together for their own mutual happiness and for the good of society. She advocated education for women, not because she wanted to turn women into men, but because "by strengthening the body and exercising the mental capacities," women would "be rendered more capable of managing [their] families, of systematizing morality, and of becoming the *friends* of [their] husbands."[41]

How did Murray defend what she surely viewed as the sordid aspects of Wollstonecraft's life? She simply explained them away. In her own eyes, said Murray, Wollstonecraft had been spiritually — if not legally — married to Gilbert Imlay, the "wretch" who took advantage of her naïveté. Although this was an error in judgment, it was hardly a mortal sin. As a self-proclaimed citizen of the world, Murray knew that marriage ceremonies differed in every country. Even some Christians thought that announcing an intention to wed was sufficient to create a marriage. The Bible itself prescribed no marriage ceremony. Admittedly, God condemned those who broke the marriage contract, but it was Imlay, not Wollstonecraft, who dissolved their union. When Imlay's fickle passions led him elsewhere, Wollstonecraft's devotion to her daughter was so great that she offered to live with him and his new mistress so that the child might have a father. Finally, she wed William Godwin, proof, surely, that she did not oppose marriage. As Murray saw it, Wollstonecraft's detractors were simply using her story for their own purposes. "Her real *crime*," she said tellingly, "*was her able defence of the sex.*"[42]

Murray also denied accusations that Wollstonecraft was a believer in total social equality. Wollstonecraft, she admitted, may have attacked invidious distinctions based on wealth and power, but she never claimed that all people were equal. She supported distinctions based on *"mental excellence."* If she wanted "to strip her sex of false refinement, of *affected imbecility,"* she never denied *"masculine superiority."* Wollstonecraft knew that "men were designed by providence to attain a greater degree of virtue than women." Thus she had never demanded total gender equality. She had only insisted "upon a similarity in *quality*, not in the *quantity* of mind," even while she disapproved efforts to conflate "the different pursuits and departments, alloted to Men, and Women." Thus, she had argued that it was a law of nature that men pursue and women yield. Women did not hunt and fish, nor did men cook and clean. In areas that were "human," however, men and women were equal.[43]

The problem for Murray, if not for Wollstonecraft, was how to devise a way to defend both equality and difference. Murray seemed to suggest that custom, education, and opportunity alone accounted for difference, that women were capable of any "human" endeavor, but in defending Wollstonecraft, she emphasized gender-based differences. Women were intellectually *equal* to men, she said, but this did not mean that their goals, their careers, their lives would be the *same* as those of men. There were "different pursuits, and departments, alloted to Men, and Women."[44] Men had the obligation to defend women from "external evils." In return, women tended to "domestic affairs." Accepting the responsibility for a well-ordered home or a well-cooked meal was a fair exchange for physical safety. If everyone did his or her part, then the duties of each were reciprocal, the relationship egalitarian.[45]

Murray never took her ideas to their logical conclusion. She loved order and abhored chaos. She longed for a society that rewarded merit without regard to gender, but she could never quite escape the sense that in some ways, and despite their common humanity, men and women were different. She might imagine a time when society would accept a "female Washington," a "she-merchant," or even a woman warrior with equanimity. She could surely contemplate a nation that honored women poets and playwrights. She could not, however, picture a world where women abandoned their duties as wives, housekeepers, and mothers. Nor could she envision a time when men might assume domestic responsibilities.

In one of her "Gleaner" essays, Murray described a farm family that descended into chaos when it abolished "the series of subordination" that made any society function smoothly. The women refused to prepare breakfast, explaining that because "equality admitteth no distinctions," they would no longer do what custom designated as women's work. The results of this democratic experiment were inevitable. Breakfast was late, the food was spoiled, the meal was a disaster. The work in the fields was equally tumultuous. With no one in charge, "anarchy" reigned, and at summer's end there were no crops to reap. A society without order, argued Murray, was one where strength was substituted for law, where brute force ruled and no one was safe. Because as a group, women were physically weaker than men, women in particular enjoyed the blessings of an orderly society where everyone knew his or her place, where each contributed to the good of the whole, and where the contributions of each member were valued.[46] "Subordination, rank and degree," said Eliza, in *Virtue Triumphant,* "are of divine origin; the lines are justly drawn; and he who breaks the Rank assigned to him by his Creator is surely an aggressor."

Judith Sargent Murray had no desire to be such an "aggressor." She valued order as much as equality, and she remained comfortable with at least some restrictions based on gender. She never wrote a single sentence, she insisted, that destroyed any "judiciously erected" barrier between the male and female world. She had no "wish to confound distinctions" or to allow women "masculine pursuits."[47] If she sometimes found it difficult to determine which pursuits were "masculine," and which "human," which distinctions were "natural," and which "artificial," she made a valiant effort to confront issues that would continue to plague the Republic long after she laid down her pen.

NOTES

[1] Linda K. Kerber, *Women of the Republic: Intellect and Ideology in Revolutionary America* (Chapel Hill: University of North Carolina Press, 1980), 11; Mary Beth Norton, *Liberty's Daughters: The Revolutionary Experience of American Women, 1750–1800* (Boston: Little Brown, 1980), 230, 254.

[2] See especially Jeanne Boydston, "The Woman Who Wasn't There: Women's Market Labor and the Transition to Capitalism in the United States," *Journal of the Early Republic* (Summer 1996): 183–206.

[3] Judith Sargent Murray, *The Gleaner: A Miscellaneous Production in Three Volumes* (Boston: L. Thomas and E. T. Andrews, 1798), 1:75.

[4] Murray, *The Gleaner* 2: 254.

[5] Judith Stevens to Winthrop Sargent, 31 July 1783, Judith Sargent Murray, Letterbook, 2:164, Mississippi Archives, Jackson, Miss.

[6] Judith Sargent Murray to Julia Maria, 12 May 1812, Letterbook, 17:113.

[7] Judith Stevens to John Murray, 30 Oct. 1779, Letterbook, 1:246, 247.

[8] Judith Sargent Murray to Mr. Sargent of Hampstead, 3 Nov. 1796, Letterbook, 10:57.

[9] Judith Sargent Murray, "Dissimilarity of minds," Poetry, 1:304, 305, Mississippi Archives, Jackson, Miss.

[10] Murray, *The Gleaner*, 2:211.

[11] See, for example *The Gleaner*, 3:197, 198. Ironically, many of Murray's republican counterparts saw gender and race as "natural" distinctions but decried "artificial" differences based on class. See Pauline Maier, "The Transforming Impact of Independence, Reaffirmed: 1776 and the Definition of American Social Structure," in *The Transformation of Early American History: Society, Authority, and Ideology,* ed. James A. Henretta et al. (New York: Knopf, 1991), 215.

[12] Murray, *The Gleaner*, 3:205.

[13] Murray, *The Gleaner*, 1:40.

[14] Murray, *The Gleaner*, 3:198.

[15] Ibid., 194.

[16] Judith Sargent Murray to Mr. Sargent of Hampstead, 2 Oct. 1798, Letterbook, 10:293.

[17] Judith Sargent Murray to Mr. Redding of Falmouth, England, 7 May 1801, Letterbook, 11:288.

[18] Murray, *The Gleaner*, 3:279–91; Nina Baym, "Introductory Essay," in Judith Sargent Murray (Constantia), *The Gleaner* (Schenectedy, N.Y.: Union College Press, 1992), xvi, xvii.

[19] Judith Sargent Murray to Winthrop Sargent, 25 Feb. 1778, Letterbook, 1:88, 89.

[20] Judith Sargent Murray to Winthrop Sargent, 28 Jan. 1796, Letterbook, 9:533.

[21] Judith Sargent Murray to Esther Ellery, 22 Apr. 1797, Letterbook, 10:102.

[22] Judith Sargent Murray to Mrs. Tenney of Exeter, 5 Jan. 1802, Letterbook, 11:323.

[23] Judith Sargent Murray to Mrs. Barrell of York, 25 Nov. 1800, ibid., 227–29.

[24] Murray, *The Gleaner*, 3:24.

[25] Murray, *The Gleaner*, 1:168.

[26] Murray, *The Gleaner*, 3:220.

[27] Ibid., 219.

[28] Murray, *The Gleaner*, 1:274.

[29] Judith Sargent Murray to John Murray, 27 Aug. 1805, Letterbook, 13:42.

[30] Judith Sargent Murray to Winthrop Sargent, 1 Nov. 1796, Letterbook, 9:598.

[31] Judith Stevens to John Murray, 30 Dec. 1798, Letterbook, 2:318.

[32] Judith Stevens to Winthrop Sargent, 15 July 1784, Letterbook 2:251.

[33] Judith Sargent Murray to Mrs. Williams, 26 July 1817, Letterbook, 20:57.

[34] Judith Sargent Murray to Mr. E_____S_____, 6 June 1783, Letterbook, 2:150.

[35] Judith Stevens to Miss Palfrey, 24 Nov. 1776, Letterbook, 1:54; Judith Sargent Murray to Anna Williams, 14 Dec. 1795, Letterbook, 8:361; Billet to Maria, 13 Mar. 1801, Letterbook, 11:271.

[36] Judith Stevens to Winthrop Sargent, 25 Feb. 1778, Letterbook, 1:90; Judith Sargent Murray to Mrs. Anna Sargent, 15 July 1793, Letterbook, 8:127.

[37] Judith Sargent Murray to Esther Ellery, 30 Jan. 1799, Letterbook, 10:346.

[38] Ruth Bloch, "The Gendered Meanings of Virtue in Revolutionary America," *Signs* 52 (1979): 500–21.

[39] Judith Sargent Murray to Mrs. K_____, 21 Apr. 1802, Letterbook, 11:343.

[40] Ibid., 343–45.

[41] Ibid., 350.

[42] Ibid., 351–53.

[43] Ibid., 348–50.

[44] Ibid., 348.

[45] Judith Sargent Murray, "The Sexes," Repository, 233; Judith Stevens to Mary Sargent Allen, 15 Sept. 1785, Letterbook, 3:13.

[46] Murray, *The Gleaner,* 1:264–74.

[47] Judith Sargent Murray to Mr. Redding of Falmouth, England, 7 May 1801, Letterbook, 11:287, 288.

PART TWO

The Documents

1

The Gleaner on Famous Literary Women
1798

In 1792, Judith Sargent Murray began submitting her essays to the Massachusetts Magazine. *Although she usually published her work under the pseudonym "Constantia," in this case she assumed the male identity of "The Gleaner." She wrote as a man, she later explained, because she feared that her work would not be taken seriously if people knew it came from a woman's pen. In 1798, Murray expanded upon her early "Gleaner" essays, turning them into a three-volume work entitled* The Gleaner. *The following selection is from "Gleaner 90," her famous four-part essay "Observations on Female Abilities." In this excerpt, she seeks to prove that women's intellectual and literary abilities are equal to men's. As the essay illustrates, Murray was well read and had more than a superficial knowledge of women's literary history. What intellectual qualities and achievements does Murray especially value in the women whose literary contributions she cites? How does she attempt to assuage possible fears that intellectual women might lose their "femininity"?*

. . . *Tenthly,* and *Lastly,* They are equally susceptible of every literary acquirement. Corinna,[1] it is said, triumphed a fifth time over the immortal Pindar,[2] who had publickly challenged her to contend with him in the poetical line. Sappho, the Lesbian poetess, was admired by the ancients—she produced many poems, and was addressed as the tenth Muse. Sulpicia, a Roman lady, who lived under the reign of Domitian, was called the Roman Sappho. Hypatia, beautiful, learned, and virtuous, the daughter of Theon, presided over the Platonic school at Alexandria, about the close of the fourth century; she was judged qualified to succeed her father in that distinguished and important office; her wisdom was held in universal esteem; and from her judgment no one thought proper to appeal: Persons cloathed in public authority, even the first magistrates, deliberated with her on the most urgent and important emergencies; this unavoidably drew around her succeeding circles of men;

---

[1]Corinna was a Greek lyric poetess who is reputed to have defeated Pindar in a poetic contest.
[2]Pindar (c. 522–443 B.C.) was considered to be the greatest lyric poet of ancient Greece.

Judith Sargent Murray, 3 vols. *The Gleaner: A Miscellaneous Production in Three Volumes* (Boston: L. Thomas and E. T. Andrews, 1798), 3:211–17.

yet she maintained her intercourse with characters of various descriptions, without the shadow of an impeachment of her reputation, until basely traduced, in a *single instance,* by bigotted and interested calumniators. Cassandra, a Venetian lady, attained an accurate skill in languages, and made great proficiency in the learning of her times; she composed with facility, both in numbers and in prose, in the language of Homer, Virgil, and Dante; she was a proficient in the philosophy of her own and preceding ages; she rendered theology harmonious; she supported theses with brilliancy; she lectured publickly at Padua; she blended the fine arts with her serious studies; and the mild complacency of her manners constituted the completion of her character: She received homage from sovereign pontiffs, and sovereign princes; and she continued an ornament of her Sex, and of humanity, one hundred and two years.

The daughter of Sir Thomas Moore,[3] Mrs. Roper, already cited under the eighth article, whose virtues were polished by literary attainments, corresponded in Latin with the celebrated Erasmus,[4] and successfully appropriated many years of her life to study. . . . Isabella of Rosera, in Spain, by her substantial arguments, natural deductions, and able rhetoric, greatly augmented the number of believing Jews; the great church of Barcelona was open for the exertion of her pulpitorial abilities; and she acquired much honour by her commentaries upon the learned Scotus.[5] France knew how to estimate the talents of the Dutchess of Retz; she pursued her studies amid the seducing pleasures of a court; and, although young and beautiful, spoke the ancient languages with propriety and elegance. Mary Stuart, queen of Scotland, possessing all the advantages of exterior, and every sexual grace, assiduously cultivated her mind: Her learning was as remarkable as her beauty; she could, we are informed, write and speak six languages; her numbers enchanted the Gallic ear; and, at an early age, she pronounced before the French Court a Latin oration, calculated to convince her hearers, that literary pursuits are proper to the Female Sex. Beauty could not plead in vain; the lovely speaker exemplified, in her own character and attainments, the truth she inculcated; she was, herself, that happy combination, the practicability of which she laboured to impress; and conviction undoubtedly irradiated the minds of her audience.

[3]Sir Thomas More (1477?–1535) was an English statesman, scholar, and martyr who served as lord chancellor to Henry VIII. He was the author of *Utopia.*
[4]Erasmus (c. 1467–1536) was a Dutch Renaissance scholar.
[5]John Duns Scotus (c. 1270–1308), a British theologian and philosopher, was especially interested in proving the existence of God.

In the thirteenth century, a young lady of Bologna, pursuing, with avidity, the study of the Latin language, and the legislative institutions of her country, was able, at the age of twenty-three, to deliver, in the great church of Bologna, a Latin oration, in praise of a deceased person, eminent for virtue; nor was she indebted for the admiration she received, to the indulgence granted to her youth, or Sex. At the age of twenty-six, she took the degree of a Doctor of Laws, and commenced her career in this line, by public expositions of the doctrines of Justinian:[6] At the age of thirty, her extraordinary merit raised her to the chair, where she taught the law to an astonishing number of pupils, collected from various nations. She joined to her profound knowledge, sexual modesty, and every feminine accomplishment; yet her personal attractions were absorbed in the magnitude and splendor of her intellectual abilities; and the charms of her exterior only commanded attention, when she ceased to speak. The fourteenth century produced, in the same city, a like example; and the fifteenth continued, and acknowledged the pretensions of THE SEX, insomuch that a learned chair was appropriated to illustrious women.

. . . Anna Maria Schurman of Cologne, appears to have been mistress of all the useful and ornamental learning of the age which she adorned: She was born in 1607; her talents unfolded with extraordinary brilliancy: In the bud of her life, at the age of six years, she cut, with her scissors, the most striking resemblances of every figure which was presented to her view, and they were finished with astonishing neatness. At ten, she was but three hours in learning to embroider. She studied music, painting, sculpture and engraving, and made an admirable proficiency in all those arts. The Hebrew, Greek and Latin languages were familiar to her; and she made some progress in the oriented tongues. She perfectly understood French, English and Italian, and expressed herself eloquently in all those languages; and she appropriated a portion of her time, to the acquirement of an extensive acquaintance with geography, astronomy, philosophy, and the other sciences: Yet she possessed so much feminine delicacy, and retiring modestly, that her talents and acquirements had been consigned to oblivion, if Vassius, and other amateurs of literature, had not ushered her, in opposition to her wishes, upon the theatre of the world: But when she was once known, persons of erudition, of every description, corresponded with her; and those in the most elevated stations, assiduously sought opportunities of seeing and conversing with her.

---

[6]Justinian (c. 483–565), probably of Slavonic heritage, was adopted by his uncle, Justin I, studied at Constantinople, and became emperor in 527. He propagated the Christian religion and commissioned the codification of Roman law, synthesizing ecclesiastical and civil law.

Mademoiselle Scudéry,[7] stimulated by necessity, rendered herself eminent by her writings. Anna de Parthenay possessed great virtues, great talents, and great learning; she read, with facility and pleasure, authors in the Greek and Latin languages; she was a rational theologician; she was a perfect mistress of music; and was as remarkable for her vocal powers, as for her execution on the various instruments which she attempted.

. . . Mademoiselle le Fevre, celebrated in the literary world by the name of Madame Dacier, gave early testimonies of that fine genius which her father delighted to cultivate. Her edition of Callimachus was received with much applause . . . she exchanged letters with Christina, queen of Sweden; she devoted herself to the education of her son and daughter, whose progress were proportioned to the abilities of their interested preceptress: Greek and Latin were familiar to her; and she was often addressed in both those languages, by the literati of Europe. Her translation of the Iliad was much admired. She is said to have possessed great firmness, generosity, and equality of temper, and to have been remarkable for her piety. . . . The character of Mary II, Queen of England, and consort to William of Nassau, is transcendently amiable. She is delineated as a princess, endowed with uncommon powers of the mind, and beauty of person. She was extensively acquainted with history, was attached to poetry, and possessed a good taste in compositions of this kind. She had a considerable knowledge in architecture and gardening; and her dignified condescension, and consistent piety, were truly admirable and praiseworthy—Every reader of history, and lover of virtue, will lament on her early exit. . . .

Anna Killigrew, and Anna Wharton, were eminent, both for poetry and painting; and their unblemished virtue, and exemplary piety, pointed and greatly enhanced the value of their other accomplishments. . . . Lady Masham,[8] and Mary Astell,[9] reasoned accurately on the most abstract particulars in divinity, and in metaphysics. Lady Grace Gethin[10] was happy in natural genius and a cultivated understanding; she was a woman of erudition; and we are informed that, at the age of twenty, "*She treated of life*

[7]Mademoiselle Madeleine de Scudéry or Sappho (1607–1701), a writer of French historical romances, created female characters who were both intelligent and rational.

[8]Lady Damaris Masham (1658–1708) wrote *Occasional Thoughts* (1700), which advocated better education for women.

[9]Mary Astell (1661–1731) wrote *A Serious Proposal to the Ladies* (1694) and *Reflections on Marriage* (1700), which argued for women's intellectual equality with men.

[10]Lady Grace Norton Gethin (1676–1697) was an English writer of comedies. Her *Reliquiae Gethinanae or Misery is Virtue's Whestone* went through three editions in four years, the last appearing in 1703.

and morals, with the discernment of Socrates, and the elegance of Xenophon"
. . . Catharine Macaulay wielded successfully the historic pen; nor were
her exertions confined to this line—But we have already multiplied our
witnesses far beyond our original design; and it is proper that we apologize to our readers, for a transgression of that brevity which we had
authorized them to expect.

2

Preface to Judith Sargent Murray's Catechism
1782

*Judith Sargent Stevens published her Universalist catechism in 1782. She
wrote it to teach the rudiments of the Universalist faith to two orphaned children for whom she and John Stevens, her first husband, had assumed responsibility. When her friends saw her effort, however, they urged her to publish
it, and she reluctantly agreed. As the preface to the catechism indicates,
Judith hesitated. Some eighteenth-century women were, indeed, publishing
poetry and essays, but the vast majority were not. Moreover, by allowing her
catechism into the public realm, Judith risked becoming involved in serious
theological controversies, an unseemly situation in the polite society of her
day. The preface reveals something of her mixed emotions even as it proclaims her identity as a woman. Its stiff, often convoluted style is at least in
part a consequence of her intellectual timidity. Note, too, the tendency to
capitalize words in midsentence. This was typical of seventeenth- and mid-
eighteenth-century practice, but was less common as punctuation and grammar became more conventional. How does Judith defend her decision against
anticipated criticism—as a woman, as a Christian, and as a mother? How
does she challenge conventional definitions of femininity?*

When a female steps without the Line in which Custom hath circumscribed her, she naturally becomes an Object of Speculation.

Judith Sargent Stevens, *Some Deductions from the System Promulgated in the Page of Divine
Revelation, Ranged in the Order and Form of a Catechism* (Norwich, Conn., Trumbull,
1782), iii–v.

The public Eye is very incompatible with the native Modesty in which our Sex are inshrined; the genial Voice of Applause is requisite to sooth us into Life: While Censure will damp the timid Ardoor, and either extinguish, or confine it to the Breast, where however, it may glow with holy Energy.

Such the Sentiments of my Soul, a very obvious Question arises—from whence proceeds my Temerity, in thus appearing before a Tribunal, where it is more than probable, I shall be accused of Arrogance, Heresy, Licentiousness, etc. etc.?

To candid Minds, only I wish to address myself: Such (the feelings of my own Heart assures me) will accept my Apology, by way of Answer to the above Query. If there is any Thing that ought, for a Moment, to take Place of those exquisite Sensations, which we boastingly term peculiarly feminine, it is surely a sacred Attention to those Interests that are crowned with Immortality. Whatsoever is essential to the ethereal Spark, which animates these transient Tenements, will exist when the Distinction of Male, and Female, shall be forever absorpt.

This Thought stimulating, hath banished that Diffidence, excited by Reflections merely sexual. Yet I do not mean to insinuate, that natural Inferiority incapacitates the female World, for any Effort, or Progress of Genius: Admitting however, the Door of Science barred to us, the Path of Truth notwithstanding, is the Page of Revelation, lies open before us: There, cloathed with becoming Reverence, we may freely expatiate: It is this Walk, aspiring as I am, I have presumed with trembling Awe to enter: My Situation in some Sort impelled the arduous Attempt. Many obvious Questions naturally arise in the Minds of Children, as Reason begins to bud and the young Idea per force will shoot.

Placed at the Head of a little Family, I beheld the Minds of my young Folks hastning towards Maturity: While I was sedulous, in preparing them to act their Parts, upon the inferior Stage of the Globe, I cou'd not but be solicitous to give them proper Conceptions, of the Father of their Spirit, their Expectations from, and Obligations to, the paternal Deity. To the Code so well digested by the Assembly of Divines, *Conscience* would not let me apply: Happily enlightened, through the Instrumentality of a favoured Servant of the Most High, I wished to convey the Instruction I had received from the Fountain of Life, through this Channel, to those under my Care: And as Retention would not at all Times favour me with an Harmony of Ideas, to help my Memory, I set about methodizing the evangelical Views of sacred Texts, which had often been inculcated upon my Mind. When they appeared in the Form of the following Essay, they were shewn to several Friends, who signified their Approbation by earnestly requesting Copies: to avoid the Trouble of furnishing which, I have consented it shoul'd be published. And this I the rather do, as I am sensible those who wish not to peruse, are still at Liberty: And those who do, are hereby presented with an Opportunity. I am well aware there are many Places, in which I might have expatiated; but it was my Study to curtail, recollecting it was for the Emolument of Children, the Piece was intended.

Insignificant however, as it may appear, the Cry of Heterodoxy may raise up an Adversary: But as I presume not to enter the Lists as a Disputant, should such an Event take Place, I shall endeavor to sooth myself, by retiring into my own Family, and observing the salubrious Effects springing from the Principles, dictated by genuine, by divine Philanthropy.

3

Upon Printing My Little Catechism
1782

Long before she considered publishing her work, Judith Sargent Murray was an inveterate writer. More than anything else, she enjoyed writing poetry. She shared some of her verses with friends, enclosing a poem or two with gifts or in letters. Others, such as the one following, she wrote simply for her own pleasure, copying them into bound volumes that she maintained throughout her life. Like most eighteenth-century poetry, Murray's verses were conventional and formulaic, moralistic and didactic. They imitated the neoclassical couplets of Alexander Pope. Judith wrote the following poem in 1782, immediately after she had published her Universalist catechism. The poem captures her sense of ambivalence, as she awaited public reaction. What hopes and fears does the poem reveal? How are her fears exacerbated because she is a woman?

> Yes there are heights I ought not to ascend,
> My arrogance I never can defend,

Judith Sargent Murray, Poetry, 1:148, 149, Mississippi Archives, Jackson, Miss.

Giddy with praise I have too high aspir'd,
My soul by false ambition hath been fir'd—
With modest blushes I should have confest,
The private walks of life for me are best,
Though sooth'd and courted—from the public view,
Of weakness conscious—I should still have flew—
But ah—alas—with eager hast[e] I've run,
Like him who seiz'd the chariot of the SUN,[1]
By love paternal he—tis true was warn'd,
But more my folly—I was doubly arm'd,
For deep conviction wav'd its hoary head,
While honest Conscience all emphatic—said—
"Untaught and simple, can you hope to find,
Candor so prevalent in human kind,
As from a *female lessons* to receive,
Must Women dictate—and must Man believe?
Beside your page, you know it cannot stand,
The Critic's eye—and his more potent hand,
Errors in style, in grammar may appear,
While you can only wash them with a tear—
And then—quoth Conscience—it is not your own
The *sentiments* will by each sight be known,
What though *your language* hath these truths arraighed
Yet still the views—But as you please—it said."
I heard, and like the youth regardless flew,
The reins I seiz'd—the prize was full in view,
Like his my fate—the goal I ne'er shall gain,
Nor yet my humble virtues now maintain,
Fame flies before me—hills and Valleys rise,
Athwart my way baleful detraction lies,
Malice, and slander—how my head runs round—
Hope how delusive is thy flattery found,
From Fancy's airy height now down I fall,
And deep oblivion's stream encircles all—
Yea each enchanting dream of future praise,
With an *immortal life* from *mortal* days.

---

[1]This is no doubt an allusion to the Greek myth of Icarus, who flew too near the sun, melting the wax of his wings, and fell into the sea.

Reflecting, during a Fine Morning, upon Existing Circumstances

Sometime in the 1770s, Judith Sargent Murray began keeping a book she called her "repository," in which she wrote short essays on subjects that attracted her fancy. Some of those essays would later appear in the Massachusetts Magazine or the Federal Orrery; others, such as the one following, were never published. Many of her early essays dealt with the American War of Independence. In "Reflecting, during a fine Morning, upon existing circumstances," she attacked the "Massachusetts Test Act," passed by the state legislature in the spring of 1779. The act confiscated the estates of all Massachusetts inhabitants who fled the state during the War, withheld their support of the patriots' military effort, or refused to take an oath of loyalty to the new government when it was tendered by local Committees of Safety. Her uncle, Epes Sargent, was one of those punished for his loyalist views.

The essay begins by contrasting images of peaceful nature, represented in scenes of order and beauty, with chaotic and bloody images of war. Perhaps because she saw firsthand how war divided entire families, Judith was particularly drawn to a popular familial metaphor: the Revolution as a "civil war" in which parents and children fought one another in deadly, unnatural combat. The main focus of the essay, however, is a vigorous defense of freedom of conscience. Her belief in the value of political and religious liberty had taken shape with her conversion to Universalism, but it was her experiences during the American Revolution that prompted her to give voice to her views. What arguments does she use to defend her friends' right to withhold their support of the patriot government? How does she use her own particular experiences to make universal judgments about human rights? How might her defense of freedom of conscience help her give voice to her views of women's rights?

It is a delightful morning, a few clouds seem to chase each other athwart the sky, but the rising sun hath dispersed those clouds and the firmament is cloathed in the brightest azure. So, just so may we not suppose that the luminous sun of righteousness will, upon that auspicious day, the Restitution of all things, gloriously dispel, the clouds clear up every doubt,

---

Judith Sargent Murray, Repository, 20–23, Mississippi Archives, Jackson, Miss.

and wipe away every tear from the faces of the then not sorrowing family of Man. The feathered songsters have been down hymning their great Creator['s] chaste and salutary influence; soft and harmonizing is the balmy breath of vernal zephyr. It seems as if Order were constituted regent of the Natural World. All but these savage Men who as if the day were too short for their hostile triumphs are already parading our streets exulting proudly while their instruments of death tower in the air. The delightful scenes of peace and security are exchanged for the horrors of war, of *civil War!*

Parents draw the sword to sheath it in the bosom of their enraged children, and children are arising at the hoary heads of those who are the Authors of their being! Oh my Country, how art thou deluged in blood! How art thou torn by internal tumult! Who but must wish for some day's Man to step between and reconcile the contending parties. Heal, heal these disorders. Our God we humbly beseech thee save . . . our World, and say to this our Nation, learn War no more. Anarchy is created . . . I tremble for myself. I tremble for my friends! Tenderly attached to many persons who are warmly engaged in opposite parties I am by consequence greatly agitated. This Massachusetts *Test Act.* Arbitrary in its designation, it encroaches even upon the liberty of inborn sentiment, and if carried into execution, it will destroy the most upright among us. Two persons I know, of unblemished integrity, they are among the dearest of my friends. They have took no active part in the present contest, they have contributed much to the public weal, yet it cannot be denied, that they do not approbate the present popular measures, but they have not presumed to oppose, they wish only to persevere in broken silence. In the decline of life, they are only solicitous to pass the remainder of their days in the bosom of their family. They do not wish to embark upon the troubled ocean of politicks. They have . . . uniformly persevered in the paths of rectitude. Their moral characters are irreproachable. They have been admired, at the head of their family, as parents, as master, as mistress. To the sons and daughters of adversity they have been most bountiful benefactors; they have dried the swollen eye of sorrow, and soothed the heart which was well near bursting with anguish. To the stranger, their hospitable Mansion was well known, the captive found a ready seat in their dwelling, and amity hath taken up her abode with them. But already have they suffered many indignities, the gothick Mob have have [sic] assaulted and insulted them and this most arbitrary act, unprecedented in civilized annals, by summoning to judgment the secrets of the soul, will compel them to wander in a state of exile, far from their peaceful home. Their integrity is unyielding, they will never sanction by their public and solemn oath sentiments which are foreign to their hearts, already their children and friends crowd around them as if the moment to bid them a last adieu was even now arrived. To banish a Man of Virtue is [impolitic?] My friends are advanced in life; they have committed no crime, their virtues are exemplary. Mere sentiment, mere opinion, these ought never to be subjected to human jurisdiction, for the free born soul will still assert its right. Yet if they must be exiled, they would consider it a mitigation of their calamity, if they should be permitted to retire to some part of America. "For Europe" they mildly observe, "will be distancing us too far from those who are very, very dear to our hearts." Surely the face of this once peaceful Village is already sufficiently changed. The habitations where friendship and her sister peace with smiling competency heretofore dwelt are now desolate forsaken and forlorn—How dreary are those deserted Mansions, once so form'd for hospitality—Can this be the cheerful Village, are these the happy dwellings—where alas! are these banished inhabitants—Were they lodged in the silent tomb, taught by reason, taught by Religion, we should gradually cease to lament them, we should hail them happy denizens of immortality. But they are driven hence by the terror of approaching desolation, they have fled to preserve their persons from the calamities of War. They are [rendered?] dependents upon the cold and stinted kindness of an unfeeling, and a mercenary World—Cease then Sovereign of our Parent Island, cease thy proclamation, lend a compassionate ear to thy petitioning subjects, thy children. See! we are harrassed, scattered, and greatly suffering—final distraction too probably awaits us. O Britain! O America! adopt, for your bleeding Countries sakes adopt conciliatory measures if ye would not that impending ruin should speedily fall upon your wretched sons, your wretched daughters—Confusion, we repeat prevails: The Legislator is powerless, the barriers of the law are thrown down Licentious with baleful influence is triumphant . . . the good are tired of this bad world, and for me, my coward soul shrinks from and trembles at the prospect before me.

5

Letter to Winthrop Sargent
February 25, 1778

As America's population became increasingly mobile during and after the Revolution, letters as a means of binding scattered families together grew more and more important. The task of writing those letters often fell to women, who could sandwich in a paragraph or two between their other household chores. In this sense, eighteenth-century letters served as substitutes for face-to-face conversations. Throughout the American Revolution, Judith Sargent Stevens wrote as often as she could to her brother Winthrop, an officer in the Continental Army. She faithfully copied all of her letters into bound "letterbooks," which she enjoyed reading from time to time, reliving past experiences and marking her progress in learning to express herself clearly and effectively. She wrote the following letter during the winter of 1778, when the new nation's prospects looked bleak. Winthrop was encamped with General George Washington's army at Valley Forge. Soldiers and officers were deserting daily, and Judith could not help but wonder if her brother should follow their example. The letter reflects her increasing frustration at her passive and relatively unimportant position. It also provides an example of her desire to "feminize" the war effort, to encourage American officers to nourish their gentler qualities despite the barbarous nature of war. What criticisms of the war does Judith include in her letter? How does she try to lay claim to some of the qualities associated with citizenship?

Impressed by the most grateful sensations, made happy by the esteem of my brother, and rejoicing in this last proof of his fraternal affection, I set me down, and with much pleasure, to acknowledge the favour, yet, almost without a subject, how shall I presume to detain your attention—? I say *presume,* for e'er you receive this letter, the vernal season[1] will be at the door[,] the skies will resume a serene aspect and all Nature will be preparing to put on the most gay attire—in consequence, the military era will commence, and contrasted to the mild atmosphere, and its peace inspiring . . . hostile fields will be displayed—Men, will array themselves in all the dreadful habiliments of War! Eagerly will they seize the deathful weapon, and prepare for the destruction of their fellow Man! What a

[1]Spring.

Judith Sargent Murray, Letterbook, 1:88–90, Mississippi Archives, Jackson, Miss.

sight—for those guardian spirits by whom it is said we are surrounded! Surely they must turn with ineffable disgust from a scene so replete with horror—Did you ever read Swift's[2] Gulliver's Travels? If you have not, I wish you would seize upon the first opportunity of devoting a small portion of your time to its perusal. But whither am I wandering[?] I meant merely to observe that as you will (to adapt my language to your feelings) e'er this letter can reach you, be engag'd in the most momentous of temporal concerns, actively engaged in struggling for the sacred rights of Mankind, you will hardly be able to loan your ear to the prattle of a female pen. You will receive from my Father, domestic, and commercial intelligence, accounts of Captives, etc. etc. What then remains for me to write? The welfare of my Country, the interests of this expansive Continent. These, I do assure you, are subjects very near my heart. I am persuaded you do not yield your reason to the tide of . . . prejudices, you will not say a female is out of her sphere, although at this . . . Crisis she should venture to press her attitudes? For are not our sex interested as wives, as Mothers and as friends? Shall we not rise or fall with those to whom, by ties the most enduring, we have eternally loved? . . . A letter written not long since by you to my Father filled me with the most corroding apprehensions. Alas! for us Moderation hath fled from our borders, she hath returned to climes more congenial with the tranquility of her temperature. It is truly distressing, truly wonderful, to see those individuals who were heretofore bound in bonds of consanguinity and united in the most endearing friendship, now kindle into the most portentious rage, upon every discovery of opposite sentiments—Those in whom bosoms once flowed the milk of human kindness, who appeared uniformly calm, uniformly benevolent, are on this fearful period actuated, by the most baleful passions—Mistrust, and malevolence, mark their conduct, and, not content with forging adamantine[3] chains for the actions of their brethren, they attempt by their test acts etc. etc. to fetter the free born Mind! Goddess of Liberty arise! in all the Majesty of thy mighty powers shine upon this benighted World, assert thy genuine sway, and let no ray of thy divinity illumine the Chaos that is so fearfully pervading. . . . Say, my dearest, are not our prospects dreary—Our Fortifications, while defended by men, who merit rank with the bravest Veterans, have yet fallen. . . . Are not our officers daily resigning? What is the inference—should it not seem that . . . this is the precise time, when the post of honour has become a private station? . . . I adore the shield to which you so piously

---

[2]Jonathan Swift (1667–1745), the English satirist and author of *Gulliver's Travels*.
[3]Rigidly firm and unyielding.

advert—the holy Redeemer is indeed inalienable—He is, truly, the substance of every figure—Let Achilles[4] boast [his] impenetrable shields—You, my brother, can, blessed be the God Man—you can exultingly say that your Almighty shield infinitely surpasses whatever the licenced pen of the Poet, hath so wonderfully filled—I admire beyond expression, this part of your letter—indeed every line which you have written is replete with incentive to gratitude. But say, my love, are the tender passions incompatible with the military character—the brave are always humane and my brother adorns the valour of the intrepid soldier with every gentler Virtue—Yes the finer feeling of benevolence as well, I am persuaded, bloom among the laurels which shall encircle your manly brow. May heaven send you in safety to your native place, may discord hasten from our globe, and benign peace, reassuming the reins of government give our youthful Warrior to repose once more under the dear covert of the paternal shade. Then will my beloved Hero joyfully breathe again his Village air, and realizing those social pleasures with which fancy haunts his solitary pillow, be as blest as he can bear . . .

[4]Greek warrior and hero of Homer's *Iliad.*

6

Margaretta Faces an Economic Crisis
1798

The popularity of the original "Gleaner" essays, published in the Massachusetts Magazine *between 1792 and 1794, owes much to the serialized story of Margaretta Melworth Hamilton. Although Judith Sargent Murray shared the prevailing prejudice against most fiction, believing that romances were likely to give young readers unrealistic expectations for their own lives, she agreed that "moral" novels peopled with virtuous heroes and heroines might have a salutary effect. The "Margaretta" series was, in effect, a thinly disguised novel. Murray takes on the persona of Mr. Vigillius, who, with his wife, Mary, adopted the orphaned Margaretta upon the death of her guardian, Mrs. Arbuthnot. Vigillius describes Margaretta's*

Judith Sargent Murray, *The Gleaner: A Miscellaneous Production in Three Volumes,* 3 vols. (Boston: L. Thomas and E. T. Andrews, 1798), 1:272–86.

education, her courtship, and her marriage to Edward Hamilton, always
emphasizing his belief that with the proper childrearing techniques, women
might become intelligent and rational beings. The following excerpt, which
appears in the first volume of The Gleaner, *describes the Hamiltons'*
dilemma as they face possible bankruptcy. Clearly autobiographical, it
paints Edward as a worthy debtor whose merchant ventures have collapsed
through no fault of his own. Murray uses her power as an author to give
her fictional characters a happy ending—one she did not enjoy herself—
through the fortuitous appearance of Margaretta's wealthy father. Murray's
message in this, as in so many of her stories and essays, is ambivalent. She
emphasizes Margaretta's rationality, her ability to cope with economic
hardships, and recognition that Edward must leave her if he is to retrieve
his economic independence. Nevertheless, her role is essentially passive. Her
father and her husband make the economic decisions, and she simply
accepts them. In what sense does Margaretta's reaction indicate that her
rationality is the result of nurture, not nature? How does her experience
reveal, perhaps unintentionally, the relatively helpless economic lot even
educated women endured?

With sensations of ineffable complacency and high glee; with feelings,
the felicity of which it would be difficult if not impossible to delineate, I
set me down, upon this 27th day of May, 1794, to recount unto the *good-
natured reader* an event, which, if I have not been extremely erroneous
in my calculations, will render him, in no inconsiderable degree, a par-
taker of my joy.

I say, good-natured reader; for, without incurring the charge of credulity,
I conceive I may fairly presume, that persons of this description have, from
time to time, been constrained to take an interest in the fate of Margaretta
Melworth Hamilton. . . . Surely it must be acknowledged that an amiable
and meritorious woman, struggling with misfortunes, is an object which
virtue must ever regard with commiseration and applause. For the officious
length of this exordium, I supplicate the indulgence of those gentle spirits, upon whose favour I have presumed; a candidate for the patronage of
benignity should hasten to gratify the feelings of susceptibility, and after
narrating a few previous arrangements, without further delay, I shall pass
on to a developement, which hath not only invested our daughter with high
affluence, but hath, moreover, restored to her a blessing, which she entertained not the smallest conception of ever being permitted to possess.

. . . Mr. Hamilton had many creditors, and they became much more
suspicious, inquisitive, and troublesome, than we had expected.

. . . It was necessary that Mr. Hamilton, who was anxious to acceler-
ate the hour that should honourably exonerate him from his embarrassments, and who was extremely desirous of making provision for the
growing family which he had in prospect, should immediately apply to
some business, which might afford an expectation of putting him in possession of wishes so indisputably laudable. A ship bound for Europe, in
which he was offered, with the probability of great commercial advantage,
a very lucrative and honorary birth,[1] propitiously presented. Of an opening so fortunate, interest loudly called upon him to avail himself; the
favourable gale of opportunity was not to be flighted. But his heart bled
for his Margaretta; yet manly decision hesitated not, and every thing was
in train for his departure. We conceived it adviseable to conceal our purpose from my daughter as long as possible; and it was not until two days
previous to the period destined for his embarkation, that I took upon
myself the painful task of disclosing to her an event, which we judged
must inevitably take place.

. . . I flatter myself, my beloved Margaretta, that your mind, equal, energetic, and considerate, would not suffer itself to be over much depressed,
should the vicissitudes of life produce contingencies, unavoidably con-
demning you to a few months absence from Mr. Hamilton; two or three
voyages might perhaps entirely retrieve his affairs, and you would ever
after have the satisfaction to reflect that you had contributed every thing
in your power; every thing which fortitude and uniform exertions could
achieve, in order to re-instate your Edward in that independence to which
he was born. I was proceeding — but I had not been sufficiently cautious.
My daughter, during my harangue, frequently changed colour; the lily
and the rose seemed to chase each other upon her now mantling, and
now pallid cheek; she trembled excessively; and upon my particular application to her, the agitation of her bosom, becoming insupportable, she
sunk breathless into the arms of that passionately beloved, and truly
afflicted husband, who hasted to prevent her fall.

"My God!" exclaimed Hamilton, "it is too much; restore, compose, and
soothe this suffering angel, too often exercised by pangs of so severe a
nature; and do, with a wretch who hath betrayed and undone her, whatever seemeth to the good."

. . . Hamilton once more kneeled before her, and the copious tears, with
which he bedewed the hand that he alternately pressed to his bosom and
to his lips, called forth a mingling stream from the eyes of the beauteous
sufferer. The scene was inexpressibly tender, but the humid drops upon
the face of my daughter annihilated at least one half of my fears upon her

[1]Berth.

account. "And can you, Sir," in a tremulous accent she exclaimed—"can you condemn my Edward to bondage, perhaps to irretrievable slavery?" What means my love? What means my love? "Ah, Sir! do you not recollect British depredations? Do you not recollect the ruthless and unrelenting rigour of that fate which awaits the captive, doomed to wear out a wretched life under the galling yoke of an Algerine despot? Might I but have been spared at this time! might a step so fatal to my peace, at least have been deferred, until the face of affairs wore, to the poor, desolate, and exiled voyager, a more confirmed aspect, I think I could have acquiesced." . . .

I was immeasurably affected; yet I knew that my daughter would soon become capable of reasoning. She possesses, in an uncommon degree, the power of accurately discussing points, in which she is the most deeply interested; but altogether unprepared for the present calamity, reason had been violently forced from the helm, and we unitedly endeavoured to restore her to that reflection, to which we well knew she was eminently adequate. The soothings of unquestioned friendship are the sweetest solace; they yield a balm which is endowed with the sovereign power of mitigation, and they are a consolation in almost every sorrow. It was necessary to bend the mind of Margaretta to our purpose, and a few hours accomplished our wishes; gradually we opened our plan; she saw the propriety of every arrangement; the necessity for the steps we had taken, and the idea, then first held up, of the possibility that the time was not far distant, which might legally immure her Hamilton within the walls of a prison, produced the expected effect. Waving her snowy hand with peerless grace, she pressed it upon her closed lips, and bowing her afflicted head, thus tacitly gave that expressive, although melancholy assent, of which, from the begin-ning, considering the justness of her way of thinking, we had made ourselves sure. Two days, as I said, only remained, and they were marked by a deeper sorrow, than any which has yet pierced the bosom of my daughter! It will not be doubted, that we called into action every motive which could give energy and firmness to her feelings; yet, while pensive resignation dwelt upon her lips, her altered countenance and debilitated form evinced the struggles of her soul. . . . Hamilton was on the eve of his departure. Yes-terday, exactly at one o'clock, we were assembled in the dining parlour. This very morning was to have witnessed the agonized moment of separation—and melancholy dejection brooded in the countenance of Margaretta.

My servant, a man whom I have loved for these forty years, entered:— "A stranger, Sir, is importunate to see you." Admit him, by all means. Margaretta was hasting from the parlour; she was solicitous to hide her grief from the observation of the uninterested; but the stranger was close upon the heels of the servant, and not being able to make her escape, she withdrew to the window.

The gentleman, the stranger, I say, entered; upon his features were imprinted the strongest marks of perturbed and tender anxiety; and, moreover, they were features *with which I was confident I had long been familiar,* although, for my soul, I could not recollect at what time, or in what place, they had met my view. He, however, fixing his inquiring eyes, with impatient solicitude, on the face of my wife, and drawing up a heavy sigh, thus laconically apologized:

"Excuse me, Madam, excuse me, Sir—but my feelings disdain ceremony." . . . "Tell me, Mr. Vigillius; tell me, ye incomparable pair! ye who have still continued the matchless guardians of my long lost and unceasingly lamented Margaretta, what apartment in this happy dwelling contains my only surviving treasure?" Margaretta, who had sought to hide her sorrow-marked visage from the gaze of a stranger, now, lost in astonishment, mechanically turning from the window, presented to his view her tearful face; she catched a glance, and, faintly shrieking, would have sunk upon the floor, had not the stranger, whom we now regarded with a kind of indignant horror, snatched her to his embrace! Our resentment, however, soon gave place to all those enraptured emotions, which the accession of high and unexpected felicity originates in the bosom, when, in a voice expressive of paternal tenderness, of paternal transport, he soothingly said—

"Compose yourself, my lovely, my admirable, my inimitable child! It is a *father's* arms that are at length permitted to enfold his long lost Margaretta!!! Arbuthnot, thou shalt no more invade my rights; it is again given me to possess my child, and all her beauteous mother stands confest! Sainted Spirit—this hour shall render thy elysian still more blessed!"

Margaretta shrunk not from his embraces: Strange as it may appear, her agitated spirit did not entirely suspend its functions; and while she seemed, in the arms of the stranger, an almost lifeless corpse, her lips yet moved, and every charming feature received an extatic kind of ejaculatory impression.

Among the trinkets belonging to her mother, which had come into her possession on the death of Mrs. Arbuthnot, was a miniature picture of her father: Perhaps there was not a single day, on which she did not gaze with filial devotion upon this picture. It was a striking likeness; and, by its general contour, her mind was strongly impressed. Hence the effect produced, by a single glance at the original; and it was a frequent observation of this picture, that occasioned the confused recollection, for which, upon the first appearance of the stranger, I was at a loss to account.

It cannot be matter of wonder, that at an interview so astonishingly interesting, not an individual retained that self-command, so requisite to common forms: At length, however, recollection resumed, in a degree, its office. . . . Mrs. Hamilton . . . quitted her seat, and suddenly kneeling before the honoured man, in this devotional attitude, with clasped hands, and in broken accents, she perturbedly questioned—"Art thou a spirit blest—dispatched from Heaven's high court, to soothe thy sorrowing child?—or art thou indeed my father? Hast thou never tasted death? and, if thou hast not, by what miracle didst thou escape those tremendous waves, which we have supposed commissioned for thy destruction?" Mr. Melworth, forsooth, to say it was he, his very self, raised his kneeling child, and again clasping her to his paternal bosom, in strains of exquisite tenderness, affectionately replied—

"Be comforted, my love; be composed, my heart's best treasure; I am indeed thy father. At a proper time, thou shalt be made acquainted with every particular; and, in the interim, as I have been informed of thy embarrassed circumstances, know, that riches, more than thou canst want, are in my gift. Thou shalt introduce me to thy worthy husband. I am apprized of the whole of thy sweetly interesting story; and thy happiness shall, if possible, be equal to thy merit." Margaretta, wild with transport, now raised her eyes and hands to Heaven, and the most extravagant and incoherent expressions of joy were upon her lips. "Then he shall not go," she exclaimed—"Avaunt, ye brooding fiends, that hover round the land of murder!—ye shall not intercept the virtuous career of Hamilton—ye shall not presume to manacle those hands that have, a thousand times, been stretched forth to wipe the tear from the face of sorrow—Avaunt, ye hell-born fiends!—Algiers, united for his destruction, shall not detain him; for lo, a blessed father descends from heaven to save his well near sinking Margaretta!"

Edward, who, from the entrance of Mr. Melworth, had remained, as it were, entranced, or petrified by astonishment, roused by his fears for the reason of Margaretta, now coming forward, prostrated himself at the feet of Mr. Melworth. No one possessed sufficient composure to introduce him—nor was this necessary; the strong sensations which pervaded his almost bursting heart, inscribing upon every manly expressive feature, veneration, joy, gratitude, and apprehension, emphatically pointed him out, and rendered a doubt impossible.

But why continue a scene, which may, *perhaps, be conceived,* but which words can never delineate? *Our mutual congratulations; our mutual expressions of felicity; the best affections of which humanity is capable; the most rapturous sensations of delight; these were all in course—and these were all afloat;* and I will only add, that Edward will not proceed on his voyage—that Margaretta is happy—that every creditor shall be amply satisfied; and I hereby advertise—let them produce their several claims; they shall receive to the last farthing, yea, and liberal interest too.

. . . And, gentle reader, for thy consolation, I give thee my word and honour, that the very next Gleaner, by recounting to thee every particular, relative to Mr. Melworth, which shall come to my knowledge, shall, if it is within the compass of my power, amply gratify a curiosity, which thou needest not hesitate to own, and which I should have been mortified in the extreme, not to have excited.

7

The Gleaner on Women's Attributes as Breadwinners

1798

This essay, taken from the third volume of The Gleaner, *is the final segment of Murray's four-part "Observations on Female Abilities." The most radical of her pronouncements on women's issues, it argues that women are capable of achieving economic independence, and hence implies that they are also able to claim the rights of citizenship for themselves. It is significant that the independent women in this essay are more daring and less conventional than any woman in the "Margaretta" series. They are forceful, active role models who are physically and mentally equal to any task. Why does Murray believe that women — married or single — need to possess remunerative skills? What traditional traits does she continue to associate with femininity, despite her praise of women who clearly lead nontraditional lives?*

Nor are the modern Fair a step behind,
In the transcendent energies of mind:
Their worth conspicuous swells the ample roll,
While emulous they reach the splendid goal.

We take leave to repeat, that we are not desirous to array THE SEX in martial habiliments; we do not wish to enlist our women as soldiers; and we request it may be remembered, that we only contend for the *capabil-*

Judith Sargent Murray, *The Gleaner: A Miscellaneous Production in Three Volumes,* 3 vols. (Boston: L. Thomas and E. T. Andrews, 1798), 3:217–24.

ity of the female mind to become possessed of any attainment within the reach of *masculine exertion*. We have produced our witnesses; their depositions have been heard; the cause is before the public; we await their verdict; and, as we entertain all possible veneration for the respectable jury, we shall not dare to appeal from their decision.

But while we do homage to the women of other times, we feel happy that nature is no less bountiful to the females of the present day. We cannot, indeed, obtain a list of the names that have done honour to their Sex, and to humanity, during the period now under observation: The lustre of those minds, still enveloped in a veil of mortality, is necessarily muffled and obscure; but the curtain will be thrown back, and posterity will contemplate, with admiration, their manifold perfections. Yet, in many instances, fame has already lifted her immortalizing trump. . . . [Murray lists some illustrious women from France and the British Isles and then continues.]

Nor is America destitute of females, whose abilities and improvements give them an indisputable claim to immortality. It is a fact, established beyond all controversy, that we are indebted for the discovery of our country, to female enterprize, decision, and generosity. The great Columbus, after having in vain solicited the aid of Genoa, France, England, Portugal, and Spain—after having combated, for a period of eight years, with every objection that a want of knowledge could propose, found, at last, his only resource in the penetration and magnanimity of Isabella of Spain, who furnished the equipment, and raised the sums necessary to defray the expenses, on the sale of her own jewels; and while we conceive an action, so honourable to THE SEX, hath not been sufficiently applauded, we trust, that the equality of the female intellect to that of their brethren, who have so long usurped an unmanly and unfounded superiority, will never, in this younger world, be left without a witness. We cannot ascertain the number of ingenious women, who at present adorn our country. In the shade of solitude they perhaps cultivate their own minds, and superintend the education of their children. Our day, we know, is only dawning—But when we contemplate a Warren,[1] a Philenia,[2] . . . &c. &c. we gratefully acknowledge, that genius and application, even in the female line, already gild, with effulgent radiance, our blest Aurora.

---

[1]Mercy Otis Warren (1728–1814), a playwright, poet, and historian, was noted especially for her history of the American Revolution.

[2]Sarah Wentworth Morton (1759–1846) was a Boston poet and novelist, a contemporary and sometime rival of Judith Sargent Murray.

But women are calculated to shine in other characters than those adverted to, in the preceding Essays; and with proper attention to their education, and subsequent habits, they might easily attain that independence, for which a Wollstonecraft[3] hath so energetically contended; the term, *helpless widow,* might be rendered as unfrequent and inapplicable as that of *helpless widower;* and although we should undoubtedly continue to mourn the dissolution of wedded amity, yet we should derive consolation from the knowledge, that the infant train had still a remaining prop, and that a mother could *assist* as well as *weep* over her offspring.

That women have a talent—a talent which, duly cultivated, would confer that independence, which is demonstrably of incalculable utility, every attentive observer will confess. THE SEX should be taught to depend on their own efforts, for the procurement of an establishment in life. The chance of a matrimonial coadjutor, is no more than a probable contingency; and if they were early accustomed to regard this *uncertain* event with suitable *indifference,* they would make elections with that deliberation, which would be calculated to give a more rational prospect of tranquillity. All this we have repeatedly asserted, and all this we do invariably believe. To neglect polishing a gem, or obstinately to refuse bringing into action a treasure in our possession, when we might thus accumulate a handsome interest, is surely egregiously absurd, and the height of folly. *The united efforts of male and female* might rescue many a family from destruction, which, notwithstanding the efforts of its *individual* head, is now involved in all the calamities attendant on a dissipated fortune and augmenting debts. It is not possible to educate children in a manner which will render them *too beneficial* to society; and the more we multiply aids to a family, the greater will be the security, that its individuals will not be thrown a burden on the public.

An instance of *female capability,* this moment occurs to memory. In the State of Massachusetts, in a small town, some miles from the metropolis, resides a woman, who hath made astonishing improvements in agriculture. Her mind, in the early part of her life, was but penuriously cultivated, and she grew up almost wholly uneducated: But being suffered, during her childhood, to rove at large among her native fields, her limbs expanded, and she acquired a height of stature above the common size;

---

[3]Mary Wollstonecraft (1759–1797), an English feminist, was the author of *The Vindication of the Rights of Woman.*

her mind also became invigorated; and her understanding snatched sufficient information, to produce a consciousness of the injury she sustained in the want of those aids, which should have been furnished in the beginning of her years. She however applied herself diligently to remedy the evil, and soon made great proficiency in writing, and in arithmetic. She reads every thing she could procure; but the impressions adventitiously made on her infant mind still obtained the ascendency. A few rough acres constituted her patrimonial inheritance; these she has brought into a state of high cultivation; their productions are every year both useful and ornamental; she is mistress of agricolation, and is at once a botanist and a florist. The most approved authors in the English language, on these subjects, are in her hands, and she studies them with industry and success.

She has obtained such considerable knowledge in the nature of soils, the precise manure which they require, and their particular adaptation to the various fruits of the earth, that she is become the oracle of all the farmers in her vicinity and when laying out, or appropriating their grounds, they uniformly submit them to her inspection. Her gardens are the resort of all strangers who happen to visit her village; and she is particularly remarkable for a growth of trees, from which, gentlemen, solicitous to enrich their fruitgardens, or ornament their parterres, are in the habit of supplying themselves; and those trees are, to their ingenious cultivator, a considerable income. Carefully attentive to her nursery, she knows when to transplant, and when to prune; and she perfectly understands the various methods of inoculating and ingrafting. In short, she is a complete *husbandwoman;* and she has, besides, acquired a vast stock of general knowledge, while her judgment has attained such a degree of maturity, as to justify the confidence of the villagers, who are accustomed to consult her on every perplexing emergency.

In the constant use of exercise, she is not corpulent; and she is extremely active, and wonderfully athletic. Instances, almost incredible, are produced of her strength. Indeed, it is not surprising that she is the idol and standing theme of the village, since, with all her uncommon qualifications, she combines a tenderness of disposition not to be exceeded. Her extensive acquaintance with herbs, contributes to render her a skilful and truly valuable nurse; and the world never produced a more affectionate, attentive, or faithful woman: Yet, while she feelingly sympathizes with every invalid, she is not herself subject to imaginary complaints; nor does she easily yield to real illness. She has lately been indisposed—and a life so valuable, when endangered, embodied a host of fears for its

safety: With difficulty she was persuaded to lie down upon her bed, and
the young woman who attended her, and to whom she had endeared herself by a thousand good offices, after softly closing the shutters and door
of her apartment, privately summoned the aid of a physician; and when
the medical gentleman made his appearance, she accompanied him to
the apartment of her friend; but behold, the bird was flown! and when pursued, she was found at a distance from her habitation, directing some
labourers, who were employed in her service, and who, she was fearful,
were not sufficiently attentive to her previous instructions. The event
proved she had acted judiciously; for, braced by the fresh air, her nerves
new strung, assumed their usual tone, her sickness vanished, and her
native vigour returned.

Although far advanced in years, without a matrimonial connexion, yet,
constantly engaged in useful and interesting pursuits, she manifests not
that peevishness and discontent, so frequently attendant on *old maids;*
she realizes all that independence which is proper to humanity; and she
knows how to set a just value on the blessings she enjoys.

From my treasury of facts, I produce a second instance, equally in
point. I have seen letters, written by a lady, an inhabitant of St. Sebastian, (a Spanish emporium) that breathed the true spirit of commerce, and
evinced the writer to possess all the integrity, punctuality and dispatch,
which are such capital requisites in the mercantile career. This lady is at
the head of a firm, of which herself and daughters make up the individuals—Her name is *Birmingham.* She is, I imagine, well known to the
commercial part of the United States. She was left a widow in the infancy
of her children, who were numerous; and she immediately adopted the
most vigorous measures for their emolument. Being a woman of a mag-
nanimous mind, she devoted her sons to the profession of arms; and they
were expeditiously disposed of, in a way the best calculated to bring
them acquainted with the art of war. Her daughters were educated for
business; and, arriving at womanhood, they have long since established
themselves into a capital trading-house, of which, as has been observed,
their respectable mother is the head. She is, in the hours of business,
invariably to be found in her compting-house; there she takes her morning repast; her daughters act as clerks, (and they are adepts in their
office) regularly preparing the papers and letters, which pass in order
under her inspection. She signs herself, in all accounts and letters, *Widow
Birmingham;* and this is the address by which she is designated. I have
conversed with one of our captains, who has often negociated with her
the disposal of large and valuable cargoes. Her consignments, I am told,

are to a great amount; and one of the principal merchants in the town of Boston asserts, that he receives from no house in Europe more satisfactory returns. Upright in their dealings, and unwearied in their application, these ladies possess a right to prosperity; and we trust that their circumstances are as easy, as their conduct is meritorious.

"Would you, good Mr. Gleaner, station us in the compting-house?" No, my fair country-women, except circumstances unavoidably pointed the way. Again I say, I do but hold up to your view, the *capability* of your Sex; thus stimulating you to cultivate your talents, to endeavour to acquire general knowledge, and to aim at making yourselves so far acquainted with some particular branch of business, as that it may, if occasion requires, assist in establishing you above that kind of dependence, against which the freeborn mind so naturally revolts. Far be it from me, to wish to *unsex* you—I am desirous of preserving, by all means, those amiable traits that are considered as characteristic—I reverence the modesty and gentleness of your dispositions—I would not annihilate a single virtue; but I would assiduously augment the faithfulness and affection of your bosoms. An elegant panegyrist of your Sex, hath assigned you the superiority in the feelings of the heart; and I cannot more emphatically conclude my subject, than in his beautifully pathetic language:

"The pleasures of women must arise from their virtues. It is by the cradle of their children, and in viewing the smiles of their daughters, or the sports of their sons, that mothers find their happiness. Where are the powerful emotions of nature? Where is the sentiment, at once sublime and pathetic, that carries every feeling to excess? Is it to be found in the frosty indifference, and the sour severity of some fathers? No—but in the warm and affectionate bosom of a *mother*. It is she, who, by an impulse as quick as involuntary, rushes into the flood to preserve a boy, whose imprudence had betrayed him into the waves—It is she, who, in the middle of a conflagration, throws herself across the flames to save a sleeping infant—It is she, who, with dishevelled locks, pale and distracted, embraces with transport, the body of a dead child, pressing its cold lips to her's, as if she would reanimate, by her tears and her caresses, the insensible clay. These great expressions of nature—these heart-rending emotions, which fill us at once with wonder, compassion and terror, always have belonged, and always will belong, only to Women. They possess, in those moments, an inexpressible something, which carries them beyond themselves; and they seem to discover to us new souls, above the standard of humanity."

8

Reasons for Lack of
Union in the Wedded State

Judith Sargent Murray believed that a good marriage offered men and women the best chance for earthly happiness, but she was also aware that marriage could be a disaster for those who wed unwisely. In the following poem, Hymen, the Greek god of marriage, explains the reason for most unhappy marriages. The problem begins in courtship, when men and women are less than honest with each other, and perhaps with themselves, about their marital expectations. Neither party is realistic; both use "flattery" and "seductive wiles," and fail to reveal their true character to their prospective partners. Not surprisingly, at honeymoon's end, bride and groom are sadly disillusioned. According to Murray, what unrealistic hopes do both men and women have concerning marriage? What might they do to avoid the disappointments described in this poem?

Say Hymen, gentle God of marriage, say,
Why from the paths of peace thy Votaries stray?
Why blasted in the long expected joy,
So soon inmingling with such sad alloy?
Why fades the roses in Adelia's cheek,
Whence springs the woes of which she dare not speak?
Where is the hope that sparkled in her eye,
Whence in the mournful oft repeated sigh?
Why stands the Lord with magisterial gate,
Imperious airs, and late assumed state?
Did not the fondest vows thy alter grace,
And joys chastized illume the blushing face?
Then why these tears of anguish, which so soon,
Portentous cloud even the *Honey Moon?* . . .
[Hymen's reply]
"Oft I have seen" with dignity he said—
"The perjur'd vow e'en in my presence made,
My wholesome laws audaciously transgress'd,
While every thought a lack of love confess'd.
The evils you lament to me are known,

Judith Sargent Murray, Poetry, 1:357–61, Mississippi Archives, Jackson, Miss.

Their vast increase of late so mighty grown.
Oft have my precepts wondering hearts assail'd,
But precepts, and examples all have fail'd . . .
The sexes were in kind compassion giv'n,
To yield upon your globe a taste of heav'n,
But erring mortals with pernicious skill,
Refuse the dictates of our soverign will,
The purposed good industriously invert,
Their utmost pow'rs of mischief they exert
With fatal zeal sweet amity they blast,
And o'er their lives thick clouds of sorrow cast.
The virgin is by soft attention woo'd,
By all the blandishments of art pursu'd,
By force of language nearly deify'd,
Beyond a doubt to god himself allied.
She fills on high some visionary throne,
While prostrate at her shrine her swain falls down . . .
Delicious flattery's seductive wiles,
The fair one of her judgment oft beguiles.
She listens, balances, and then believes,
To her fond heart the youth belov'd receives,
And e'er the indissoluable knot is tied,
With mutual art their mutual faults they hide.
The Virgin eager to commence a bride,
Hushes each fear, and lays each doubt aside,
Bright hope predicts a long unrival'd reign,
Despotic o'er the husband as the swain!
That he will ne'er his righteous sway controul,
But hail her lasting Empress of her soul.
He, too, impatient waits the destin'd hour,
Which gives, and guarantees his Lordly pow'r.
He fancies all those virtues grace her mind,
Which form her modest, tender, gentle, kind,
That mellowing love will gild each added year,
And in prospective halcyon days appear.
Thus each expects a mild submissive friend,
And disappointment will on each attend.
The marriage day the fateful veil removes
And lo! the Godess a mere Woman proves!
Sighs, flattery, and oaths are now no more,
The obsequious Lover ceaseth to adore.

The Angel trembling on his tongue is change'd
The plainest words in common order ranged.
He dies no more though absent from her sight,
But seeks in varied life some near delight.
Amaz'd and shock'd the weeping fair beholds,
The long dark scroll her added life unfolds.
Tears course each other down her cheek,
The swollen eyes the tale of sorrow speak . . .
Baleful recrimination then begins,
And wedded happiness that moment ends.
Thus air built Castles tumble from their base,
And Clouds and Darkness occupy their place . . ."

9

Margaretta Faces a Marital Crisis
1798

The following selection from the first volume of The Gleaner *employs a plot technique common to eighteenth-century novels, letters between the protagonists to move the story along. Women writers were especially fond of the "epistolary novel" form, whose chatty, informal quality masked their lack of familiarity with grammatical rules. Moreover, literate women were accustomed to writing letters, and they found it a relatively unintimidating model.*

In this episode of the "Margaretta story," Mr. Vigillius describes a major crisis in his daughter's marriage. It is Mary Vigillius who first notes that "all was not right at Margaretta's." Margaretta turns to Mary for advice when she believes that her husband, Edward, has fallen in love with his stepsister and ward, Serafina Clifford. Mary urges Margaretta to "reverence herself" and to question the "despotic" custom that puts the onus on women for marital failure, but she also tells her to be more realistic, to expect less passion from her husband, and to work harder to make Edward happy. Fortunately, Margaretta later discovers that she has misinterpreted Edward's behavior. She finds out that Edward faces economic disaster. Serafina has offered him the proceeds of her own inheritance so that he will be able to

Judith Sargent Murray, *The Gleaner: A Miscellaneous Production in Three Volumes,* 3 vols. (Boston: L. Thomas and E. T. Andrews, 1798), 1:188–99.

*take care of his wife and child. Edward has refused. What does Murray's
depiction of Margaretta's crisis reveal about her views on the possibility of
marital happiness based on love alone? On balance, does Mary's advice to
her daughter reinforce more traditional views of women's role or does it pave
the way for equality and autonomy in marriage?*

"All is not right at Margaretta's"—said my poor Mary, some nights since,
as she laid her head upon her pillow. It was an involuntary expression,
and from the fullness of her heart it escaped her. She would gladly have
recalled it, or at least have palliated its effects, but it was too late, for the
impression was indelibly made—*all is not right at Margaretta's!* Her
words reverberated through the inmost recesses of my soul; they seemed
to possess a deadly power, which, at a single blow, annihilated the seren-
ity of my bosom. . . .

I had observed, that a kind of pensive melancholy had for some time
clouded the fine open countenance of my wife; that her wonted equanimity was interrupted; that her slumbers were disturbed and broken and
that the admirable regularity of her movements were evidently discom-
posed. As I possessed a perfect confidence in her prudence, I had for-
borne to press her upon so distressing a change, well knowing, that
whenever it was advantageous or proper, discretion would not fail of
prompting her to pour into my ear the sorrows of her heart.

Maternal affection had armed her with an anxious and vigilant attention to her daughter; . . . Whenever Mary occasionally looked in upon her
Margaretta, if her visit was unexpected, she was sure to find her bathed
in tears; and the apologies which she seemed to study, but ill concealed
the discomposure of an agonized bosom.

Mary, with all her penetration, could not divine the cause of an event,
which she so greatly deplored; she imagined that her daughter was in possession of every thing which could conduce to the most pleasing kind of
tranquillity; and she conceived that the grateful affections of her heart
ought to be in constant exercise. Competency beamed its regular, mild, and
equal blessings upon her; her infant was not only lovely and promising, but
he seemed almost exempted from those disorders, which are usually attendant upon his imbecile age; her own health was uniformly good; and though
Edward Hamilton partook, of course, the morbid contagion of her grief, yet
he was still the pensively pleasing and entertaining companion.

Mary concluded, that nothing remained, but for Margaretta to reas-
sume the accustomed equability of her temper, in order to the perfect
restoration of that sunshine, which had for a season illumed her hours;

and tenderly interested, while her heart was torn by anxiety, she could not forbear to interrogate—but the only replies she could obtain were sighs and tears, interrupted by broke[n] assurances, that indeed she was—she was very happy; and that she supplicated her dear Mamma to put upon every appearance the most candid construction. Her mother, however, made wise by the observations she had collected from books, from the study of her fellow mortals, and from a large share of natural discernment, could not be thus easily deceived.

Curiosity was, upon this occasion, her smallest inducement; and she trembled at the impervious darkness of a cloud, which she rationally apprehended involved the dearest hopes of her Margaretta! Baffled in repeated attempts to fathom a mystery, which had yielded her bosom a prey to the keenest anguish, she changed the mode of her attack; and, addressing her daughter by letter, in the language of discretion, in the language of tenderness, she penned the feelings of her soul.

To Mrs. Hamilton

Is it possible for Margaretta Hamilton to conceive her mother a calm spectator of that corroding inquietude, which is gradually and too surely undermining the peace of a child, who is, she had almost said, dearer to her than any other human being? As I have not been stimulated by an idle wish to obtain your secret, I am hurt that my inquiries have proved so ineffectual. Can Margaretta wish to veil herself from the eye of the guardian friend of her early years? Believe me, I seek only to probe the wound, that I may the more assuredly arrest the progress of the envenomed poison, and be enabled to judge what prescription may operate as a specific. . . .

When we gave our Margaretta to Edward Hamilton, *we conceived that we had yielded her to the man of her heart;* and, believing him to be every way worthy, we congratulated ourselves upon the establishment of the felicity of our child. What, my love, can have produced a change so affectingly agonizing? Whenever you *appear* tolerably composed, it is *evident* that you are *acting* a part.

I tremble lest your father should penetrate the thin disguises which you assume; and, sanguine as his expectations in regard to you have been, it is difficult to say, what serious consequences his disappointment might produce.

Oh, my child, my soul is torn by the most fearful conjectures! will you not endeavour to assuage the sorrows of my heart? will you not at least relieve me from the pangs of suspense? Can it be, that Mrs. Hamilton is so far subjected to sexual weakness, as to have delivered herself up to the most alarming chagrin, merely because, perhaps, she receives not from the husband such *adulatory devoirs* as distinguished the lover? Surely I ought to regard this idea as inadmissible; and yet, the strongest minds may have their moments of imbecility; and, my Margaretta, all accomplished, all lovely as she is, must nevertheless still be considered as a young and inexperienced woman.

If this is indeed the source of your perturbed anxiety, I persuade myself that some such reflections as the following, will ere long awaken you to reason.

It is impossible to change the order of nature. Delighted admiration of pleasing novelties, is the spontaneous growth of every bosom; a second view finds us more calm; a third, a fourth, may possibly rouse us to pleasure; but a constant repetition will create that indifference, which will constitute a perfect contrast to the keen edge of our new-born feelings. The impassioned ardours of the soul must of necessity subside; *they are but created to expire:* But I pity the mind which prefers not the calm rational affections that succeed, to all the hurricane of the passions.

Love, as it is commonly described, is undoubtedly a short-lived being; it is a luxurious glutton, that invariably gormandizeth to its destruction; but from its perfumed ashes ariseth a star-gemmed soother, that the wedded pair may either crush in the birth, or agree to cherish, as the security of their mutual happiness. Esteem may sometimes be traced as the *parent,* but I think it will be found that it is oftener the *offspring* of love. Young esteem, entwined by smiling confidence, enwreathed with sweet complacency, how fragrant is its rosy breath, how necessary to the hymeneal career, and how much is it in the power of the affianced friends to render its existence permanent!

Behold your Edward in a large circle of ladies; doubtless, he is all attention; his features are animated; and if they are young, beautiful and sentimental, he is all soul; he seems to tread on air, and he hath no eyes or ears, but for them; he will address to them the most refined gallantries, and he will appear lost amid a constellation so splendid. But think you, my love, that he would experience sensations thus highly wrought, were he to mingle every hour in their society? and would you wish to exchange for such *mental gewgaws,* if I may so express myself, the solid pleasures of endearing familiarity; the advantages resulting from unbroken confidence, from a social intercourse, uninterrupted by the fopperies of language, and from all the matchless and serene enjoyments which wedded friends may know?

Are you not apprehensive that the continued clouds which gloom your lovely face, may prematurely destroy your bloom, and, by imperceptible degrees, alienate the affections of your husband? If once you relinquish your place in his bosom, it will require a series of the most arduous efforts to restore you to the possession you will have thus imprudently abdicated!

I am not an advocate for undue gentleness, or submissive acquiescence; such conduct may border upon meanness; a woman should be *just too, she should reverence herself:* I am far from conceiving that the female world, considered in the aggregate, is inferior to the male; but custom hath established a certain order in society, and custom is a despot, whose chains, I am fearful, it will be in vain that an individual will assay to burst.

I know too, that it is for the interest of every person who singly considers either him or herself, to cultivate an *equal* and *serene* temper of mind. If you array yourself in the garments of tranquillity, if you seek to clothe yourself with innate cheerfulness, *habit* will at length render you in *reality complacent,* and it will not be you who will derive the smallest share of advantage therefrom.

In short, my dear girl, you have every inducement to call forth your most unremitted exertions. Parents tenderly anxious for your welfare — ... a husband acknowledged as highly deserving, and a beauteous infant, whose little eyes are raised to you for protection, for instruction, and for peace: ... Speak, I conjure you, speak; and let your communications mitigate the pangs, which cease not to lacerate the bosom of your afflicted and commiserating mother.

The evening of the day, which has presented the foregoing address, returned Mary the subjoined reply.

To My Dear and Honoured Mother

Pitying angels — and must I then speak? assuredly I must — every consideration unquestionably points out an explanation.

I have sank, mortifyingly sunk, in the estimation of her whose *approbation* I would die to preserve; and I have inflicted upon her the severest anguish; yet, probably, her tender bosom may be disburthened, by a knowledge that her Margaretta is not altogether so culpable as she hath apprehended: And duty seems to impel an unreserved confidence; for the honoured woman, to whom I am primarily indebted for every thing that can render life valuable, hath commanded me to be explicit,

But stop! — can duties clash? Ought the deferrent female to accuse him to whom she hath voluntarily yielded her most sacred and solemn vows? Can Margaretta criminate her Edward!!!!

Yet, possibly, what I have to urge in my own defence, may not exhibit my Hamilton in a censurable point of view; from a mutable being we are not to expect immutability; and, if my conjectures have their foundation in truth, though I may be wretched, I will not be unjust. It is necessary that I justify myself to my mother; but I will not dare to cast a shade upon the character of a man, whom I regard as the first of created beings.

Hardly three months after our marriage had elapsed, when Edward exhibited marks of a growing and deep-felt inquietude! an impenetrable gloom over-shadowed every feature! Had you witnessed, as I have done, and still do, the lasting and serious sorrows of his bosom, your maternal remonstrance would have been addressed to him, rather than to your unfortunate child. Often hath he regarded me with a fixed and melancholy attention: and when, alarmed and terrified, I have sought the cause of his mysterious deportment, as if unable to command his grief, he hath fled with precipitation from my importunities. To induce him to disclose the fatal secret of his heart, no means within my power have been left unassayed; and although failing in my well intended efforts, I have still endeavoured to soothe and woo his steps to the sweet and flowery paths of peace.

With the severe eye of unrelenting rigour, I have examined my own conduct: Probably I am under the domination of *self-partiality;* for, in regard to him, I cannot view myself as reprehensible either in thought, word, or deed.

When, by your direction, I announced to him my expectation of presenting him with a little being, who would bring into the world with it, its claims to his fondest affections, — Oh, Madam! instead of the effect which we naturally imagined, the sorrows of his heart became ungovernable; with convulsed and agonized emotions, he clasped his hands — Never shall I forget his exclamation; it sounded like a death-warrant to my ear— *"Gracious God! wretch, wretch that I am!"*—What he would have added, I know not; for, overpowered by my grief and my surprise, I sunk lifeless at his feet; and when, by his endeavours, and those of the attendants whom he summoned to my relief, I was recalled to sense and to recollection, I found him kneeling by my bed side, assiduously and tenderly employed in my restoration, and his transports at beholding me, as he expressed himself, once more open my eyes to love and to him, at seeing the bloom again revisit my cheeks, were, he declared, the most exquisite he had ever experienced!

You will not doubt, that I seized this tender moment, to expostulate with him relative to his heart-affecting and soul-piercing expressions of grief, and continued melancholy; but, although he beheld me, as I then supposed, with unabating affection, although he soothed my spirit by the most delicate and unequivocal assurances, he nevertheless turned a deaf ear to the voice of my supplication! . . .

Fearful of disgusting him by my persecutions, I banished from my lips every expression of my anxiety; and, as far as was in my power, I dismissed from my features the inquietude of my bosom. I studied, by my every movement, his pleasure; and I flattered myself, that the birth of my child, by giving a new turn to his ideas, would restore my felicity. It is true that I had nothing to complain of, except the corroding grief, with which he evidently struggled, and which, notwithstanding his efforts to conceal it, was generally the companion of his private hours: For the rest, I judged myself in possession of his heart, and his deportment was descriptive of the most refined and faithful attachment.

Thus passed the days, until the arrival of my pangful hour. You, dear Madam, were a witness to the distressing agitation of his soul, during that perilous and tremendous period; you heard and repeated his fervid vows for my safety; they were music in my ears; doubtless they were sincere, for the heart of Edward Hamilton is as tender as it is manly. You also witnessed the rapt sensation of his grateful spirit, when he received his son; you heard and marked the paternal blessings, which he poured upon his youngling head; and, it is true, that the little creature is as dear to him, as the vital spark which warms him to existence — *but alas! this is the sum total of my enjoyments!* The anguish of heart, which is destroying the *father of my child,* seems daily to augment! The tears, of which he is apparently unconscious, often bedew the face of my infant! Frequently, as if by mutual consent, we gaze in silent sorrow upon the dear innocent, and when Hamilton supposes himself unobserved, his eyes and hands are raised toward heaven; and in all the majesty of innate woe, he pathetically makes his appeal to the Searcher of all hearts, while rectitude, it should seem, is the motto of his life.

Yet, I will not withhold some circumstances, that have produced inferences, which my full soul hath recoiled at admitting. Alas, my mother! will you not esteem me wretched, when I confess to you, that I have but too much reason to suppose *myself the origin of his misfortune.*

Some weeks after the birth of my little William, I was alarmed by the frequent absence of Hamilton; and as I *forbore any remarks thereon, being unwilling to embitter, by my expostulations, the few moments which he allowed me,* I continued ignorant of the manner in which he appropriated his time. *Accident,* at length, informed me that all those hours of which he had robbed me, were devoted to Serafina! and from her he always returned a prey to the deepest and most fearful chagrin.

The shock which my tenderness and my sensibility received, in a moment so replete with anguish, I assay not to describe; but reason, I bless God, darted athwart the region of my soul her beamy influence. Serafina was the sister of my heart; she was a lovely and an amiable woman. Edward and Serafina had been educated together from early life; their habits of intimacy were confirmed; and I considered, that if her society possessed more charms than mine, Edward was unfortunate, but not culpable.

I immediately formed the resolution of soliciting her to become an inmate in our house; and when I made my proposal to Hamilton, *he received it with more satisfaction than my feelings could well tolerate;* he kissed my hand with rapture; a gleam of joy vermilioned his cheek, and he flew to acquaint Miss Clifford with the wishes which I had expressed.

Serafina too demonstrated the highest complacency; a residence with her Margaretta, she was pleased to say, would complete her felicity; and she could not hesitate, when a situation every way eligible was tendered to her acceptance.

Our plan was no sooner concerted than put into execution: Miss Clifford was established in this mansion, and Hamilton no longer wandered abroad! When I am present, Hamilton hath never, for a single moment, abated his marked attentions to me; and he regards Serafina in his accustomed manner; but if I unexpectedly join them, although they have apparently been engaged in the most affectingly interesting conversation, they are immediately silent, embarrassed and uneasy!

The fine eyes of Serafina are often drowned in tears, and the grief of Hamilton seems to know no bounds! Two weeks since, upon the morning of the day on which you surprised me yielding up my whole soul to sorrow, supposing Hamilton in his closet, I took my needle-work, with a design, while sitting beside him, to make one more effort to allure him into the sweet and flowery walks of tranquillity. He was not there—but an open piece of paper lying upon his scritoire, written by the hand of Serafina, in which I saw my name in large characters inscribed, caught my attention. I read it   its contents are indelibly engraven upon the tablets of my heart; and, with a trembling hand, I transcribe them for your perusal.

"That I love not my own soul better than I do my Edward Hamilton, I trust he will always believe. I have received his *expostulatory letter,* and by that *love which we mutually avow,* I conjure him to consider, weigh, ponder, and reflect. *Can Edward consign Margaretta to ruin? Can he be forgetful of the interest and well-being of his infant son?* If Hamilton will give these claims their *due weight,* I persuade myself that he will then listen to the voice of prudence—of that prudence which is, *in this instance,* regent in the bosom of

SERAFINA CLIFFORD"

I read, I say—and the agony of my spirit was inexpressible—with a wild air I turned toward the window; and, as if fate had determined to make me completely wretched, I beheld Edward and Serafina, arm under arm, walking down the gravel-walk of our little flower garden: This, at such a moment, was too much. With precipitate and unequal steps, impassioned almost to frenzy, I hasted from the closet, flying, as for refuge, to my own. It was at this distressing juncture, that you, Madam, looked in upon me; you saw, and your eye condemned the irregular expressions of a sorrow to which you was a stranger; but I flatter myself that you will, in future, rather pity than censure your Margaretta.

. . .—Thus, dear and honoured Madam, you will see that I have no common cause of sorrow—that I am not so very faulty as you conceived. Thus have I entitled myself to your advice; and thus you will be induced to pity your

MARGARETTA HAMILTON

10

Lines Written While Rocking the Cradle of My Julia Maria

December 8, 1791

When Julia Maria Murray was born on August 22, 1791, her mother was overjoyed. She had helped raise two orphan children, and was devoted to various cousins, nieces, and nephews. The happiness she derived from her attention to other people's children, however, had never been sufficient to assuage Murray's desire for a child of her own. Indeed, she believed that a childless woman was almost unnatural. As the following poem indicates, she took pleasure in the most ordinary tasks associated with motherhood, investing them with an emotional significance that would have puzzled her ancestors. The poem also depicts an understanding of human nature at variance with the Puritan focus on original sin and human depravity. What words does Murray use to describe her daughter's essential characteristics? Do you think that she would have described a son in the same way?

Judith Sargent Murray, Poetry, 3:337–39, Mississippi Archives, Jackson, Mississippi.

My Maria—careful joy—
All my moments you employ—
Time advanceth not for me,
Tis devoted all to thee;
Circle'd in my fond embrace,
As thy features I retrace,
Fancying charms before unknown,
Quite enthusiastic grown,
Beauteous Helen[1]—I exclaim,
Though most unlike the Grecian dame—
Virtue shall be my Julia's guide,
Prudence watching by her side;
Through every ordeal she shall pass,
Confess'd the fair accomplished lass;
And though a Paris[2] may assail,
Never, shall his arts prevail,
With virgin pride her breast shall glow,
Serene as truth her passion flow.
Thus while I snatch the ardent kiss,
Repeating oft the fragrant bliss,
Or while I yield the honied stream,
Of golden scenes I fondly dream;
With roses strewing every hour,
Which rears to life my pretty flow'r,
Gaily futurity expands,
And tiptoe Hope with chaplet stands,
Its perfum'd sweets diffusing round.
Tis thus the Cherub in my arms,
My pleas'd imagination warms
Arresting every rising thought,
With busy plans and wishes fraught:
Each day successive as it moves,
My labor unremitted proves,
Just as I said—her opening worth,
Only of three short months the growth,
My every Movement hath purloin'd,
Morn, noon, and night to her resign'd:
For though the little charmer sleeps,

[1] Helen of Troy was the beautiful heroine of Homer's *Iliad*.
[2] Abductor of Helen, whose action precipitated the Trojan War.

And silence its soft vigil keeps,
Some skirt, or vest my worth supplies,
And see that cap unfinish'd lies:
Something presents which must be done,
This robe completed—that begun;
So that it is exceeding plain,
I can no leisure hour obtain.
Well be it so—content am I—
My moments pass serenely by,
No Flowerist with half my glee,
Expects his opening buds to see,
Or builds though high he mounts in air,
His Castles more than half so fair . . .

11

Margaretta's Education

1798

In her seventh "Gleaner" essay, Judith Sargent Murray broached the subject that was dearest to her heart—the education of women. Her own daughter was a little over a year old when the essay first appeared in November of 1792, and as she described the educational program devised by Mary Vigillius, she surely imagined that she herself would employ similar methods with Julia Maria. The plan contained Murray's essential beliefs. It emphasized the importance of a mother's early influence on her children. It made a strong case for the value of a broad education for all women. And it contended that an educated woman would be an ideal Republican woman. She would be rational, benevolent, fond of life's simple pleasures, and not likely to be led astray by frivolous, worldly temptations. Later "Gleaner" essays would call upon Americans to endow their daughters with a classical education, yet Margaretta, it is interesting to note, became proficient in only two languages: the conventional English and French. Why did Mary Vigillius initiate a correspondence with Margaretta, when they lived under the same roof? What was the Vigilliuses' attitude toward allowing Margaretta

Judith Sargent Murray, *The Gleaner: A Miscellaneous Production in Three Volumes,* 3 vols. (Boston: L. Thomas and E. T. Andrews, 1798), 1:66–76.

to read novels? How does Vigillius defend Mary's educational plan from charges that intelligent women would become "unsexed"?

. . . When we returned home,[1] we fitted up a little chamber, of which we constituted Margaretta the sole proprietor; my wife informing her that she should establish a post betwixt her apartment and her own, that if they chose, upon any occasion, to separate, they might with the greater convenience open a correspondence by letter. The rudiments of Margaretta's education had been attended to; in her plain work she had made considerable proficiency; she could read the seventh, tenth, eleventh and twelfth chapters of Nehemiah, without much difficulty; . . . but Mary very soon sketched out for our charge rather an extensive plan of education; and as I was not entirely convinced of the inutility of her views, the natural indolence of my temper induced me to let the matter pass, without entering my caveat by way of stopping proceedings; and indeed, I think the propriety of circumscribing the education of a female, within such narrow bounds as are frequently assigned, is at least problematical. A celebrated writer, I really forget who, hath penned upon this subject a number of self-evident truths; and it is an incontrovertible fact, that to the matron is entrusted not only the care of her daughter, but also the forming the first and oftentimes the most important movements of that mind, which is to inform the future man; the early dawnings of reason she is appointed to watch, and from her are received the most indelible impressions of his life. Now, was she properly qualified, how enviable and how dignified would be her employment. The probability is, that the family of children, whom she directed, supposing them to possess common capacities, being once initiated into the flowery paths of science, would seldom stop short of the desired goal. Fine writing, arithmetic, geography, astronomy, music, drawing; an attachment to all these might be formed in infancy; the first principles of the fine arts might be so accommodated, as to constitute the pastime of the child; the seeds of knowledge might be implanted in the tender mind, and even budding there, before the avocations of the father permitted him to combine his efforts. Affection for the sweet preceptress, would originate a strong predilection for instructions, that would with interesting tenderness be given, and that would be made to assume the face of entertainment, and thus the young proficient would be, almost imperceptibly, engaged in those walks, in which an

---

[1]The Vigilliuses were returning from a trip to South Carolina, where they had first encountered the orphaned Margaretta and agreed to adopt her.

advantageous perseverance might rationally be expected. A mother, who possesseth a competent knowledge of the English and French tongues, and who is properly assiduous about her children, I conceive, will find it little more difficult to teach them to lisp in two languages, than in one; and as the powers of the student advanceth, certain portions of the day may be regularly appropriated to the converting in that language which is not designed for the common intercourses of life. Letters, in either tongue, to the parent, or fictitious characters, may be alternately written, and thus an elegant knowledge of both may be gradually obtained. Learning, certainly, can never with propriety be esteemed a burthen; and when the mind is judiciously balanced, it renders the possessor not only more valuable, but also more amiable, and more generally useful. Literary acquisitions cannot, unless the faculties of the mind are deranged, be lost: and while the goods of fortune may be whelmed beneath the contingencies of revolving time, intellectual property still remains, and the mental funds can never be exhausted. The accomplished, the liberally accomplished female, if she is destined to move in the line of competency, will be regarded as a pleasing and instructive companion; whatever she does will connect an air of persuasive elevation; whatever she may be adventitiously called, genuine dignity will be the accompaniment of her steps; she will always be attended to with pleasure, and she cannot fail of being distinguished; should she, in her career of life, be arrested by adverse fortune, many resources of relief, of pleasure, and of emolument, open themselves before her; and she is not *necessarily* condemned to laborious efforts, or to the drudgery of that unremitted sameness, which the ro[u]tine of the needle presents.

But whatever may be the merits of the course which I am thus *apparently* advocating, without stopping to examine the other side of the question, I proceed to say, that the plan of education adopted for Margaretta was, as I have already hinted, sufficiently extensive, and that Mrs. Vigillius (to address my good wife, in her dignified character of governante, with all possible respect) having instructed her pupil in the grand fundamental points of the philanthropic religion of Jesus, was never easy while any branch of improvement, which could by the most remote construction be deemed feminine, remained unessayed; and I must in justice declare, that the consequence, by producing Margaretta at the age of sixteen, a beautiful and accomplished girl, more than answered her most sanguine expectations.

Of needle work, in its varieties, my wife pronounced her a perfect mistress; her knowledge of the English, and French tongues, was fully adequate to her years, and her manner of reading had, for me, peculiar charms;

her hand writing was neat and easy; she was a good accomptant, a tolerable geographer and chronologist; she had skimmed the surface of astronomy and natural philosophy; had made good proficiency in her study of history and the poets; could sketch a landscape; could furnish, from her own fancy, patterns for the muslins which she wrought; could bear her part in a minuet and a cotillion, and was allowed to have an excellent hand upon the piano forte. We once entertained a design of debarring her the indulgence of novels; but those books, being in the hands of everyone, we conceived the accomplishment of our wishes in this respect, except we had bred her an absolute recluse, almost impracticable; and Mrs. Vigillius, therefore, thought it best to permit the use of every decent work, causing them to be read in her presence, hoping that she might, by her suggestions and observations, present an antidote to the poison, with which the pen of the novelist is too often fraught. The study of history was pursued, if I may so express myself, systematically: To the page of the historian one hour every day was regularly devoted; a second hour, Mary conversed with her adopted daughter upon the subject which a uniform course of reading had furnished; and a third hour Margaretta was directed to employ, in committing to paper such particular facts, remarks and consequences deduced therefrom, as had, during the hours appropriated to reading, and conversing, most strikingly impressed her mind; and by these means the leading features of history were indelibly imprinted thereon. Mrs. Vigillius also composed little geographical, historical, and chronological catechisms, or dialogues, the nature of which will be easily conceived; and she pronounced them of infinite advantage in the prosecution of her plan; she submitted likewise, at least once every week, to little voluntary absences, when my boy Plato, being constituted courier betwixt the apartments of my wife and daughter, an epistolary correspondence was carried on between them, from which more than one important benefit was derived; the penmanship of our charge was improved; the beautiful and elegant art of letter writing was by degrees acquired; and Margaretta was early accustomed to lay open her heart to her maternal friend.

Persons when holding the pen, generally express themselves more freely than when engaged in conversation; and if they have a perfect confidence in those whom they address, the probability is, that, unbosoming themselves, they will not fail to unveil the inmost recesses of their souls—thus was Margaretta properly and happily habituated to disclose, without a blush, each rising thought to her, on whom the care of preparing her for the great career of life had devolved.

No, Mr. Pedant, she was not unfitted for her proper sphere; and your stomach, however critical it may be, never digested finer puddings than those which I, with an uncommon zest, have partook, as knowing they were the composition of her fair hand—yes, in the receipts of cookery she is thoroughly versed; she is in every respect the complete housewife; and our linen never received so fine a gloss as when it was ironed and laid in order by Margaretta. Mrs. Vigillius was early taught the science of economy, and she took care to teach it to her daughter; and being more especially economical of time, she so arrangeth matters as never to appear embarrassed, or in a hurry, having always her hours of leisure, which she appropriates to the contingencies of the day. It is true, she does not often engage in visits of mere ceremony, seldom making one of any party, without some view either to her own emolument, or that of those about her; and with regard to dress, she spends but little time in assorting an article which is, it must be confessed, too generally a monopolizer of a blessing, that can hardly be too highly estimated. She doth not think it necessary to have her dishabille for the morning, her robe-de-chambre for noon, and her full trimmed polanee or trollopee, for the evening. The morning generally, except in cases of any particular emergency, presents her dressed for the day; and as she is always elegant, of course she can never be preposterous, extravagant or gaudy. It will be hardly necessary to add, that Miss Melworth was, and is, her exact copiest; and indeed she is so warmly attached to my dear Mary, that I verily believe it would have been in her power to have initiated her into the devious paths of error; and this is saying a great deal of a mind which possesseth such innate goodness, as doth that which inhabits the gentle bosom of my Margaretta. . . .

But while we have been assiduously employed in cultivating the mind of Margaretta, we have been endeavouring to eradicate the seeds of that over-weening self conceit, which, while it would induce an ostentatious exhibition of those talents, natural, or adventitious, which she may possess—like a rampant weed would impede and overshadow the growth of every virtue. Against pride and affectation we have been careful to guard her, by constantly inculcating one grand truth; a truth, to the conviction of which every ingenuous mind must be ever open. Her person, the symmetry of her features, the rose and lily of her complexion, the *tout ensemble* of her exterior, the harmony of her voice, &c. &c.—these are the endowments of nature—while the artificial accomplishments with which she is invested, resulting wholly from accident, and being altogether independent of her own arrangements, confer upon her no real or intrinsic merit.

We are daily assuring her, that every thing in future depends upon her own exertions, and that her character must be designated by that confutent decency, that elegant propriety, and that dignified condescension, which are indeed truly estimable. We have apprized her, that in every stage of her journey through life, she will find friends — or a social intercourse with the circles in which she may be called to move — constituting one of her principal enjoyments, and that if she is not eager for admiration, if she avoids making a display of superior abilities, she will escape those shafts of envy which will otherwise be too surely aimed at her peace; and secure to herself the complacent feelings of those with whom she may be conversant.

Margaretta hath a becoming spirit, and dissimulation is a stranger to her heart; she is rather cheerful than gay; she never diverts herself with simplicity and ignorance; *double entendres* she detests; she is not an adept in the present fashionable mode of playing upon words, and she never descends to what is called jesting; she can deliver herself upon any subject, on which she ventures to speak, with great ease; but in large or mixed companies she engages in conversation with manifest reluctance; and I have heard her declare, that she hath frequently, when encircled by strangers, felt alarmed at the sound of her own voice; she never comments upon those blunders which are the result of a neglected education, nor will she lend her smiles to those who are thus employed; and she observes, that such kind of peccadillos have upon her no other effect, than to excite in her bosom the sensation of gratitude.

With the laws of custom, or fashion, she is thoroughly acquainted, and she consents to follow them as far as they square with the dictates of rectitude; but she never sacrifices to their documents either her humanity, or her convenience; she regards, as extremely venial, an ignorance of their despotic institutions; (indeed the multifarious requirements of mere ceremony, strike her in so trifling a point of view, that she conceives it rather a matter of course that they should sometimes be omitted) and she prefers plain manners to all the glitter of a studied or laboured address.

But it is against the unaccountable freaks of the capricious, that all the artillery of that humour, of which she possesses a natural fund, is levelled; frank and ingenuous herself, she laughs at the vagaries of the whimsical, and her heart is ever upon her lips; she reflects much, and her judgement is fashioned by reason; she cannot be seen without pleasure, nor heard without instruction.

But I am rather describing what Margaretta *is* than what she *was,* at the period of her history to which we are arrived. Three or four years have matured her talents, presenting the daily improving and promising girl, a truly lovely and accomplished woman, abundantly answering the fondest expectations which were formed of her.

12

Letter to Winthrop Sargent

September 1803

If Margaretta's education achieved the goals Mr. and Mrs. Vigillius had in mind, Judith Sargent Murray discovered that in the real world, even the best intentions could lead to mixed results. Sometime in 1800, Winthrop Sargent's stepchildren — David, James, and Anna Williams — arrived in Boston, where Judith promised to supervise their education. David and James attended New Hampshire's Phillips Exeter Academy, expecting to matriculate at Harvard thereafter. While Judith wrote constantly to the boys, their tutors, and the heads of the families with whom James and David boarded, the experience was a disaster. The boys changed lodging three times, never finding quarters that suited them. They neglected their lessons, borrowed excessively, and were involved in one scrape after another. James never attended Harvard, and David remained there only until he was expelled in December 1807. Anna, on the other hand, presented no problems, and Judith was pleased with her progress. The following letter was written in 1803, as Judith admitted to her brother and his wife what she had been trying to conceal from them for two years: James and David were not doing well at school, and their behavior outside the classroom left much to be desired. How does Murray account for her nephews' deficiencies? Why does she think home schooling is preferable to institutional learning? How does she use her experience with the boys to plead for the value of education for women?

To my beloved brother,

    Urged by affectionate sympathy for you, and for my very dear sister, I follow my communication of the 29th by such a statement of facts, and

Judith Sargent Murray to Winthrop Sargent, [Sept. 1803], Letterbook, 12:874–79, Mississippi Archives, Jackson, Miss.

such hints as I flatter myself may efface the impression made by, or at least mitigate the, sufferings consequent upon Judge T[enny's] unfeeling representation. It should always be remembered, that under the dominion of imperious necessity, your sons were much longer neglected, than in other circumstances they would have been, and it seems rational, and just, to revert, not so much to their time of life, as to the period where their education systematically commenced. I am told that the regulations in the Exeter Academy, defer instructing a latin scholar in the english tongue, until the last year of tutelage — David, and James, were placed in the Academy with little or no knowledge of grammar, and with not much more than the rudiments of writing, since which, they have been uniformly engaged in construing latin, and while writing their exercises, all their facilities being occupied by this to them, arduous task, it should not be a matter of wonder that they do not attend to the formation of their letters — Indeed a habit of negligence in their hand writing, is unavoidably induced, and while no kind friend is constantly at their elbow with line, upon line, and precept, upon precept their retrocession in this art, should be calculated upon as a natural event. When my children write their exercises upon the french language, I am almost momentarily enforcing my wishes, that they would not forget the necessity of attending to the construction of their letters, and to the orthography[1] of their english, as well as french, and I enjoin it upon them to exhibit to me every written exercise never omitting to applaud or condemn, as I have occasion. Literary people insist, that latin is the best foundation which the grammarian can possibly lay — I have not the arrogance to contend this point, but I take leave to observe, that while shaping the adamantine rock, and deploying in laying the mass of materials, the progress is much more slow, and imperceptible, than when constructing the lighter and more obvious parts of an edifice — the application is easy — the ultimatum may be happy, although the first steps are thorny, and tedious. I have been constant in my inquiries relative to the progress made by the children in their study of the latin tongue, and even Judge T[enney] has uniformly assured me, that *David's* acquirements fully equalled his preceptor's expectations — Yet he has written to you that the preceptor despaired of making anything of them — his testimony then is contradictory, and by consequence if not inadmissable, is certainly of little value — Yet I make an extract from a letter received from the Judge dated the 31st ult. "It would gratify you Madam to know, that David's conduct, as far as it has fallen under my observation, to come to

[1]Spelling.

my knowledge (except in the instance of his quarrel with the parson) has been proper, and manly and since his last visit to you at Boston, Mr. Abbot[2] speaks well of his application, and progress." I forbore to mention to you, my dear, this same Mr. Rowland, because I conceived that distance from the scene of action combining with parental solicitude, might swell the magnitude of an offence that I did not consider as very enormous, but as the humane Judge has mentioned the business, without narrating the particulars, it may be well to state accurately, an affair which, originating in a sudden ebullation of youthful passion, received its stimulus from a premature exercise of the rights of Man. While Mr. Rowland continued single, under the auspices of the well disposed person who superintended his household, his mansion continued a pleasant residence for the children — but Mr. Rowland's marriage introduced new regulations, and peace, and plenty, as far as it related to the boarders, were vanished from his abode. David was ordered to study in the parlor, this amidst the interruption of conversation, he found impossible, and so he retreated into the kitchen, when a disturbance among the children, in which he was no way interested,[3] was imputed to him, and he was preemtorily commanded to return to the parlor — a consciousness of innocence, stimulated him to disobey a summons, which he imagined originated in a supposition of offence, and the enraged priest collared, and struck him! When David, indignant at this procedure, quitted his house, and as Judge T[enney] was then at Washington, selected for himself another lodging. It appears to me, upon this representation, that although candour may find some thing to blame, yet, even justice in its most rigid constructions, will not pronounce him guilty of a very heinous misdemeanor. It must be confessed that James is not altogether so studious as David, no one denies him capacity but I am told the preceptor complains, that he has not as yet found the road to his mind, yet that there is such a road, cannot be disputed. Since the receipt of your last favour, I have taken the liberty to address Mr. Abbot upon this very important subject — when his responses are received, they shall, together with my letter, be laid before you.

I have no hesitancy in replying to your question, "would it not be advisable to take these children under my own eye, with the aid of an able Preceptor" — assuredly my dear it would — I should not choose to educate a *solitary* pupil, as for obvious reasons, that grand engine, emulation, would be wanting, but the powerful stimulus is as effectually supplied by

[2]David's tutor at Phillips Exeter Academy.
[3]Involved.

two as by twenty students. A parent is ever the most interested in the progress of the child, and a tutor hourly under the eye of a judicious and well informed father, would assuredly achieve every thing within the compass of human ability. To say truth, the chance of children in full schools is very slender; they are not apprized of the value of those golden moments which they squander—the attention of the Preceptor is necessarily divided, and subdivided, and if the pupil wants application, and receives no aid from the parent, the consequence is inevitable—the child must be thrown upon the world, uneducated, or at best but superficially taught—and hence we are crowded upon, in every circle, by swarms of illiterate pretenders; while the *real scholar* is regarded as a prodigy, and can scarcely fail of being hailed as the . . . man of art. A learned, painstaking, and upright Man, who has long been the principal of an Academy, recently observed—"We can do no more than assign the several tasks, with directions in the pursuit—our pupils must furnish Genius, and application, if they be deficient in these, so multiplied are the claims upon us, and such is the necessity of impartiality, that we have no remedy, the *neglig[e]nt* must remain uninformed." I make it an invariable rule not to commit to other hands, anything that I am qualified to teach my children myself, and I know that they advance with abundantly more rapidity, when I am myself their instructor. Anna begins to read with tolerable facility, and even elegance, but as she sensibly observes, she did not get this at school—In the . . . Academy, she makes one of a large class of children who read alternately—among a multitude, the worst examples are no doubt exhibited—Cadences, accents, emphasis, and even pauses, are . . . violated, and it is hardly in the power of a single individual to call to order a little army of offenders—No day passes in which Anna, and Julia Maria, do not read in concert with me, and I scrupulously mark the smallest error—If I were capable of instructing them in every branch of education, it would contribute inexpressibly to my felicity, a Mother is certainly the most proper preceptress for her children, and it [is] for this reason that I would educate a daughter, upon the most liberal plan, since, whether established in a family of her own or otherwise, it is scarcely possible she should not be more or less employed, in teaching the young idea how to shoot—It is not then the exclusive emolument of the little female we are to consult—posterity will reap the benefit of our labours, their salutary effects may ameliorate society, and looking with a benign influence upon the community at large, they may powerfully influence movements the most important, even to the latest period of time—But during my first years, although our parents were, as you know, the best of human being[s], they yet did homage to the shrine of fashion. Custom tyranises

over the strongest minds—It was the mode to confine the female intellect within the narrowest bounds, and by consequence, I was robbed of
the aids of education—I shall feel the effects of this irrational depriva-
tion, as long as I shall continue an inhabitant of this world—I am thus
unqualified to preside as the unassisted instructress of my children, assis-
tants are indispensable, and did I possess affluence, teachers in all those
branches of science, in which I contemplated initiating my young people,
should reside constantly in my family—Forgive my loquacity, the subject is interesting, and your anxieties and interrogations have drawn me
forth—I repeat that I shall be well pleased to render my services to your
children, and this I can do both with convenience and very high gratification to myself. . . .

God I trust has preserved to you the Infant Washington,[4] of whom, in
your last letter, you were so apprehensive—Embrace your lovely friend,
and my other treasures in your possession, in my name—Mr. Murray and
my children unite with me in tender expressions of affectionate love, and
duty, to our friends at Bellmont, at the Vale, and at Mount Airy—And I
pray you to accept for yourself the fond regards of your ever affectionate
sister.

[4]Winthrop's son.

13

Letter to Reverend Redding
May 7, 1801

*In the letters she writes to relatives and friends, Judith Sargent Murray's
prose seems flowery and stilted to a modern ear. When she corresponds with
strangers, especially with strangers whose approval she seeks, her style
becomes even more convoluted and artificial. Still, despite her attention to
the rules of grammar and spelling, even in the following letter—obviously
written with considerable care—she often substitutes dashes for periods*

Judith Sargent Murray to Rev. Mr. Redding, 7 May 1801, Letterbook, 11:287–88, Mississippi Archives, Jackson, Miss.

and continues to capitalize the occasional noun in mid-sentence for no apparent reason.

Murray wrote to the Reverend Redding hoping that he would help her dispose of the remaining unsold copies of The Gleaner. *Thus the letter exhibits a fawning quality, as Murray praises Redding's ability while denigrating her own. Nevertheless, she cannot altogether hide her pride in her own authorship or her determination to defend her views on women's equality. Like many American writers, she blames her literary failures on the tendency of her countrymen to prefer work emanating from European pens. But what is perhaps more significant, she takes considerable pains to correct what she believes to be Redding's false impressions about her understanding of women's role. She refers him to one of her essays in* The Gleaner, *pointing to what is arguably the most conventional portion of her four-part essay on female abilities. In this passage, Murray contends that women are, indeed, more modest, more gentle, and more affectionate than men, even as she claims that these virtues lead logically to the natural attributes associated with motherhood. (See Document 7.) How does Murray explain most differences between men and women? What evidence can you find in this letter to indicate that Murray still hopes for literary fame?*

Rev. and dear Sir,

Although I have hitherto been unfortunate in my attempts to address you, yet stimulated by your late highly flattering favour, the pen of acknowledgement is again in my hand — Gratitude is respectful and ardent in its dictates, and every sentiment of propriety, combines to enforce the immediate necessity of the tributary lines. Your approbation, my respected panagyrist,[1] confers a gratification of no common description — It is true that the voice of undue commendation will tinge the honest cheek, with the blush of conscious demerit — we inhale with rapture the fine effluvia, and great is the inquietude, of that virtue, which can cheerfully assist in removing from the perception of its Encomiast,[2] the illusive veil. No my good, and revered friend (I exult that you permit the sacred appelation) I cannot allow your plea of incapacity — your letters communicate pleasure, and confer distinction, and I can never be unmindful of benefits. While I contend for the general elevation, or equality of

[1] A panegyrist is one who praises another in an oration or in writing.
[2] One who praises.

my sex, I know how to appreciate my own abilities, and I cheerfully sub-
scribe to the confession of individual inferiority — the office of Caterer for
the sentimentalist, is, in my opinion, a dignified office, and the acknowledgment that I have added a single item to the catalogue of delicacies,
which already amply enriches the refined, and [mental?] Conniseur, is a
guerdon[3] that I have not ceased with continued solicitude to desire —
judge then, with what pride I trace in the pages of Mr. R[edding] that
potent word *originality* — this word is the talisman of my literary wishes,
and in proportion as my claims, thereto obtain, or diminish my fond
expectations are invigorated, or become paralyzed — Continue to me,
Dear Sir, the patronage of your friendship, and I shall then boast of an
asylum in the bosom of information and fortune. America seems to be
singularly deficient, in every species of remuneration, to her literary children: if she designs to cast an eye upon the tasks of Genius her glance
is frigid, or fastidious, and thus the most glowing efforts are too often rendered torpid — works of unquestionable merit are almost totally
neglected, and in such a defection of attachment to indigenous productions it is not wonderful[4] that I have not yet been able to dispose of the
first edition of the Gleaner, although it contained no more than 1000
copies — yet America can seize with avidity, every European publication
that appears in our mother tongue, and new editions from your writers
are daily issuing from our presses — I am free to own, that this fact
evinces a superiority of national taste, but conscious as an individual, that
the investigation of my essays, should connote much of candour, I am
induced to wish that with national taste, we also combined national *partiality* — An analysis, written upon your side the Atlantic, would be a
favourable event to an American Author but perhaps our productions, seldom meet the eye of a British Reviewer. I am told that it is customary to
forward to these gentlemen Critics copies of every production, and under
this impression, I take leave to address to your care, and subject to your
direction, a set of the Gleaner and if through your instrumentality, I may
dispose of the remainder of my volumes or come into possession of that
portion of celebrity, to which my humble effort may be legitimately entitled, I shall owe to you, my respected friend an obligation of a very important and pleasing kind. I am, my dear Sir, apprehensive that you do not
accurately comprehend my ideas relative to the sexes, I have conceived
that the distinction male, and female, does not exist in *Mind,* and it
appears to me that my opinion is sanctioned by the imposing authorities

[3] Reward.
[4] Surprising.

of nature, reason, and scripture—I have thought that the disimilarity confessedly apparent, was merely artificial, entirely the result of education, variety of pursuits, and uncounted accidental occurences and, to corroborate this sentiment, I have addressed a number of proofs which as they are of high credibility, must while they remain uncontroverted, be considered as conclusive—but I do not recollect ever to have penned a sentence, which could justify the shadow of suspicion that I was seeking to throw down barriers, most judiciously erected, to destroy the distinction of character, or to create that confusion which would no doubt be consequent upon the rushing together or mingling of those departments, now so advantageously, and so properly assigned to the male and female world—A lover of system, I am constantly fond of regularity, and that order, and subordination, are the stamina of civilized life, is an undeniable position—a careful perusal of the pages which I have had the temerity to submit to the public upon this subject, will, I imagine, convince Mr. R[edding] that I entertain no wish to confound and destroy distinctions, that I do not assert the *eligibility* of giving to women masculine pursuits. I only contend for the *practicability* of their attaining, as far as it depends upon mind, the loftiest heights—yet all those acquirements which are supposed within the grasp of a masculine understanding—nor, although as you observe these Columbian States may produce no female Washington, can a conviction of radical inferiority be from this circumstance fairly deduced—Exigencies of the magnitude with those that claimed the immortal Mind must call us forth, propriety must mark our steps, and an elevated stand in the temple of fame be constituted our goal, e'er an argument can be raised upon this foundation—But as a testimony that I know how to appreciate, and that I do indeed glory in the appropriate excellence of my sex, I again refer to the essays I have penned upon this question of equality—particularly to pages 223, and 224 of the Gleaner, third volume, beginning with —No my fair Country women—and so on to the conclusion of the ninety-first Essay— My eagerness to vindicate myself from the censure implied in your remarks, has produced this letter of egotism, and if I may judge of the future, by the past, it will be perused with abundant partiality—Was the profile that you honored with a place in your literary recess, endowed with sensibility it would evince much of gratitude—I gladly rank you among my most respected Correspondents—I dwell with pleasure upon the idea of that congeniality between us, which you have so flatteringly supposed and I joyfully anticipate the blissful period, when disembodied spirits shall meet and by mingling the sacred pleasures of the soul, shall incalculably enhance their value—in one word, when we shall *know* as we are *known*—I drop a tear over the premature removal of your lovely daughter—a recollection of her filial piety and of her early and fervent devotion to her Creator, must be to her sorrowing mother and to yourself, an exhaustless source of consolation—The promise of her budding life was indeed fair—when children of such hopes are cut off, the anguish of a parent's heart must be immeasurable, but in the paradise of paternal Deity, the beauteous flower will securely expand—in a situation so frigid, and so remote as in the steril[e] soil of this our world, it would have been confined and injured in its growth, and when succeeding events shall reunite the dispersed human family, you will no doubt acknowledge the wisdom of that regulation, which, early emancipating your darling child, bestowed upon the faculties a heavenly completion. . . .

14

On the Equality of the Sexes
1790

Judith Sargent Murray (then Judith Stevens) wrote an essay entitled "The Sexes" in 1779 and copied it into her "Repository." In 1790, she submitted it, with some alterations and additions, to the Massachusetts Magazine, *which published it in two installments in March and April of that year. Murray's defense of women's intellectual equality in the essay rests on her belief that women are endowed with the qualities of imagination, reason, memory, and judgment. Her claim that women are naturally rational creatures was particularly notable, at a time when many observers insisted that women were naturally emotional, even passionate, but never reasonable. Her early conviction that women's deficiencies were a product of their limited educational opportunities was not only reminiscent of the views of philosopher John Locke, but anticipated the work of the English feminist Mary Wollstonecraft. The appended letter extract challenged the views of New England's religious establishment; she used her ingenuity to defend the biblical Eve against traditional accusations that her sin in the Garden of Eden was the source of all human degradation and misery. How does Mur-*

Judith Sargent Murray, "On the Equality of the Sexes," *Massachusetts Magazine*, March 1790, 132–35, April 1790, 223–26.

ray use conventionally negative descriptions of women to her own advantage? What weaknesses does she concede might be attributed to women? Why are they not especially important?

Is it upon mature consideration we adopt the idea, that nature is thus partial in her distributions? Is it indeed a fact, that she hath yielded to one half of the human species so unquestionable a mental superiority? I know that to both sexes elevated understandings, and the reverse, are common. But, suffer me to ask, in what the minds of females are so notoriously deficient, or unequal. May not the intellectual powers be ranged under their four heads—imagination, reason, memory and judgement. The province of imagination has long since been surrendered up to us, and we have been crowned undoubted sovereigns of the regions of fancy. Invention is perhaps the most arduous effort of the mind; this branch of imagination hath been particularly ceded to us, and we have been time out of mind invested with that creative faculty. Observe the variety of fashions (here I bar the contemptuous smile) which distinguish and adorn the female world; how continually are they changing, insomuch that they almost render the whole man's assertion problematical, and we are ready to say, *there is something new under the sun.* Now, what a playfulness, what an exuberance of fancy, what strength of inventive imagination, doth this continual variation discover? Again, it hath been observed, that if the turpitude of the conduct of our sex, hath been ever so enormous, so extremely ready are we that the very first thought presents us with an apology so plausible, as to produce our actions even in an amiable light. Another instance of our creative powers, is our talent for slander; how ingenious are we at inventive scandal? what a formidable story can we in a moment fabricate merely from the force of a prolifick imagination? how many reputations, in the fertile brain of a female, have been utterly despoiled? how industrious are we at improving a hint? suspicion how easily do we convert into conviction, and conviction, embellished by the power of eloquence, stalks abroad to the surprise and confusion of unsuspecting innocence. Perhaps it will be asked if I furnish these facts as instances of excellency in our sex. Certainly not; but as proofs of a creative faculty, of a lively imagination. Assuredly great activity of mind is thereby discovered, and was this activity properly directed, what beneficial effects would follow. Is the needle and kitchen sufficient to employ the operations of a soul thus organized? I should conceive not. Nay, it is a truth that those very departments leave the intelligent principle vacant, and at liberty for speculation. Are we deficient in reason? We can only reason from what we know, and if opportunity of acquiring knowledge hath been denied us, the inferiority of our sex cannot fairly be deduced from thence. Memory, I believe, will be allowed us in common, since every one's experience must testify, that a loquacious old woman is as frequently met with, as a communicative old man; their subjects are alike drawn from the fund of other times, and the transactions of their youth, or of maturer life, entertain, or perhaps fatigue you, in the evening of their lives. "But our judgment is not so strong—we do not distinguish so well." Yet it may be questioned, from what doth this superiority, in thus discriminating faculty of the soul, proceed. May we not trace its source in the difference of education, and continued advantages? Will it be said that the judgment of a male of two years old, is more sage than that of a female's of the same age? I believe the reverse is generally observed to be true. But from that period what partiality! how is the one exalted and the other depressed, by the contrary modes of education which are adopted! the one is taught to aspire, and the other is early confined and limited. As their years increase, the sister must be wholly domesticated, while the brother is led by the hand through all the flowery paths of science. Grant that their minds are by nature equal, yet who shall wonder at the *apparent* superiority, if indeed custom becomes *second nature;* nay if it taketh place of nature, and that it doth the experience of each day will evince. At length arrived at womanhood, the uncultivated fair one feels a void, which the employments allotted her are by no means capable of filling. What can she do? to books, she may not apply; or if she doth, *to those only of the novel kind,* lest she merit the appellation of a *learned lady;* and what ideas have been affixed to this term, the observation of many can testify. Fashion, scandal and sometimes what is still more reprehensible, are then called in to her relief; and who can say to what lengths the liberties she takes may proceed. Meantime she herself is most unhappy; she feels the want of a cultivated mind. Is she single, she in vain seeks to fill up time from sexual employments or amusements. Is she united to a person whose soul nature made equal to her own, education hath set him so far above her, that in those entertainments which are productive of such rational felicity, she is not qualified to accompany him. She experiences a mortifying consciousness of inferiority, which embitters every enjoyment. Doth the person to whom her adverse fate hath consigned her, possess a mind incapable of improvement, she is equally wretched, in being so closely connected with an individual whom she cannot but despise. Now, was she permitted the same instructors as her brother, (with an eye however to their particular departments) for the employment of a rational mind an ample field would be opened. In astronomy she might catch a glimpse of the immensity of the Deity, and thence she would form amazing conceptions of the august and supreme Intelligence. In geography she would admire Jehova in the midst of his benevolence; thus adapting this globe to the various wants and amusements of its inhabitants. In natural philosophy she would adore the infinite majesty of heaven, clothed in condescension; and as she traversed the reptile world, she would hail the goodness of a creating God. A mind, thus filled, would have little room for the trifles with which our sex are, with too much justice, accused of amusing themselves, and they would thus be rendered fit companions for those, who should one day wear them as their crown. Fashions, in their variety, would then give place to conjectures, which might perhaps conduce to the improvement of the literary world; and there would be no leisure for slander or detraction. Reputation would not then be blasted, but serious speculations would occupy the lively imaginations of the sex. Unnecessary visits would be precluded, and that custom would only be indulged by way of relaxation, or to answer the demands of consanguinity and friendship. Females would become discreet, their judgments would be invigorated, and their partners for life being circumspectly chosen, an unhappy Hymen would then be as rare, as is now the reverse.

Will it be urged that those acquirements would supersede our domestick duties, I answer that every requisite in female economy is easily attained; and, with truth I can add, that when once attained, they require no further *mental attention*. Nay, while we are pursuing the needle, or the superintendency of the family, I repeat, that our minds are at full liberty for reflection; that imagination may exert itself in full vigor; and that if a just foundation early laid, our ideas will then be worthy of rational beings. If we were industrious we might easily find time to arrange them upon paper, or should avocations press too hard for such an indulgence, the hours allotted for conversation would at least become more refined and rational. Should it still be vociferated, "Your domestick employments are sufficient"—I would calmly ask, is it reasonable, that a candidate for immortality, for the joys of heaven, an intelligent being, who is to spend an eternity in contemplating the works of Deity, should at present be so degraded, as to be allowed no other ideas, than those which are suggested by the mechanism of a pudding, or the sewing of the seams of a garment? Pity that all such censurers of female improvement do not go one step further, and deny their future existence; to be consistent they surely ought.

Yes, ye lordly, ye haughty sex, our souls are by nature *equal* to yours; the same breath of God animates, enlivens, and invigorates us; and that we are not fallen lower than yourselves, let those witness who have greatly towered above the various discouragements by which they have been so heavily oppressed; and though I am unacquainted with the list of celebrated characters on either side, yet from the observations I have made in the contracted circle in which I have moved, I dare confidently believe, that from the commencement of time to the present day, there hath been as many females, as males, who, by the *mere force of natural powers,* have merited the crown of applause; who *thus unassisted,* have seized the wreath of fame. I know there are who assert, that as the animal powers of the one sex are superiour, of course their mental faculties also must be stronger; thus attributing strength of mind to the transient organization of this earth born tenement. But if this reasoning is just, man must be content to yield the palm to many of the brute creation, since by not a few of his brethren of the field, he is far surpassed in bodily strength. Moreover, was this argument admitted, it would prove too much, for occular demonstration evinceth, that there are many robust masculine ladies, and effeminate gentlemen. Yet I fancy that Mr. Pope, though clogged with an enervated body, and distinguished by a diminutive stature, could nevertheless lay claim to greatness of soul; and perhaps there are many other instances which might be adduced to combat so unphilosophical an opinion. Do we not often see, that when the clay built tabernacle is well nigh dissolved, when it is just ready to mingle with the parent soil, the immortal inhabitant aspires to, and even attaineth heights the most sublime, and which were before wholly unexplored. Besides, were we to grant that animal strength proved anything, taking into consideration the accustomed impartiality of nature, we should be induced to imagine, that she had invested the female mind with superiour strength as an equivalent for the bodily powers of man. But waving this however palpable advantage, for *equality* only, we wish to contend.

CONSTANTIA

By way of supplement to the foregoing pages, I subjoin the following extract from a letter wrote to a friend in the December of 1780.

AND now assist me, O thou genius of my sex, while I undertake the arduous task of endeavouring to combat that vulgar, that almost universal errour, which hath, it seems enlisted even Mr. P_____ under its banners. The superiority of your sex hath, I grant, been time out of mind esteemed a truth incontrovertible; in consequence of which persuasion, every plan of education hath been calculated to establish this favourite tenet. Not long since, weak and presuming as I was, I amused myself with selecting some arguments from nature, reason and experience, against this so generally received idea. I confess that to sacred testimonies I had not recourse. I held them to be merely metaphorical, and thus regarding them, I could not persuade myself that there was any propriety in bringing them to decide in this *very important debate.* However, as you, sir, confine yourself entirely to the sacred oracles, I mean to bend the whole of my artillery against those supposed proofs, which you have from thence provided, and from which you have formed an intrenchment *apparently* so invulnerable. And first, to begin with our great progenitors; but here, suffer me to promise, that it is for mental strength I mean to contend, for with respect to animal powers, I yield them undisputed to that sex, which enjoys them in common with the lion, the tyger, and many other beasts of prey; therefore your observations respecting *the rib, under the arm, at a distance from the head, &c.&c.* in no sort militate against my view. Well, but the woman was first in the transgression. Strange how blind *self love* renders you men; were you not wholly absorbed in a partial admiration of your own abilities, you would long since have acknowledged the force of what I am now going to urge. It is true some ignoramuses have, absurdly enough informed us, that the beauteous fair of paradise, was seduced from her obedience, by a malignant demon, *in the guise of a baleful serpent;* but we, who are better informed, know that the fallen spirit presented himself to her view, *a shining angel still;* for thus, saith the criticks in the Hebrew tongue, ought the word to be rendered. Let us examine her motive— Hark! the seraph declares that she shall attain a perfection of knowledge; for is there aught which is not comprehended under one or other of the terms *good* and *evil.* It doth not appear that she was governed by any one sensual appetite; but merely by a desire of adorning her mind; a laudable ambition fired her soul, and a thirst for knowledge impelled the predilection so fatal in its consequences. Adam could not plead the same deception; assuredly he was not deceived; nor ought we to admire his superiour strength, or wonder at his sagacity, when we so often confess that example is much more influential than precept. His gentle partner stood before him, a melancholy instance of the direful effects of disobedience; he saw her not possessed of that wisdom which she had fondly hoped to obtain, but he beheld the once blooming female, disrobed of that innocence, which had heretofore rendered her so lovely. To him then deception became impossible, as he had proof positive of the fallacy of the argument, which the deceiver had suggested. What then could be his inducement to burst the barriers, and to fly directly in the face of that command, which *immediately* from the mouth of Deity *he* had received, since, I say, he could not plead the fascinating stimulus, the accumulation of knowledge, as indisputable conviction was so visibly portrayed before him. What mighty cause impelled him to sacrifice myriads of beings yet unborn, and by one impious act, which *he saw* would be productive of such fatal effect, entail undistinguished ruin upon a race of beings, which he was yet to produce. Blush, ye vaunters of fortitude; ye boasters of resolution; ye haughty lords of the creation; blush when ye remember, that he was influenced by no

other motive than a bare pusillanimous attachment to a woman! by sentiments so exquisitely soft, that all his sons have, from that period, when
they have designed to degrade them, described as highly feminine. Thus
it should see, that all the arts of the grand deceiver (since means adequate
to the purpose are, I conceive, invariably pursued) were requisite to mis-
lead our general mother, while the father of mankind forfeited his own,
and relinquished the happiness of posterity, merely in compliance with the
blandishments of a female.

15

The Gleaner Contemplates the Future Prospects of Women in this "Enlightened Age"

1798

Murray's "Observations on Female Abilities" in the third volume of The
Gleaner *begins where "On the Equality of the Sexes" left off. In this essay, she
amasses an enormous amount of concrete detail to prove the general points
she made earlier. Murray was clearly optimistic about the prospects of American women in 1798, imagining that a new era of gender equality was dawning in this "younger world." Once again, as in her other essays on women's
issues and in her Margaretta story, Murray argues that women are rational
beings, capable of exhibiting the traits associated with Republican citizenship.
Once again she maintains that educated women make the most virtuous
mothers and wives. At the same time, she continues to insist that women can
be brave, strong, and heroic as well as modest, religious, and chaste. How
does Murray's description of Spartan women call into question the notion that
women are naturally fitted for motherhood? Why does she think that it is as
dangerous for society to elevate women as it is to degrade them?*

Amid the blaze of this auspicious day,
When science points the broad refulgent way,

Judith Sargent Murray, *The Gleaner: A Miscellaneous Production in Three Volumes,* 3 vols.
(Boston: L. Thomas and E. T. Andrews, 1798), 3:188–96.

Her iron sceptre prejudice resigns,
And sov'reign reason all resplendent shines.

The reader is requested to consider the four succeeding numbers as supplementary to an Essay, which made its appearance, some years since, in a periodical publication of a miscellaneous nature. The particular paper to which I advert, was entitled, *The Equality of the Sexes;* and however well I may think of that composition, as I do not conceive that the subject is exhausted, I have thought proper, treading in the same path, to set about collecting a few hints, which may serve as additional, illustrative, or ornamental.

And, first, by way of exordium,[1] I take leave to congratulate my fair country-women, on the happy revolution which the few past years has made in their favour; that in these infant republics, where, within my remembrance, the use of the needle was the principal attainment which was thought *necessary* for a woman, the lovely proficient is now permitted to appropriate a moiety of her time to studies of a more elevated and elevating nature. Female academies are every where establishing, and right pleasant is the appellation to my ear.

Yes, in this younger world, "the Rights of Women" begin to be understood; we seem, at length, determined to do justice to THE SEX; and, improving on the opinions of a Wollstonecraft, we are ready to contend for the *quantity,* as well as *quality,* of mind. The younger part of the female world have now an inestimable prize put into their hands; and it depends on the rising generation to refute a sentiment, which, still retaining its advocates, grounds its arguments on the incompatibility of the present enlarged plan of female education, with those necessary occupations, that must ever be considered as proper to the department and comprised in the duties of a judiciously instructed and elegant woman; and, if our daughters will combine their efforts, converts to the new regulations will every day multiply among us. To argue against facts, is indeed contending with both wind and tide; and, borne down by accumulating examples, conviction of the utility of the present plans will pervade the public mind, and not a dissenting voice will be heard.

I may be accused of enthusiasm; but such is my confidence in THE SEX, that I expect to see our young women forming a new era in female history. They will oppose themselves to every trivial and unworthy monopolizer of time; and it will be apparent, that the adorning their persons is not with them a *primary* object. They will know how to appreciate personal advantages; and, considering them as bestowed by Nature, or Nature's God, they will

---

[1] Beginning or introduction.

hold them in due estimation: Yet, conscious that they confer no *intrinsic* excellence on the *temporary* possessor, their admeasurement of *real virtue* will be entirely divested of all those *prepossessing ideas,* which originate in a beautiful exterior. The noble expansion conferred by a liberal education will teach them *humility;* for it will give them a glance of those vast tracts of knowledge which they can never explore, until they are accommodated with far other powers than those at present assigned them; and they will contemplate their removal to a higher order of beings, as a desirable event.

Mild benignity, with all the modest virtues, and every sexual grace — these they will carefully cultivate; for they will have *learned,* that in no character they can so effectually charm, as in that in which nature designed them the *pre-eminence.* They will accustom themselves to reflection; they will investigate accurately, and reason will point their conclusions: Yet they will not be assuming; the characteristic trait will still remain; and retiring sweetness will insure them that consideration and respect, which they do not presume to demand. Thinking justly will not only enlarge their minds, and refine their ideas; but it will correct their dispositions, humanize their feelings, and present them the *friends of their species. The beauteous bosom will no more become a lurking-place for invidious and rancorous passions;* but the mild temperature of the soul will be evinced by the benign and equal tenour of their lives. Their manners will be unembarrassed; and, studious to shun even the *semblance of pedantry,* they will be careful to give to their most systematic arguments and deductions, an unaffected and natural appearance. They will rather *question* than *assert;* and they will make their communications on a supposition, that the point in discussion has rather *escaped the memory* of those with whom they converse, *than that it was never imprinted there.*

It is true, that every faculty of their minds will be occasionally engrossed by the most momentous concerns; but as often as *necessity* or *propriety* shall render it incumbent on them, they will *cheerfully* accommodate themselves to the more *humble duties* which their situation imposes. When their sphere of action is enlarged, when they become wives and mothers, they will fill with honour the parts allotted them. Acquainted, theoretically, with the nature of their species, and experimentally with themselves, they will not expect to meet, in wedlock, with those faultless beings, who so frequently issue, armed at all points, from the teeming brain of the novelist. They will learn properly to estimate; they will look, with pity's softest eye, on the natural frailties of those whom they elect partners for life; and they will regard their virtues with that sweet complacency, which is ever an attendant on a predilection founded on love, and happily combining esteem. As mothers, they will assume with alacrity their arduous employment, and they will cheerfully bend to its various departments. They will be primarily solicitous to fulfil, in *every instance,* whatever can *justly* be denominated *duty;* and those intervals, which have heretofore been devoted to frivolity, will be appropriated to pursuits, calculated to inform, enlarge, and sublime the soul — to contemplations, which will ameliorate the heart, unfold and illumine the understanding, and gradually render the human being an eligible candidate for the society of angels.

Such, I predict, will be the daughters of Columbia; and my gladdened spirit rejoices in the prospect. A sensible and informed woman — companionable and serious — possessing also a facility of temper, and united to a congenial mind — blest with competency — and rearing to maturity a promising family of children — Surely, the wide globe cannot produce a scene more truly interesting. See! the virtues are embodied — the domestic duties appear in their place, and they are all fulfilled — morality is systematized by religion, and sublimed by devotion — every movement is the offspring of elegance, and their manners have received the highest polish. A reciprocation of good offices, and a mutual desire to please, uniformly distinguishes the individuals of this enchanting society — their conversation, refined and elevated, partakes the fire of genius, while it is pointed by information; and they are ambitious of selecting subjects, which, by throwing around humanity, *in its connexion,* additional lustre, may implant a new motive for gratitude, and teach them to anticipate the rich fruition of that immortality which they boast. Such is the family of reason — of reason, cultivated and adorned by literature.

The idea of the incapability of women, is, we conceive, in this *enlightened age,* totally *inadmissible;* and we have concluded, that establishing the *expediency* of admitting them to share the blessings of equality, will remove every obstacle to their advancement. In proportion as nations have progressed in the arts of civilization, the value of THE SEX hath been understood, their rank in the scale of being ascertained, and their consequence in society acknowledged. But if prejudice still fortifies itself in the bosom of any; If it yet enlisteth its votaries against the said despot and its followers, we produce, instead of arguments, *a number of well attested facts,* which the student of female annals hath carefully compiled.

Women, circumscribed in their education within very narrow limits, and constantly depressed by their occupations, have, nevertheless, tinged the cheek of manhood with a guilty suffusion, for a pusillanimous capitulation with the enemies of their country. Quitting the loom and the distaff, they have beheld, with indignation, their husbands and their sons flee in battle: With clasped hands, and determined resolution, they have placed themselves in their paths, obstructing their passage, and insisting, with heroic firmness, on their immediate return to death or conquest!

They have anxiously examined the dead bodies of their slaughtered sons; and if the fatal wounds were received in front, thus evincing that they have bravely faced the foe, the fond recollection of their valour has become a source of consolation, and they have sung a *requiem* to their sorrows! Women, in the heat of action, have mounted the rampart with undaunted courage, arrested the progress of the foe, and bravely rescued their besieged dwellings! They have successfully opposed themselves to tyranny and the galling yoke of oppression! Assembling in crowds, they have armed themselves for the combat—they have mingled amid the battling ranks—they have sought heroically—and their well-timed and well-concerted measures have emancipated their country! They have hazarded the stroke of death in its most frightful form; and they have submitted to bonds and imprisonment, for the redemption of their captive husbands!

The character of the Spartan women is marked with uncommon firmness. At the shrine of patriotism they immolated nature. Undaunted bravery and unimpeached honour, was, in their estimation, far beyond affection. The name of Citizen possessed, for them, greater charms than that of Mother; and so highly did they prize the warrior's meed,[2] that they are said to have shed tears of joy over the bleeding bodies of their wounded sons!

When Europe and Asia were infested by armed multitudes, who, emigrating for purposes of devastation and settlement, perpetrated the most ferocious acts, among all those various tribes of unprincipled invaders, *no discriminating line seems to have marked the sexes;* wives submitted to similar hardships with their husbands; equally they braved the impending danger; and their efforts and their sufferings were the same: Nor can their habits of endurance and patient fortitude admit a rational doubt.

The women of Hungary have rendered themselves astonishingly conspicuous in their wars against the Ottoman Empire—But proofs abound; and numerous actions might be produced to evince, that courage is by no means *exclusively* a masculine virtue. Women have frequently displayed an intrepidity, not to be surpassed by men—neither is their bravery the impulse of the moment. They not only, when trained by education, and inured by subsequent habit, rise superior to the fears of death; but, with unimpassioned and sedate composure, *they can endure life*— they can struggle with the fatigues and inconveniences—they can fulfil the duties, and they can support the irremediable calamities of war. They have achieved the most surprising adventures; indulgencies have been

[2]A reward.

extended to them on the well-fought field; and they have expired with the weapons of death in their hands! Actuated by devotional zeal, and stimulated by the sublime expectation of an opening heaven, and a glorious immortality, they have rushed into the flames, have ascended the scaffold, have suffered the dismemberment of their bodies, have submitted to the tortures of dislocation, and to the most excruciating racks, in defence of the truth! not hath the voice of murmuring or complaint escaped their lips!

Women have publickly harangued on religion—they have presented themselves as disputants—they have boldly supported their tenets—they have been raised to the chair of philosophy, and of law—they have written fluently in Greek, and have read with great facility the Hebrew language. Youth and beauty, adorned with every feminine grace, and possessing eminently the powers of rhetoric, have pathetically conjured the mitred fathers and the Christian monarchs to arm themselves for the utter extirpation of the enemies of their holy religion.

In the days of knight-errantry, females, elevated by the importance with which they were invested, discriminated unerringly between the virtues and the vices, studiously cultivating the one, and endeavouring to exterminate the other; and their attainments *equalled the heroism of their admirers;* their bosoms glowed with sentiments as sublime as those they originated; generosity marked their elections; the impassioned feelings, the burst of tenderness, were invariably blended with honour; and every expression, every movement, was descriptive of the general enthusiasm. Pride, heroism, extravagant attachments; these were common to both sexes. Great enterprizes, bold adventures, incredible bravery—in every thing the women partook the colour of the times; and their taste and their judgment were exactly conformed. Thus the sexes are congenial; they are copyists of each other; and their opinions and their habits are elevated or degraded, animated or depressed, by precisely the same circumstances.

The Northern nations have generally been in the habit of venerating the Female Sex. Constantly employed in bending the bow, in exploring the haunts of those animals, who were the victims of their pleasures and their passions, or of urging against their species the missive shafts of death, they nevertheless banished their ferocity, and assumed the mildest manners, when associating with their mothers, their sisters, their mistresses, or their wives. In their ample forests, their athletic frames and sinewy arms were nerved for battle, while the smiles of some lovely woman were the meed of valour; and the hero who aspired to the approbation of the beautiful arbitress of his fate, authorized his wishes, and established his pretensions, by eminent virtue, and a long series of unbroken attentions.

A persuasion, that the common Father of the universe manifests himself more readily to females than to males, has, at one period or another, obtained, more or less, in every division of the globe. The Germans, the Britons, and the Scandinavians—from these the supposition received an early credence. The Grecian women delivered oracles—the Romans venerated the Sibyls—among the people of God, the Jewish women prophesied—the predictions of the Egyptian matron were much respected—and we were assured, that the most barbarous nations referred to their females, whatever they fancied beyond the reach of human efforts: And hence we find women in possession of the mysteries of religion, the *arcana* of physic, and the ceremonies of incantation. Writers assert, that several nations have ascribed to women the gift of prescience, conceiving that they possessed qualities approximating to divinity; and the ferocious German, embosomed in his native woods, renders a kind of devotional reverence to the Female Sex.

Such is the character of those periods, when women were invested with *undue elevation;* and the reverse presents THE SEX in a state of humiliation, altogether as unwarrantable. The females among the savages of our country, are represented as submitting to the most melancholy and distressing oppression; slaves to the ferocious passions and irregular appetites of those tyrannical usurpers, who brutally and cruelly outrage their feelings. They encounter for their support, incredible hardships and toils, insomuch that, weary of their own wretched existence, the women on the banks of the Oronoko, urged by compassion, not unfrequently smother the female infant in the hour of its birth; and she who hath attained sufficient fortitude to perform this *maternal* act, esteems herself entitled to additional respect. Commodore Byron,[3] in his account of the inhabitants of South-America, informs us, that the men exercise a most despotic authority over their wives, whom they consider in the same view they do any other part of their property, and dispose of them accordingly: Even their common treatment of them is cruel; for, although the toil and hazard of procuring food lies entirely on the women, yet they are not suffered to touch any part of it, till their imperious masters are satisfied, and then he assigns them their portion, which is generally very scanty, and such as he has not an appetite for, himself.

Thus have THE SEX continued the sport of contingencies; unnaturally subjected to extremes; alternately in the mount of exaltation, and

[3]Commodore Byron was John Byron (1723–1786), grandfather of the English poet Lord Byron (1788–1824).

in the valley of unmerited degradation. Is it wonderful, then, that they evince so little stability of character? Rather, is it not astonishing, that their attainments are so numerous, and so considerable? Turning over the annals of different ages, we have selected a number of names, which we purpose, in our next Essay, to cite, as vouchers of THE SEX'S merit; nor can we doubt, that their united suffrages will, on a candid investigation, effectually establish the female right to that *equality with their brethren, which, it is conceived, is assigned them in the Order of Nature.*

A Judith Sargent Murray Chronology (1751–1820)

1751

Judith Sargent is born on May 1.

1753

Winthrop Sargent, Jr., is born.

1755

Esther Sargent is born.

1768

Fitz William Sargent is born.

1769

Judith Sargent marries John Stevens.

1774

John Murray arrives in Gloucester.

1776

The Declaration of Independence is signed.

1777

Fifteen Universalists form Gloucester's Independent Church of Christ, the first Universalist Church in America.

1781

Gloucester's Universalists refuse to pay taxes to support the First Parish Church.

1782

Judith Sargent Stevens publishes her Universalist catechism.

1783

The Peace of Paris officially ends the American Revolution.

1784

Judith Sargent Stevens publishes "Desultory thoughts upon the utility of encouraging a degree of self-complacency, especially in female bosoms."

1786

John Stevens faces bankruptcy.

1787

The Constitutional Convention meets in Philadelphia.
John Stevens dies in St. Eustatius.

1788

Judith Sargent Stevens marries John Murray.

1789

The French Revolution begins with an assault on the Bastille.
George Murray is stillborn on August 5.

1790

Judith Sargent Murray publishes "On the equality of the sexes."
Catherine Macaulay publishes her *Letters on Education.*

1791

Julia Maria Murray is born on August 22.

1792–94

Judith Sargent Murray publishes her "Gleaner" and "Repository" essays in the *Massachusetts Magazine.*

1792

The Massachusetts General Assembly acts on the Gloucester Universalists' request for a charter of incorporation and grants toleration to the church, which ends all law suits against it.
Mary Wollstonecraft publishes *A Vindication of the Rights of Woman.*

1795

Judith Sargent Murray's *The Medium* or *Virtue Triumphant* is performed at Boston's Federal Street Theater.

1796

Judith Sargent Murray's *The Traveller Returned* is performed at Boston's Federal Street Theater.

1798

Judith Sargent Murray publishes her three-volume work, *The Gleaner.*

1799

William Godwin's *Memoirs of Mary Wollstonecraft Godwin* (1798) is published in Philadelphia.

1805

Mercy Otis Warren publishes her *History of the American Revolution.*

1808

Judith Sargent Murray's *The African* is performed at Boston's Federal Street Theater.

1812

Julia Maria Murray marries Adam Bingaman.

1813

Julia Maria Bingaman gives birth to Charlotte Bingaman.

1815

John Murray dies.

1816

Judith Sargent Murray publishes *Life of John Murray, by himself. With a continuation by Mrs. Judith Sargent Murray.*

1818

Judith Sargent Murray, Julia Maria Bingaman, and Charlotte Bingaman move to Natchez, Mississippi.

1820

Judith Sargent Murray dies.

Selected Bibliography

BACKGROUND AND GENERAL WORKS

There is only one biography of Judith Sargent Murray. Vena Bernadette Field's *Constantia: A Study of the Life and Works of Judith Sargent Murray, 1751–1820* (Orono: Maine University Press, 1931) was written before the recovery of Murray's Letterbooks and consequently relies on printed sources. Both Sharon Harris, in *American Women Writers to 1800* (New York: Oxford University Press, 1996) and *Selected Writings of Judith Sargent Murray* (New York: Oxford University Press, 1995), and Nina Baym, in her Introduction to the Union College Press edition of Murray's *The Gleaner* (Schenectady, 1992), have written short biographies that make some use of the manuscript collection available at the Mississippi Archives in Jackson, Mississippi.

One way to appreciate Judith Sargent Murray's contributions to her society is to compare her with some of her contemporaries. Particularly fine studies of elite American women include Joy Day Buel and Richard Buel, Jr., *The Way of Duty: A Woman and Her Family in Revolutionary America* (New York: W. W. Norton, 1984); Elaine Forman Crane, ed., *The Diary of Elizabeth Drinker: The Life Cycle of an Eighteenth-Century Woman* (Boston: Northeastern University Press, 1994); Edith B. Gelles, *Portia: The World of Abigail Adams* (Bloomington: Indiana University Press, 1992); and Rosemarie Zagarri, *A Woman's Dilemma: Mercy Otis Warren and the American Revolution* (Wheeling, Ill.: Harlan Davidson, 1995).

Christine Leigh Heyrman's *Commerce and Culture: The Maritime Communities of Colonial Massachusetts, 1690–1750* (New York: W. W. Norton, 1984) provides an excellent analysis of the early history of Gloucester, Massachusetts. For a more traditional approach, see John J. Babson, *History of the Town of Gloucester* (Gloucester: Proctor Brothers, 1960). From Daniel Vickers, *Farmers and Fishermen: Two Centuries of Work in Essex County, Massachusetts, 1630–1830* (Chapel Hill: University of North Carolina Press, 1994), students will gain an appreciation of Gloucester's fishing industry. For excellent analyses of the rise in "gentility" in America beginning in the last quarter of the eighteenth century, see Richard Bushman, *The Refinement of America: Persons, Houses, Cities* (New York: Knopf, 1992), and John F. Kasson, *Rudeness and Civility: Manners in Nineteenth Century Urban America* (New York: Hill and Wang, 1990).

RELIGION

Religion was central to the lives of eighteenth-century women. For Judith Sargent Murray, whose conversion to the Universalist religion informed her view of gender relations, it was particularly important. For the effect of Puritanism on women, see Mary Maples Dunn, "Saints and Sisters: Congregational and Quaker Women in the Early Colonial Period," *American Quarterly* 30 (1978): 582–601; Margaret Masson, "The Typology of the Female as a Model for the Regenerate: Puritan Preaching, 1690–1730," *Signs* 2 (1976): 304–15; Gerald F. Moran and Maris A. Vinovskis, "The Puritan Family and Religion: A Critical Reappraisal," *William and Mary Quarterly,* 3rd ser., 39 (1982): 29–63; and Laurel Thatcher Ulrich, " 'Vertuous Women Found': New England Ministerial Literature, 1668–1735," *American Quarterly* 28 (1976): 20–40. Works touching on the history of the Universalist religion include Ernest Cassara, *Universalism in America: A Documentary History* (Boston: Beacon Press, 1971); Richard Eddy, *Universalism in Gloucester, Massachusetts* (Gloucester: Proctor Brothers, 1892); Nathan O. Hatch, *The Democratization of American Christianity* (New Haven: Yale University Press, 1989); Stephen A. Marini, *Radical Sects of Revolutionary New England* (Cambridge: Harvard University Press, 1982); and Russell E. Miller, *The Larger Hope: The First Century of the Universalist Church in America* (Boston: Unitarian Universalist Association, 1979). John D. Cushing, "Notes on Disestablishment in Massachusetts, 1780–1833," *William and Mary Quarterly* 3rd ser., 26 (1969): 169–90, gives a lucid explanation of the Gloucester Universalists' role in the movement toward separation of church and state in the Bay Colony. For an understanding of the interrelationship between women and religion in the revolutionary era, see Susan Juster, *Disorderly Women: Sexual Politics and Evangelicalism in Revolutionary New England* (Ithaca: Cornell University Press, 1994); Barbara E. Lacey, "The World of Hannah Heaton: The Autobiography of an Eighteenth-Century Connecticut Farm Woman," *William and Mary Quarterly* 3rd ser., 45 (1988): 280–304; Richard Shiels, "The Feminization of American Congregationalism, 1730–1835," *American Quarterly* 33 (1981): 46–62; and Laurel Thatcher Ulrich, " 'Daughters of Liberty': Religious Women in Revolutionary New England," in *Women in the Age of the Amer-*

ican Revolution, ed. Ron Hoffman and Peter J. Albert (Charlottesville: University Press of Virginia, 1989).

WOMEN AND THE AMERICAN REVOLUTION

Two books have set the standard for our understanding of the effect of the American Revolution on women: Linda Kerber, *Women of the Republic: Intellect and Ideology in Revolutionary America* (Chapel Hill: University of North Carolina Press, 1980), and Mary Beth Norton, *Liberty's Daughters: The Revolutionary Experience of American Women, 1750–1800* (Boston: Little, Brown, 1980). Some of the best of Kerber's many articles on women and the revolutionary period have been conveniently published in *Toward an Intellectual History of Women: Essays by Linda K. Kerber* (Chapel Hill: University of North Carolina Press, 1997). Neither Kerber nor Norton contend that American women experienced great gains as a result of the Revolution, but there are those historians who argue that women gained almost nothing in the postwar period and that in some ways their position declined. See especially Elaine F. Crane, "Dependence in the Era of Independence: The Role of Women in a Republican Society," in *The American Revolution: Its Character and Limits,* ed. Jack Greene (New York: New York University Press, 1987): 253–75; and Joan Hoff Wilson, "The Illusion of Change: Women and the American Revolution," in *The American Revolution: Explorations in the History of American Radicalism,* ed. Alfred F. Young (Dekalb: University of Northern Illinois Press, 1976): 383–446. For the importance to women of the republican notions of "independence" and "virtue," see Joan R. Gunderson, "Independence, Citizenship, and the American Revolution," *Signs* 13 (1987): 59–77; and Ruth H. Bloch, "The Gendered Meanings of Virtue in Revolutionary America," *Signs* 13 (1987): 37–59. See also Alfred F. Young, "The Women of Boston: 'Persons of Consequence' in the Making of the American Revolution, 1765–1776," in *Women and Politics in the Age of the Democratic Revolution,* ed. Harriet B. Applewhite and Darlene G. Levy (Ann Arbor: University of Michigan Press, 1990): 181–226.

WOMEN AND ECONOMICS

There have been many excellent books and articles analyzing the economic position of women in the postrevolutionary era. A good place to begin is with Marylynn Salmon, *Women and the Law of Property in Early America* (Chapel Hill: University of North Carolina Press, 1986). Jeanne Boydston, *Home and Work: Housework, Wages, and the Ideology of Labor in the Early Republic* (New York: Oxford University Press, 1990), analyzes the changing nature of, and attitudes toward, "women's work."

Women in the Age of the American Revolution, ed. Ron Hoffman and Peter J. Albert, includes a number of excellent essays discussing the legal rights of women—especially their right to property—in the Revolutionary era. See particularly, Daniel Scott Smith, "Inheritance and the Social History of Early American Women," 45–66; Gloria L. Main, "Widows in Rural Massachusetts on the Eve of the Revolution," 67–90; David E. Narrett, "Men's Wills and Women's Property Rights in Colonial New York," 91–133; Carole Shammas, "Early American Women and Control Over Capital," 134–54; and Salmon, "Republican Sentiment, Economic Change, and the Property Rights of Women in American Law," 447–78. For women's experience as widows, see Alexander Keyssar, "Widowhood in Eighteenth-Century Massachusetts: A Problem in the History of the Family," *Perspectives in American History* 8 (1974): 83–119. Both Lisa Wilson Waciega, "A 'Man of Business': The Widow of Means in Southeastern Pennsylvania, 1750–1850," *William and Mary Quarterly* 3rd ser., 44 (1987): 40–64; and Susan Branson, "Women and the Family Economy in the Early Republic: The Case of Elizabeth Meredith," *Journal of the Early Republic* 16 (1996): 47–71, indicate that Judith Sargent Murray's interest in the complexities of banks, investments, and stocks was not unusual.

COURTSHIP AND MARRIAGE

A good many studies exist concerning the role that courtship and marriage played in women's lives. See Stephanie Coontz, *The Social Origins of Private Life: A History of American Families, 1600–1900* (London: Verso Press, 1988), for an overview of changes in the American family and its role. Lee Virginia Chambers-Schiller, *Liberty a Better Husband: Single Women in America: The Generations of 1780–1840* (New Haven: Yale University Press, 1984), reminds us that even in the late eighteenth century, some women consciously opted for a single life. See Ellen K. Rothman, *Hands and Hearts: A History of Courtship in America* (New York: Basic Books, 1984), for changes in courtship practices in the late eighteenth and early nineteenth centuries. Jan Lewis, "The Republican Wife: Virtue and Seduction in the Early Republic," *William and Mary Quarterly* 3rd ser., 44 (1987): 689–721, discusses the relationship between republicanism and changing attitudes toward the institution of marriage. For alterations in divorce laws, see Nancy F. Cott, "Eighteenth-Century Family and Social Life Revealed in Massachusetts Divorce Records," *Journal of Social History* 10 (1976): 20–43; and "Divorce and the Changing Status of Women in Massachusetts," *William and Mary Quarterly* 3rd ser., 33 (1976): 586–614.

MOTHERHOOD

Even more work has been done on views of motherhood in the eighteenth and nineteenth centuries. For an analysis of the changes in those views, see especially Ruth H. Bloch, "American Feminine Ideals in Transition: The Rise of the Moral Mother, 1785–1815," *Feminist Studies* 4 (1978): 101–26; Nancy Schrom Dye and Daniel Blake Smith, "Mother Love and Infant Death, 1750–1920," *Journal of American History* 73 (1986): 329–53; Jan Lewis, "Mother Love: The Construction of an Emotion in Nineteenth-Century America," in *Social History and Issues in Human Consciousness: Some Interdisciplinary Connections,* ed. Andrew E. Barnes and Peter N. Stearns (New York: New York University Press, 1989): 209–29. Studies of important developments in the birthing process include Nancy Schrom Dye, "History of Childbirth in America," *Signs* 6 (1980): 97–108; Sylvia D. Hoffert, *Private Matters: American Attitudes toward Childbearing and Infant Nurture in the Urban North, 1800–1860* (Urbana: University of Illinois Press, 1989); Catherine M. Scholten, *Childbearing in American Society, 1650–1850* (New York: New York University Press, 1985); and Laurel Thatcher Ulrich, *A Midwife's Tale: The Life of Martha Ballard, Based on Her Diary, 1785–1812* (New York: Random House, 1991). Jacqueline S. Reiner, "Raising the Republican Child: Attitudes and Practices in Post-Revolutionary Philadelphia," *William and Mary Quarterly* 3rd ser., 39 (1982): 150–63, is a useful study of childrearing techniques in this period. The classic analysis of "republican motherhood" comes from Linda Kerber, *Women of the Republic* as well as her "The Republican Mother: Women and the Enlightenment—An American Perspective," *American Quarterly* 28 (1976): 187–205. Rosemarie Zagarri, "Morals, Manners and the Republican Mother," *American Quarterly* 44 (1992): 26–43, offers a persuasive argument that the Scottish Enlightenment provided the philosophical roots of republican motherhood.

EDUCATION

The mid-eighteenth century witnessed important changes in attitudes toward women's education. Lawrence A. Cremin, *American Education: The National Experience, 1783–1876* (New York: Harper and Row, 1989), provides the standard overview. For discussions of women's literacy, see Kenneth Lockridge, *Literacy in Colonial New England* (New York: W. W. Norton, 1974); E. Jennifer Monaghan, "Literary Instruction and Gender in Colonial New England," *American Quarterly* (1988): 18–41; and Robert B. Winans, "The Growth of a Novel-Reading Public in Late Eighteenth-Century America," *Early American Literature* 9 (1975): 267–75. Mary

Kelley's " 'Vindicating the Equality of Female Intellect': Women and Authority in the Early Republic," *Prospects: An Annual of American Cultural Studies* 17 (1992): 1–27, discusses the rationale for women's education in the postrevolutionary era. For Judith Sargent Murray's views of women's education, see Madelon Cheek, " 'An Inestimable Prize,' Educating Women in the New Republic: The Writings of Judith Sargent Murray," *Journal of Thought* 20 (1985): 250–62.

WOMEN AND LITERATURE

There has been an explosion in studies analyzing the role of "the book" in eighteenth-century culture, particularly women's culture. Begin with Cathy N. Davidson, *The Revolution and the Word: The Rise of the Novel in America* (New York: Oxford University Press, 1986); Richard D. Brown, *Knowledge Is Power: The Diffusion of Information in Early America, 1700–1865* (New York: Oxford University Press, 1989); and Michael Warner, *The Letters of the Republic: Publication and the Public Sphere in Eighteenth Century America* (Cambridge: Harvard University Press, 1990). See also William J. Gilmore, *Reading Becomes a "Necessity of Life": Material and Cultural Life in Rural New England, 1780–1830* (Knoxville: University of Tennessee Press, 1989). For information on letter writing and the epistolary novel, see Janet Gurkin Altman's *Epistolarity: Approaches to a Form* (Columbus: Ohio University Press, 1992); *The Familiar Letter in the Eighteenth Century,* ed. Howard Anderson, Philip B. Daghlian, and Irvin Ehrenpreis (Lawrence: University Press of Kansas, 1966); and Ruth Perry, *Women, Letters and the Novel* (New York: AMS Press, 1980). Nina Baym, in *American Women Writers and the Work of History, 1790–1860* (New Brunswick, N.J.: Rutgers University Press, 1995) and "Between Enlightenment and Victorian: Toward a Narrative of American Women Writers Writing History," *Critical Inquiry* 18 (1991): 22–41, analyzes the work of women historians, including Mercy Otis Warren and Judith Sargent Murray, in the early Republic. See also Mary Kelley, "Designing a Past for the Present: Women Writing Women's History in Nineteenth-Century America," American Antiquarian Society *Proceedings* 105 (Worcester: American Antiquarian Society, 1996): 315–46. For an understanding of eighteenth-century poetry, see Gordon E. Bigelow, *Rhetoric and American Poetry of the Early National Period* (Gainesville: University of Florida, 1960). For eighteenth-century women poets, see Pattie Cowell, "Early New England Women Poets: Writing as a Vocation," *Early American Literature* 29 (1994): 103–21. Frank Choutreau Brown, "The First Boston Theatre on Federal Street," *Old Time New England* 36 (1945): 1–7, gives a short history of Boston's first theater, while Arthur H. Quinn's *A History of the American Drama from the Beginning to the Civil War* (New York: Harper and Brothers, 1923) offers a general analysis of the growth of the American theater in the early years. See Kenneth Silverman, "The Economic Debate Over the Theater in Revolutionary America," in *The American Revolution and Eighteenth-Century Culture: Essays from the 1976 Bicentennial Conference of the American Society for Eighteenth-Century Studies,* ed. Paul J. Korshin (New York: AMS Press, 1976): 219–40, for an excellent analysis of the Federalist-Republican debate over the theater. Amelia Howe Kritzer, in "Playing with Republican Motherhood: Self-Representation in Plays by Susanna Haswell Rowson and Judith Sargent Murray," *Early American Literature* 31 (1996): 150–66, examines Murray's treatment of women in her two plays. Analyses of *The Gleaner* include Nina Baym's Introductory Essay to *The Gleaner* (Schenectady: Union College Press, 1992); Madelon Jacoba, "The Novella as Political Message: *The Margaretta Story,*" *Studies in the Humanities* 18 (1991): 146–64; and Kirstin Wilcox, "The Scribblings of a Plain Man and the Temerity of a Woman: Gender and Genre in Judith Sargent Murray's *The Gleaner,*" *Early American Literature* 30 (1995): 121–44.

GENDER STUDIES

Historians are now beginning to develop analytic tools for understanding changing gender roles and attitudes in America. Useful overviews of the direction in which women's history is going may be found in Kathleen M. Brown, "Brave New Worlds: Women's and Gender History," *William and Mary Quarterly* 3rd ser., 50 (1993): 311–28, and Joan Cashin, Introduction to the Special Issue on Gender in the Early Republic, *Journal of the Early Republic* 15 (1995): 353–58. Ruth H. Bloch, "Untangling the Roots of Modern Sex Roles: A Survey of Four Centuries of Change," *Signs* 4 (1978): 237–52; Nancy F. Cott, *The Bonds of Womanhood, 'Women's Sphere' in New England, 1780–1835* (New Haven: Yale University Press, 1977); and Mary Beth Norton, "The Evolution of White Women's Experience in Early America," *American Historical Review* 89 (1984): 593–619, lay out a general overview of the nature and direction of the changes in women's lives in early America. See also Carroll Smith-Rosenberg, "Domesticating 'Virtue': Coquettes and Revolutionaries in Young America," in *Literature and the Body: Essays on Populations and Persons,* ed. Elaine Scarry (Baltimore: Johns Hopkins University Press, 1988). Thomas Laqueur, *Making Sex: Body and Gender from the Greeks to Freud* (Cambridge: Harvard University Press, 1990), and Londa Schiebinger, *The Mind Has No Sex? Women in the Origins of Modern Science* (Cambridge: Harvard University Press, 1989), discuss the growing belief in women's physical and mental inequality in the late eighteenth century from a transatlantic perspective. Nancy F. Cott's "Passionlessness: An Interpretation of Victorian Sexual Ideology, 1790–1850," *Signs* 4 (1978): 219–36, helps explain why women found notions that they were "naturally" more sexually pure than men increasingly attractive. Michelle Rosaldo, in her "Women, Culture, and Society: A Theoretical Overview," in *Woman, Culture and Society,* ed. Michelle Rosaldo and Louise Lamphere (Stanford: Stanford University Press, 1974): 17–42, was one of the first scholars to enunciate the classic understanding of gender-based "separate spheres." See Linda Kerber, "Separate Spheres, Female Worlds, Woman's Place: The Rhetoric of Women's History," *Journal of American History* 75 (1988): 9–39, for a critical analysis of the historical use of "separate spheres" as an analytic tool. For women's political role, see Linda Kerber, *Women of the Republic,* and Mary Beth Norton, *Liberty's Daughters,* as well as Anne M. Boylon, "Women and Politics in the Era Before Seneca Falls," *Journal of the Early Republic* (1990): 363–82; and Mary G. Dietz, "Context Is All: Feminism and Theories of Citizenship," *Daedalus* 116 (1987): 1–24. Chados Michael Brown, "Mary Wollstonecraft, or, The Female Illuminati: The Campaign Against Women and 'Modern Philosophy' in the Early Republic," *Journal of the Early Republic* 15 (1995): 389–424, and R. M. Janes, "The Reception of Mary Wollstonecraft's *A Vindication of the Rights of Woman,"* *Journal of the History of Ideas* 39 (1978): 293–302, both analyze her impact in America.

Index